Wolfe

W9-ASQ-162

# Painting for All

# PAINTING
# FOR ALL

A complete guide for the amateur and
student artist

*

MERVYN LEVY

Odhams Books Limited     Long Acre, London

DEDICATION

*For Dylan Thomas with whom I shared so many of*
*"the lamb white days . . ."*

*Reprinted November, 1958*
*Reprinted July, 1959*
*Reprinted November, 1959*
*Reprinted August, 1960*
*Reprinted March, 1962*
*Reprinted September, 1964*

*Made and Printed in Great Britain by C. Tinling & Co., Ltd.,*
*Liverpool, London and Prescot.*
*T.964.R6.N.*

# Contents

5

*The joy is in the doing,
and the revelation in the act . . .*

# Illustrations in Colour

*All pictures in colour are reproduced by courtesy of the Trustees of the Tate Gallery*

# Illustrations in Monochrome

# ILLUSTRATIONS IN MONOCHROME

* Reproduced from "My Life's History" by Grandma Moses (André Deutsch)

# ILLUSTRATIONS IN MONOCHROME

# ILLUSTRATIONS IN MONOCHROME

11

# ACKNOWLEDGEMENTS

The author and publishers wish to express their appreciation of the considerable help extended to them by individuals and organizations in many parts of the world in illustrating this book, and in particular would like to thank the following for their courtesy in allowing paintings to be reproduced from their collections and galleries: Ashmolean Museum, Oxford; B. T. Batsford, Ltd.; Burrell Collection—Glasgow Art Gallery; Sir Chester Beatty Collection; Cone Collection—Baltimore Museum of Art; Contemporary Art Society; Courtauld Institute; Directors and Trustees of the British Museum; Directors and Trustees of the National Gallery of Ireland; Directors and Trustees of the National Gallery, London; Directors and Trustees of the Tate Gallery, London; Directors and Trustees of the Victoria & Albert Museum; Dr. Huw T. Edwards, LL.D.; French Reproduction Rights, Ltd.; Galerie St. Etienne; Emanuel Hoffman Institute; Glasgow Art Gallery; Grandma Moses Properties Inc.; Hermitage Museum, Leningrad; Iveagh Bequest, Kenwood; Elis Jenkins, Esq.; Keith Warner Collection; Kunsthistorischen Museum, Vienna; Kunstmuseum, Basle; London County Council; Louvre, Paris; Luxembourg Museum, Paris; Mansell Collection; Museum of Modern Art, Paris; Museum of Modern Art, New York; National Museum of Wales; Mrs. K. M. Nevinson; Miss Catherine Powell; Prado, Madrid; Royal Library, Windsor Castle; Soprintendenza alle Gallerie di Firenze; Uffizi Gallery, Florence; Vatican Library, Rome; Wallace Collection, London.

The author wishes also to thank the following for invaluable assistance: The Borough of Camberwell for permission to reprint part of the author's Introduction to the Exhibition "Fire In The Hold" presented at the South London Art Gallery in March, 1957; Stephen Bone, Esq., Art Critic of the *Manchester Guardian*, R. O. Dunlop, Esq., R.A., and Colin Moss, Esq., A.R.C.A. (Lond.) for the contributions which appear in their names.

The authors and publishers of the following works, have provided the writer with the most valuable information, and from many of the publications listed quotations have been used: *Artists on Art* by Robert Goldwater and Marco Treves (Kegan Paul); *Aesthetics and History* by Bernard Berenson (Constable); *The Demon of Progress in the Arts* by Wyndham Lewis (Methuen); *Modern English Painters: Lewis to Moore* by Sir John Rothenstein (Eyre and Spottiswoode); *The Principles of Art* by R. G. Collingwood (Clarendon Press Oxford); *The Meaning of Art* by Sir Herbert Read (Faber and Faber); *The March of the Moderns* by William Gaunt (Jonathan Cape); *The Artist at Work* by Ruhemann and Kemp (Penguin Books); *Picasso: Fifty Years of his Art* by A. H. Barr (Museum of Modern Art, New York); The Director and Trustees of the Whitechapel Art Gallery for permission to quote from R. H. Wilenski's Introduction to the Merlyn Evans Exhibition, Whitechapel Art Gallery, October 1956; *Classic Art* by Heinrich Wölflinn (Phaidon Press), and to J. M. Dent and Sons for permission to quote from the poem "Fern Hill" by Dylan Thomas.

## INTRODUCTION

# The Creative Idea in Art

To THOSE of you who pick up this book for the first time, whether in a bookshop, a library, or perhaps from the bookshelf of a friend—from whom you should borrow it at once—I would say simply this; if you are not yet painting for pleasure, start now. The initiates among you will require no bolstering from me, no reassuring that painting is the most rewarding and fruitful of all hobbies. To have taken up painting, no matter at what age, or point in one's life, is to have entered into a new, and deeper awareness of the whole meaning of existence, to have tasted spiritual refreshment, and to have found the perfect form of creative relaxation.

For those of you who have already begun to explore the rich depths of seeing, and imagining, of thought, and feeling—for painting is all of these—I hope this book will provide fresh, or more compact information, and stimulation from new directions; information about the history and the theory of painting, helpful notes on techniques and materials, and stimulation in the realm of ideas. Creative thought is the keystone of good painting, and technical skill unsupported by a lively and inventive imagination has the hollow ring of a society portrait in which truth has been sacrificed for the sake of superficial appearances. Vanity is perhaps the most sterile of all vices.

"Can't you do *anything* with my daughter's nose?" I was once asked by a distraught mother. I had been commissioned to paint the portrait of a girl of seventeen with a delightful hook nose of gargantuan proportions, and, quite naturally, I gave this feature its rightful prominence, painting with reverence and enthusiasm a worthy mate for Cyrano's proboscis. I chose a three-quarter aspect which displays the nose to its best advantage, rather than a full face which, while presenting a foreshortened version of the offending member would not in my opinion have been anything like as stirring. It was a nose of great personality and I wished neither to curb nor suppress its presence. I did even more however—I wilfully exaggerated its size in order to intensify the portrait, a method employed more conspicuously by the cartoonist whose art depends entirely upon the

13

exaggeration or modification of salient physical characteristics. But the sitter and her parents were greatly distressed both by the literal, and the psychological truth, and insisted that the nose was not as bad as it had been painted. Nonetheless, I stuck resolutely to my guns, and to mama's plea—"Can't you do *anything* with my daughter's nose?" I replied that it was surely a nose to be proud of, and that from my point of view it would have to remain, at least in my painting, as I *knew* it to be. Needless to say the portrait was refused, and I never received my fee.

So much for truth and the interpretive approach in professional portraiture. Had I acquiesced to the demands of vanity I might conceivably have eked out some sort of hypocritical likeness. Average sitters are always prepared to accept flattering versions of themselves even when they know them to be untrue. But the truth, unless you are a "beauty", is a different matter. In the worst kind of professional portrait painting the basic idea is perverted and used to suppress and diminish, rather than to intensify truth. On the other hand, *the creative idea* is the force that distinguishes the true artist, for not only does it represent the unique conception of the painter, but enables him to approach the unique truth at the heart of his subject. This is particularly evident in great portraiture where the painter's insight into the mysteries of the sitter's personality is often crystallized through distortion, or exaggeration. But the painter must first arrive at an assessment of the sitter's personality; is it weak, strong, cruel, vain, mean, or generous? It is of course an intuitive as well as an intellectual process, this relentless search for the truth. Having made the assessment, the creative idea determines the representation.

I offer as evidence of the creative idea in action, two portraits. (Facing page 49) In both you will observe the use of exaggeration to intensify both particular personality, and general type.

Augustus John's portrait of the Welsh poet, Dylan Thomas, is of special interest since I can speak with authority of its resemblance to the sitter. It was painted at a time when the poet and myself were sharing a flat in Chelsea[1]. It is a fine likeness in spite of the fact that in reality the overall shape of Thomas's head was noticeably squarish, rather than delicately elongated as it appears in John's painting. This particular distortion invests the poet with an ethereality he did not possess in the flesh. The conception of the poet type (Shelley, Keats), as frail, slim, delicate, wan, other-worldly, has been used as the creative idea behind the Thomas portrait with great success. Although the features are unmistakably those of the poet—the vast pools of the eyes, the fleshy, voluptuous nose and mouth—the shape of the head is most certainly *not* his, but that of the poet

[1] Dylan Thomas and myself were born in Swansea. We were contemporaries at the Swansea Grammar School, and between the years 1932–36, shared an empty flat in Coleherne Road, Chelsea. Our furniture consisted mainly of orange boxes.
See *Dylan Thomas: Letters to Vernon Watkins*, Dent and Faber (1957): page 97.

archetype. Yet how much better is this study as a psychological interpretation, for this creative distortion.

Now look at Rembrandt's portrait of an old woman and note how he has symbolized the *spirit of age* by exaggerating a common characteristic of elderly faces—the collapse of the shape of the face into a sagging, puffy, amorphous mass. This portrait contrasts strikingly with John's conception of the spirit of youth, with its firm, taut, shapely features.

Here then are two portraits, both of distinct individuals, yet both embracing within their basic conception the substance of the most far reaching thoughts and ideas: powerful enough to promote in the spectator compelling, and profound reflections.

The great portrait painter speaks not only of the individual, but of humanity, and of human type. The small, vanity appeasing "society portrait" can speak only lies about the individual. It promotes no thought, and possesses no meaning beyond its immediate, and mercenary objective. The true work of art continues to unfold and create within the personality of the spectator. It is a continuous *coming into being*. Picasso has described the creative process and the function and character of the work of art in a statement he made to the writer Christian Zervos, in 1935. . . .

"A picture is not thought out and settled beforehand. While it is being done it changes as one's thoughts change. And when it is finished it still goes on changing, according to the state of mind of whoever is looking at it. A picture lives a life like a living creature, undergoing the changes imposed on us by our life from day to day. . . ."

None of this however is possible if the work itself is *dead*. Where the creative idea is absent, or for mercenary reasons intentionally held in check—the true aesthetic sin—as in the stereotyped professional portraiture that litters the large-scale annual exhibitions of the Royal Academy, the Royal Society of Portrait Painters, and so on, we arrive at a type of painting against which the beginner must be firmly warned. It is frequently presented to the amateur painter as a valid model by bad teachers and instructional journals who set out, not to assist the beginner in the quest for his own unique artistic personality, but to provide him with a package deal in ready-made dodges. Like a box of artistic conjuring tricks. Thus he can learn, parrot-wise, to "draw" and "paint" in the manner of his instructors; faces, trees, clouds, water, smoke, reflections in glass and silverware. A whole range of such neatly worked out, but utterly soulless "just copy me" exercises are regularly foisted upon the unsuspecting beginner.

There is of course only one way of painting water, or of drawing cats, and that is your own inimitable way. True, there are certain basic principles and rules that all artists may learn to their advantage—the fundamentals of anatomy, perspective, and colour theory, for instance—yet even before these basic principles are learned the beginner is well advised to explore the latent possibilities of his unique vision and style. These, contrary to the methods of bad instruction, cannot be taught. The good teacher will stimulate and excite the student into those mental and technical explorations that alone can reveal the right road for the individual.

Beyond that he may teach, as my colleagues and myself have endeavoured to do in this book, certain common laws, but my first concern is to prevail upon you either to begin painting, or to deepen your interest in a superb pastime by approaching the whole problem of painting, perhaps from a more thoughtful angle.

With this in mind I have begun my introduction on the assumption that thought, and what I have called "the creative idea" are more important in art than any facility, however skilful, for representing appearances. In itself, technical proficiency is a slippery mask that can deceive none but the inexpert, and the plebeian mentality.

I am writing at the moment while on holiday in Puerto Soller, a tiny Mallorcan sea-port. The little town is still largely unspoiled, and not yet so popular with tourists as to have sold out its soul to the devils of commerce. It has of course its quayside stalls, its shops, and its itinerant beach-traders, but there is nothing yet that savours of the brash, vulgar commercialism that has eaten the heart out of so many, once beautiful, continental towns, and cities. Here, the local people, the peasants and the fisher-folk still live simply—beyond the claws of television— singing and dancing in their leisure hours, and producing, apart from their exquisite lace, and needlework, a stream of delightful clay figurines, streaked with bright colours and depicting the day to day activities of the villagers, in which horses, and donkeys, and motor-scooters play a conspicuous part. In all of these works, the creative idea plays its part, if here, instinctively. For these are not, as you can see, at all concerned with superficial appearances, but with spirit; the true work of art is not an appearance—but an *essence*. They symbolize with a jaunty abandon the spirit of a gay, and happy people, for whom work and play are curiously inter-related. (See picture facing page 104).

They produce also decorative pots which embrace more typically perhaps even than the figurines the qualities and character of these island folk. The key shape is simple, as the basic life of the people themselves. The bird forms symbolize the imagination, the floral rosettes their love of decoration, and the masks of human faces their passion for acting, make-believe, and drama.

Mallorcan folk art is an expression of the living, creative soul of a community; a manifestation of life without which no social group can realize itself to the full. This is what modern *pleasure painting* in the more complex and sophisti-

**LANDSCAPE WITH BATHERS**     Richard Wilson, R.A. (1714–1782)

A superb example of picture making (see Chapter One) and colour perspective. As colour recedes into the distance it grows paler in tone, and colder in hue.

**DAMP AUTUMN**     Ivon Hitchens (1893–     )

In this fragile, misty portrayal, the painter has distilled an essence: the gossamer ephemerality of autumn.

*Left:* **NUDE**     **Amedeo Modigliani (1884–1920)**

An imaginative interpretation of the figure in which the Italian born painter combines the elongation of form (note the head in particular) to which he was so deeply attracted in African Negro sculpture, with the rich, sensual colour that is characteristically his own. Compare the poetic aspect of the Modigliani, with the purely factual observations of Forain.

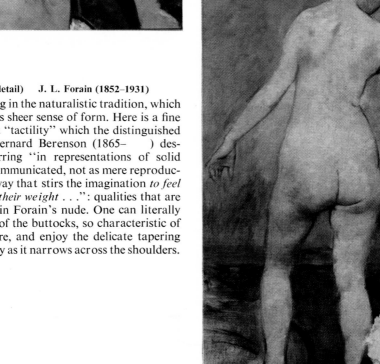

*Right:* **NUDE (detail)**     **J. L. Forain (1852–1931)**

A figure painting in the naturalistic tradition, which is notable for its sheer sense of form. Here is a fine example of that "tactility" which the distinguished art historian Bernard Berenson (1865–   ) describes as occurring "in representations of solid objects when communicated, not as mere reproductions, but in a way that stirs the imagination *to feel their bulk, heft their weight* . . .": qualities that are clearly evident in Forain's nude. One can literally *feel* the weight of the buttocks, so characteristic of the female figure, and enjoy the delicate tapering away of the body as it narrows across the shoulders.

cated societies of northern Europe is striving towards today. For not only does a community need its highly skilled professional artists, it needs also to realize its creative potential as an integrated, purposeful group, through the practice of its folk, or "people's art". That communities in modern industrial Europe have largely ceased in recent times to practise those forms of communal self-expression common to less "civilized" communities, is the source, I have no doubt, of much of our current psychological apathy, and discontent. The spiritual malaise which afflicts Western man today is largely the result of our having abandoned those forms of life-enhancing self-expression that stabilize more primitive societies. We have ceased even to make our own pleasures in the context of the family circle, preferring to squat in the sty of contentment, luxuriously appointed with every soul-killing device—for that is what the modern "civilized" home has become— while the mind slips cosily into the slime of "entertainment", softening and crumbling beneath the dead caresses of radio and television, until we are left with a nation of cows at gates staring with blank eyes into nothing[1].

Happily, as I say, there are signs of a spiritual renascence, of the emergence of a new kind of folk art, peculiar to our time, and to the type of society in which we live. That so many people from all walks of life have taken up painting for pleasure is proof enough that society today needs an outlet for its creative potential. Social psychologists of the future may well interpret the current popular enthusiasm for painting as the first tangible manifestation of a spiritual revolt against an era of soulless materialism.

Where priests and politicians the world over have failed so wretchedly throughout the ages to assist humanity in its struggle towards true civilization— the rejection of war for instance—where these "experts" have failed, can art succeed? I think yes. It very nearly did in Greece during the golden age. Certainly there is no more humanizing, no more civilizing force in life, than art. But it is not enough to leave it all to the professionals. God's plan is that of a continuous sequence of creation, and it is only by participating *ourselves* in this destiny that we can aspire to the enlightenment of mind and spirit from which alone can spring the fullest realization of ourselves, and of the miraculous universe in which we are set. When all men are in possession of this revelation of goodness, grace, and beauty, they will not wish any longer to injure, or to kill one another. That is why it is especially important today that people should practise a creative art, and what with more pleasure, or to more purpose, than painting?

To those of you who are not yet painting, I say, begin. To those of you who, in spite of all that I have so far said may ask "but why should I *personally* start painting?", I would say—because you are alive, and because life means

[1] See also Appendix.

B
17

creation. If we do not create as individuals, we cannot create as a society, and a society that does not create, must of necessity, die.

There is more evidence of the Creator's intention in the tiny, creating society of Puerto Soller, Mallorca, than you will find, at present, in the sick, apathetic societies of northern Europe, for all their labour-saving devices, and mechanized entertainments.

It matters not how well you paint—only that you should; for painting is the opening of doors that would otherwise remain closed. You only have to put it to the test to find out.

Men have always painted pictures and carved images. Nothing is more fundamental than the desire to express ourselves in pictorial terms. By his very nature man is a creative, and inventive animal. Whether employed as a magic symbol in cave painting, or as the means of spiritual regeneration in our own time, the creative image is our link with God. Today, surely, we need that link more than ever. The late Professor Collingwood, sometime Professor of Philosophy in the University of Oxford and a great authority on art and aesthetics, wrote in *The Principles of Art* (1938): "Art is the community's medicine for the worst disease of mind, the corruption of consciousness".

This age has ample need for such medicine, for never has consciousness been the subject of such a many pronged attack by the forces of material corruption. That is why you should paint—and why I know you *will*.

"Pick up your brushes and start to paint, and when you have finished, put them down." Rembrandt is reputed to have said this to a student who sought his advice. I would say the same to you; for in the doing is the goodness, and in the act the revelation. . . .

\* \* \*

I have endeavoured from the outset to relate painting to ideas. This I think is vital. There are of course, other, more practical issues of great importance in painting, and to this end I have thought it wise to invite other experts to contribute chapters on such specialist subjects as painting in oils, painting landscape, portrait painting, and so on. These contributions from R. O. Dunlop, R.A., painter, Stephen Bone, art critic of the *Manchester Guardian*, and Colin Moss, A.R.C.A., a practising teacher of drawing and painting, will do much to provide you with points of practical interest, with information about techniques and materials—and with still more, and perhaps different ideas, from my own.

MERVYN LEVY

# CHAPTER 1

# The Art of Picture Making

## COMPOSITION

COMPOSITION is the science of harmonious design, and as such, it ranks as the one indispensable element in the work of art. Whether the painter is working three-dimensionally, in the more flat, decorative manner of the early Italian masters[1], or in the manner of an artist like Henri Matisse who frequently abandoned the conventions of academic space and form for the sake of two-dimensional pattern and design, composition is the one quality which all great painting, irrespective of the dissimilarities of individuals or schools, must, and does possess. (See picture facing page 105).

Once the artist has decided upon a subject, his next problem is the planning of its composition. No matter how intensely he may feel about his subject, or how energetically he pursues its translation into paint, the ultimate success or failure of his efforts will depend entirely upon composition; upon whether or not the elements, or parts of the subject are satisfactorily organized in relation to one another. Now balance and rhythm are an essential part of the scheme of composition, which must contrive to hold the eye of the spectator securely in the picture. To this end it is essential to decide upon one element in particular which shall form the nucleus of the scheme, and towards which the eye of the spectator shall be compulsively directed. To appreciate this, you have only to consider "The Birth of Venus" by the Florentine master, Sandro Botticelli (facing p. 24). Immediately, the eye is compelled towards the Venus; whatever else of interest the eye may discover later—and there is of course much—the first reaction on looking at this picture is to rivet all one's attention upon the central figure: or *is* it a central figure? It is in fact just sufficiently *off* centre to destroy that tedious symmetry which should always be avoided when planning a composition. The element of *asymmetry* is here subtly intensified by the gentle angle at which the

[1] In the widest sense, the term "early Italian masters" includes all those typical forms of medieval painting (fresco, manuscript, and panel painting) that flourished in Italy between the fifth and sixth centuries, and the close of the fourteenth century. Giotto (*c.* 1266–1337) is usually considered to mark the initial stages of the transition form the medieval "flat", to the Renaissance "round".

figure of the Venus leans away from the vertical. The lesson is clear. Never set the main focus of interest exactly at the centre of the composition.

Let us consider just why it is that the eye is compelled, over and over again, to return to the Venus, and in particular to her face. The answer quite simply lies in the fact that the eye is *commanded* to the intended goal by the rhythms and actions of the balancing groups on either side, all of which converge upon the goddess. The rhythms and lines of force in the figure on the right, from the tips of her toes, through the powerful compulsion of the outstretched arm, conspire to direct the eye to the face, while the figures on the left of the picture, placed with superb asymmetry, make quite certain that the eye does not escape its destiny; they do in fact, quite literally, blow the eye back to the heart of this miraculous composition. The main direction is pointed by the figure on the right, while those on the left ensure the eye's captivity, and the continuance of its homage to Venus. Even the more static elements, the sharp promontories of land, and the foliage, play their part in pointing to the goal.

Rhythm, action, and movement are not in themselves sufficient: the dynamic must be offset by the static, the restless by the still, the curve by the straight. This contrast of action and repose, known technically as *contrapposto*[1], is a vital element in the art of composition. In Botticelli's masterpiece, the dynamic rhythms of the figures are balanced and offset by the repose of the horizon line and the verticals of the slender tree trunks, by the strip of light colouring in the foreground, and by the rushes in the opposite corner. I have analysed the *contrapposto* of the painting on the page opposite.

Now observe the level at which the horizon line divides the picture. In composition, no horizontal or vertical line should be permitted to divide the picture space into equal halves. Here, the horizon cuts the picture just sufficiently above half-way, to approach the ideal of the *Golden Section*[2]. He has also exercised another important rule of composition: the breaking of any long, monotonous line, a principle demonstrated here by the placing of the flowers which cut the horizon as they fall.

Simplicity of conception is also a vital element in the art of picture making. Botticelli's masterpiece is disarmingly simple; the shapes and forms are clearly conceived, and orientated with great clarity. There is no confusion, no uncertainty of intention. Like all the purest forms of greatness in the arts, the consummate masterpiece seems so obvious that the student is certain he has only, in this case,

---

[1] Also, see Glossary.

[2] A geometrical proportion which has for centuries been regarded as a universal law, governing the harmony of proportion both in art, and in nature. The common formula is, "to cut a finite line so that the shorter part is to the longer part as the longer part is to the whole". *See Glossary.*

An analysis of the dynamic and static elements in "The Birth of Venus" by Botticelli.

to pick up his brushes and compose a similar *tour de force* himself. It is not of course quite as easy as all that: but there is no reason why the study and analysis of such a work as this should not help the painter materially to improve upon, and perfect, his own powers of composition. Many people of course possess an instinctive sense of composition, a feeling for balance being a common characteristic of the art of children, and of amateurs. But this crude, unshaped potential can only be extended to its maximum limits by the planned application of the scientific rules of picture making. Composition is something of an exact science and, as such, it possesses a distinct mathematical flavour. Certainly the problem of organizing the various elements in the "The Birth of Venus" has been solved as mathematical problems are, by a precise working out of the correct answer. Botticelli's composition is the perfect solution of his particular problem: there could not conceivably be a better answer. And so it is with all great composition; the master arrives at *an absolute*.

This one painting demonstrates the basic principles of picture making, and you can learn sufficient from a study of this work to provide you with all the guidance you could possibly need when composing a subject of your own choice.

Let me now summarize these principles. Composition depends upon the following qualities, and rules:

(a) *Balance*: of shapes, forms, colours and tones. The balance of light and dark.

(b) *Rhythm*.

(c) *Contrapposto*, or contrast: the opposition of the dynamic and the static, of the straight and the curve, of action and repose.

(d) *Asymmetry*.

(e) The breaking of long, monotonous lines.

(f) Ensuring that the picture is not divided either vertically, or horizontally, into equal halves.

(g) *Proportion*: The division of any given whole into something approaching the ideal of the Golden Section: something a little more than a third of any given length.

(h) The organization of important rhythms and directions so that they lead the eye to the main feature, or "heart" of the composition.

(i) Fundamental simplicity of conception.

Many authorities take this matter of picture making a stage further in their analysis of the works of the masters, and relate the application of basic principles to the creation of certain *types* of composition. Perhaps the most perennial of these is that based either wholly, or in part, upon the pyramid, or triangle. In fact the essence of composition is geometry, and most of the great Italian paintings can be analysed into a series of broad geometric components, one of which predominates as the key proposition in a substantially mathematical scheme. In the more static type of composition it is the cube, square, or rectangle that predominates, as in Duccio's "Christ Healing the Blind Man" (facing page 25). But in the painting of later periods, it is the relatively dynamic pyramid that assumes command. Consider El Greco's "Agony in the Garden", painted about 1585. Here is an extremely dramatic composition in which geometric shapes play a distinct part. The triangle is the predominant motif, and I have indicated the extent of its participation in the scheme with an analytical sketch. Even "The Birth of Venus" is loosely pyramidal in conception, the three groups converging from their wide base to an apex. As an architectural feature in composition, the pyramid is probably the most powerful of all geometric elements, combining as it does, solidity with grace. When, as in "The Agony in the Garden", or in Rembrandt's "The Adoration of the Shepherds", a series of triangular shapes are orientated in opposition to one another, the result is one of great strength. In the Rembrandt, the main group is enclosed within a triangle, but there are, as you will see from my analytical sketch, many other triangular elements involved. The pyramidal type of composition constitutes the basis of many of Raphael's Madonnas, and is indeed, a common feature in Renaissance painting. The "Madonna and Child"

As this analysis shows Rembrandt's "The Adoration of the Shepherds" is a composition based on the opposition of triangular shapes. (Facing page 48).

from the School of Verrocchio (between pp. 24-25) is a clear example of how the pyramid can be used to effect a composition of great force, and simple dignity.

Now picture making of this rather severe, formal type, common as I say, especially to the Renaissance, is known as "closed composition". But there is no

Geometric shapes play a distinct part in the composition of El Greco's "The Agony in the Garden": see page 22.

reason why the principles of picture making should not be applied in terms of an "open composition". In such a picture there is far less sense of constriction, and the "open composition" lends itself, obviously, to the land, or seascape, where a feeling of space is all important.

The late Sir Charles Holmes (1868–1936), sometime Director of the National Gallery, drew a clear distinction between *unity* and *infinity* in composition. Structural unity is of course essential in the planning of a composition, but a sense of infinity must be rated as an element of great importance, particularly in landscape, where the "architecture" of picture making should unobtrusively underlay the expansiveness and infinity which is the most fundamental property of nature. Hence the "open composition" in which unity of design and a sense of infinity are successfully wed. Consider the seascape by Eugène Boudin (1824–98). Here, by the French master, is a fine, open composition, based, nonetheless, on the classical rules of picture making. There is balance, rhythm in the brisk, bustling figures which contrive to engage the attentions of the spectator, and a subtle opposition of the straight lines of foreshore and horizon with the arcs of the parasols and dresses. Long, monotonous lines are cunningly broken, and the sense of exhilarat-

*Above:* **THE BIRTH OF VENUS**
**Sandro Botticelli (c. 1444/5–1510)**

Although in many of his works Botticelli might be said to epitomize the spirit of the Renaissance, both in the departure of his subject content from the purely religious conventions of the medieval period and in his application of anatomy and perspective, he symbolizes also the conflict between narrow medievalism and the free spirit of the new humanism. Torn between the secular patronage of the Medici and his fanatical devotion to the religious reformer Savonarola, he painted little after the execution of the fiery preacher in 1498. *The Birth of Venus* was painted for a country villa of the Medici, and is typical of the vogue for Neo-Pagan subjects that flourished among a cultivated minority of Florentine citizens.

*Right:* **THE CORONATION OF THE VIRGIN**
**Lorenzo Monaco (c. 1370–1425)**

In the work and personality of Lorenzo Monaco, also a Florentine painter, there is no conspicuous conflict. His art is solidly rooted in the conventions of the medieval idiom and in direct descent from the formalism of the Byzantine style. By comparison with Botticelli the figures of Monaco are stiff and wooden, although a certain rhythm and movement in the conception of his draperies suggests an interest in aesthetic problems for their own sake. In this respect Monaco is part of the transition between the Middle Ages and the Renaissance.

*Left:*
**MADONNA AND CHILD**
**School of Verrocchio (15th century)**

*Opposite:*
**THE VIRGIN OF THE ROCKS**
**Leonardo da Vinci (1452–1519)**

It is easy to see in the *Madonna and Child* many affinities with the art of Leonardo. He was himself a pupil of Andrea del Verrocchio (1435–88) from whose workshop this superb example of Renaissance classicism emanates. In both the pictures here reproduced the composition is based on the triangle, a favourite device of Renaissance masters—notably Raphael—while the ideations of the Madonnas, the angels, and the children, are strikingly similar. In the conception of Leonardo however, the sense of transcendent vision reaches its apogee. Against the grace, and suppleness, of the figures in *The Virgin of the Rocks*, even the "Verrocchio" Madonna appears curiously wooden. The Leonardo on the other hand seems illumined by the soft glow of an inner fire—pure, and divine. Here is a master whose vision of an ultimate, impersonal majesty is perhaps the most glorious in the history of European painting.

*Right:*
**A DANCE TO THE MUSIC OF TIME**
**Nicolas Poussin (1594–1665)**

Poussin composed his pictures in "the grand manner". This he described as consisting of "subject-matter, thought, structure, and style. The first thing is that the subject-matter shall be grand. . . ."

*Above:* **THE AGONY IN THE GARDEN**
**El Greco (1541–1614)**

*Left:* **CHRIST HEALING THE MAN BORN BLIND**
**Duccio (c. 1255–1319)**

In the work of El Greco the religious subject receives a highly personal interpretation: its emotive and mystical aspects are intensified by a curious elongation of form, and the use of bright, astringent colours. Duccio's imagery, on the other hand, in spite of an early attempt to grapple with the problems of perspective, stems directly from the rigid and stereotyped forms of the Byzantine style.

ing spaciousness—of *infinity* in fact—has been accentuated by the way in which the artist has contrived the maximum expanse of sky. (Facing page 97).

The same sense of infinity pervades Ruben's "Autumn: The Chateau de Steen" (1636) in which, by comparison with Boudin's "La Plage", the proportion of land to sky has been inverted. The horizon cuts the picture space close to the ratio of the Golden Section, drawing the eye upwards, and away into the distance, like a magnet. The composition is based on a powerful zig-zag motif, while the sense of extension beyond the limits of the picture itself is suggested by the long, free flowing lines that sweep across the middle-distance. The cart making its way *out* of the picture, also contributes to this atmosphere of the infinite—of space beyond the mere physical limits of the painting. The picture is rich in compositional features, notably the opposition of the straight and the curve in the tree trunks. (Facing page 97).

### THE QUALITIES OF PAINTING

Picture making is not simply a matter of rules and principles; in themselves they do not make the living work of art. The consummate painting is animated by a number of factors additional to those of composition, and to these, relatively intangible qualities, we can attribute the inward life of the work of art.

The qualities about which I now wish to speak comprise the instinctive side of painting. Closely related to the unique personality of the artist, they determine the nature of those differences in conception, feeling, and style, which make one painter immediately distinguishable from another. Tintoretto, Constable, and Degas, for the sake of an immediate comparison, are all masters of composition in the more formal, and abstract sense of the word, but there is no doubt about which master is which. In spite of constants in the art of composition, they are, in other respects, completely dissimilar. What then are these additional factors that complete the work of art? We can list them as follows:

(a) Originality of Conception.

(b) Tactile Values.

(c) The power to arouse *empathy* in the spectator.

(d) Paint Quality, or *Matière*.

The need for originality of conception speaks for itself, but the remainder of these values need definition especially since the terms involved are technical.

Tactility in painting is the sense of what things really *are*. Stone, flesh, wood, water, silk, iron, and so on, any of which might be represented in paint, must *feel* to the beholder, what they are in reality. Looking at the flesh of a thigh in a painting it must literally *feel* warm, and soft. Iron, on the other hand, must *feel* hard, and cold. Mood and atmosphere too, must feel what they are. A windy March day in a Constable must feel different from a hot June day in a Monet. *Tactile Values*, as tactility is known technically, comprises the total experience, both physical and imaginative, of apprehending in a painting, the awareness of distance, space, and mass; of warmth and coolness, stillness and noise, hard and soft. A great authority on matters of aesthetics, Bernard Berenson has described tactile values as follows:

> "Tactile values occur in representations of solid objects when communicated, not as mere reproductions (no matter how veracious), but in a way that stirs the imagination to feel their bulk, heft their weight, realize their potential resistance, span their distance from us, and encourage us, always imaginatively, to come into close touch with, to grasp, to embrace, or to walk around them."
>
> ("Aesthetics and History")

Now *empathy* is really an extension, a deepening of the condition of tactile values. It is the power, possessed in the highest degree by the greatest artists, of arousing in the spectator a sense of absolute identification with the painter's work. A "becoming one" with the work of art. Empathy is in fact an act of love in which both the spectator and the artist must participate equally. Initially, the onus is upon the painter, who must stimulate in the beholder, like a good lover, the desire for union. He must ravish the eye, and the senses, with such skill, as to bring about the desired result. The spectator in turn will respond to the advances of the painter and, by the application of his own imaginative powers, bring the experience to a consummation. Indeed, the paradise of human love, at the moment of its consummation, is very close to the nirvana of aesthetic bliss—the "becoming one" with the work of art. In both experiences there is the projection of self, and the *annihilation* of self, in union with the object of adoration, and through the beloved, with the infinite bliss of God beyond.

Everyone must surely have experienced this becoming one with the work of art, when listening to music, an art form whose appeal to the emotions is perhaps more immediate than that of any other. How blissfully when listening, perhaps to Tchaikovsky, or Chopin, can one glide into the heart of the music, losing oneself utterly, in the magic of the composer's spell. One literally ceases to be oneself, and becomes the music. Great writing, and great painting, can inspire the same sense of identification in the reader, or the beholder. Through tactility, one is aware in painting, of the physical properties of the subject; through empathy, of their emotive significance. Empathy means "feeling into"—the projection of personality *into* the object of contemplation: i.e. the work of art. The result of this "feeling into" is the creation in the spectator of an emotional identification of the "self" with the work of art. Empathy, if you like, is an extreme form of sympathy. Just as "sympathy" means feeling *with*, so "empathy" means feeling *into*. The difference is that between feeling by proxy, or feeling second-hand, and feeling *itself*.

The most characteristic aspect of the work of art, so far as individuality is concerned is its *paint quality*, or *matière*. The way in which an artist handles his paint, and brushes, is as distinctive, and revealing, as his handwriting. Herein is contained the essence of his nervous energy, and those peculiarities of style which are the tangible evidence of his distinction from all others. All the qualities I have spoken of so far are in themselves abstractions which can only be given form by the way in which the artist uses his materials. The softness of flesh, or the hardness of stone, depend upon two things in particular—*texture*, and *brush-work*. These are the main properties of paint quality. Together they combine to effect the *matière* of a painting, an expression which is used when referring to the intrinsic qualities of the physical surface of a painting irrespective of subject content.

Paint is an organic substance: it lives like flesh, possessing in itself, a wide range of subtleties. The great manipulators of oil paint, masters like Rembrandt, and Van Gogh who use the medium to the full extent of its rich potential, are those painters who can exert the maximum sense of tactility, and so promote in the spectator, the maximum empathetic responses. When an artist, working in oils— and I think we should agree that this is the really great medium for the painter— composes his pictures with an eye for design and pattern, rather than for feeling, and when moreover, he uses the rich, full medium of oil paint so thinly (Matisse is a case in point) that texture and brush-work are effaced, his work will inevitably lose much of its potency. Oil paint is a medium which must be used *thickly*. Contrasts in texture, and the living force of the brush-stroke, are an intrinsic part of the spirit of the medium. In every master of the oil medium, from Titian to Augustus John, evidence of the part played by texture and brush-work, is overwhelming.

Get into the habit of studying oil paintings at close quarters, purely from the point of view of assessing the full significance of paint quality. Look at as many original paintings by masters of the medium, as you can, remembering of course that the technique of oil painting such as we understand it today, was not perfected until painters like Titian, in particular, used it for the first time, with real thickness. He was perhaps the first master to employ contrast in paint texture, to explore the possibilities of "thick and thin", a system of painting developed to the highest extent by Rembrandt, in whom we can study the use of a thick impasto to suggest form—that of flesh, or drapery for instance—offset by thinly painted shadows, and other, less substantial features.

Get into the habit of thinking of paint as the living flesh in which the artist fashions the tangible form of his idea. The sculptor uses clay, or stone: the painter can do no better than to use the full, rich plasticity of thick oil paint. Look for all this when you study painting. Almost every sizable town in the country has an art gallery, and every art gallery is sure to sport a few works by artists of repute. Many of the nation's smaller galleries possess masterpieces too—not everything of importance is in London, by any means, although naturally, if you live in the metropolis, your opportunities for the study of oil painting are greatly increased.

The science of composition then is something you can learn; the additional qualities common to the consummate work of art being a matter of personality. One might, for instance, employ the pyramidal type of composition common in Raphael, but only a fool would seek to emulate the brush-work of Rubens. That would be as absurd as trying to write a letter in the style of someone else's handwriting.

The object of the study of the masters is not to facilitate their imitation, but to illumine the possibilities of one's own potential. Blatant copying from great painters—the stupid sitting in galleries and imitating like a parrot—I have always held to be a bad thing; an analytical appreciation of the whys and wherefores of their "know how", an absolutely indispensable aspect of 'the student's evolution; the student, professional or amateur.

Looking at much of the painting of our own, immediate period, you may well feel that it fails to make good if measured against the standards set out in this chapter. So it does.

This is an age in which, after a burst of genuine experiment and exploration (the chapter on Modern Art will tell you all about the relevant aspects of the modern movement), painting has declined during the past twenty years, sometimes into mere charlatanism—a paying game which any impudent fraud can exploit, simply by cooking up a sufficiently *outré* stunt, something so "advanced" that the intellectual snob can batten on to it, and for the sake of his own ends, seek to attribute to it, meanings that in itself it does not of course possess. Sometimes this delusion is genuine, in which case, as a sort of psychological blindness it is to be pitied. But often it is part of the unscrupulous plot to foist upon a small, gullible, yet influential and affluent section of the community—there's no fool like a wealthy fool!— that form of "advanced" art which the wealthy, for some peculiar reason imagine to be their own special province. When such is the case, the perpetrators of these abominable aesthetic crimes must be roundly condemned. Not because they catch the sucker, but because their insidious influence tends to corrupt and debase the standards of genuine art and criticism. The result is, as the two following examples show, that even where artist and critic are sincere, the layman is too often given by way of "explanatory" commentary the sort of verbal drivel that leaves him more baffled and mystified than ever. And you may also bear in mind that any art which needs the support of another to explain, or in any way to qualify its existence has already failed in the first function of the work of art—*articulation*. In art, that which cannot speak for itself has nothing to say.

At a recent London one-man exhibition[1], a young Frenchman exhibited a number of hardboard squares painted in single flat colours—blue, red, orange, and so on. These paintings were covered by a typical piece of fatuous literary nonsense, written by a French critic, Pierre Restany:—

"Each of these propositions defines a visual field, a coloured area, cleared of every graphic transcription and is thereby liberated from the time-element and consecrated to the uniform expression of a certain tonality. Beyond Mr. Know-all and nothing, common prey to visual deceptions, the old *habitués* of the informal will agree on the definition of a 'nothing' in their senseless attempt of wishing to raise to the power of $+^{\circ\circ}$ the dramatic (and by now classical) adventure of Malevich's square".

I have quoted merely an extract from a much lengthier introduction to the exhibition in question. Do not worry if you can make no sense of this jargon: it is quite meaningless, and as perfect an illustration of my point as you could hope to find. The following extract from an introduction by Mr. Denis Bowen to a recent exhibition of paintings by a Miss M. Beaumont-Hill[2] runs it very close. Having explained that Miss Beaumont-Hill has developed "a novel and personal way of handling paint", the writer goes on:

"This imagery is brought into action by these coagulations of energies emerging within a viscous tracery of veined protrusions as if they were injections into ectoplasmic space."

\*      \*      \*

I make no bones of my condemnation of deliberate extremism in painting. It was important in this chapter on picture making to contrast the emptiness of the stunt painter, so rife today, with the fertility of those true artists for whom painting is a rich composite of inspiration and craft. Nor is there any reason why order and discipline should extinguish the pure, free flowing fires of passionate self-expression. No painter ever worked with greater freedom and passion than Van Gogh, yet every, racing, fiery brush-stroke that consumed his canvas is determined by the clarity of the underlying idea, and by the artist's certainty that what he has to say *must* be expressed with lucidity, and with *economy*. There are no superfluous brush-strokes in Van Gogh, any more than in Rembrandt. Nothing is a matter of

[1] Monochrome Propositions—Yves Klein. Gallery One. June, 1957.
[2] New Vision Centre, Marble Arch, London. October 1957.

chance. In both painters, passion and clarity are complementary; spontaneity and economy of means, synonymous.

If, when composing your own pictures, you bear in mind the principles and the ideas that I have outlined in the present chapter, remembering also that the driving force behind *all* pictures that really have something to say, is *the idea* (I called this the creative idea in my introduction), then you have already taken the first step in the art of picture making.

*Composition* is a means towards the expression, aesthetically, of the creative idea; *tactility*, *empathy*, and *matière* are the qualities which give it life. The first step in picture making is to find the right idea, in relation to the right subject. We shall consider this problem at length in a later chapter.

# CHAPTER 2

# Painting in Opaque Water-colours

OPAQUE water-paints are unquestionably the best medium in which to commence painting for pleasure. Not because they are more sympathetic than oils—indeed in some ways they are less so—but because their use demands a minimum of equipment, and a relatively small initial outlay in expense. They also possess a rude, hearty strength, which as we shall see, is fundamentally consistent with the early stages of pleasure painting. Although even professional students will find in the use of this relaxing medium the perfect antidote for the exactments of academic study. It will provide them with a release from tension, and a general refreshment that will send them back to their more disciplined studies, with renewed interest, and increased vigour.

I am not concerned in this chapter with such matters as the choice of suitable subjects for painting, or with the form of your personal style; these are issues for subsequent consideration. In this first chapter on painting I want simply to introduce to you a striking, and spirited medium.

Opaque water-paints differ radically from the transparent variety in possessing *body*. Thus, they present the beginner with a definite substance, and this in itself is a satisfying thing. The creative experience is perhaps richest when we can express ourselves in a medium that yields co-operatively to our touch. For this reason both clay, and oil colour, are deeply rewarding media since they can be moulded and shaped into the required form: *caressed* into the required form I should perhaps say, since creative self-expression is an act of love. Opaque water-colours also possess some of this tangible plasticity. *Transparent* water-colours on the other hand present a number of drawbacks to the beginner. Their relative thinness, and lack of body, make them an extremely difficult, and consequently frustrating medium for any but the accomplished technician. In the hand of the inexperienced, this thin, delicate medium lends itself only to weak, inconclusive results. I am not of course arguing that ultimate strength depends upon the use of thick, dark lines, and pure, bright colours; that would be like saying that the best pianist is the one who makes the most noise. But I do suggest that the natural

31

strength of opaque water-colours will provide you with a robust and fluent vehicle for the expression of your *feelings*, and in your first pictures the free flow of pure emotion is far more important than any attempt to grapple with the problems of technical accomplishment. Bold, spontaneous, free-expression is the first step, and it is for this reason that I have distinguished between the advantages, and the disadvantages of the two types of water paint.

Whatever refinements of technique or style you may achieve in the course of time, the first thing is to commit yourself, up to the hilt—to take the plunge, fearlessly, and with abandon. Unless you do so at the outset, a fear that haunts and inhibits so many artists, will hamper, and frustrate you too. The fear of making a mess, of spoiling a piece of paper, is the inevitable, and limiting consequence of approaching the problems of painting the wrong way round. Only the practise of freedom can lead you to the *need* for discipline, and order. Technical mastery is the result of endless mistakes, although many beginners seek to achieve this mastery in their first picture. It is far more important to learn how to express your feelings in the early stages, for unless a painting is illuminated by this inward fire, not all the technical mastery in the world will give it life. So get your feelings flowing freely first of all, and commit them through the sheer exuberance of the unacademic approach. The bold touch is essential at the outset, and the bolder the medium, the greater the support it will lend to your passion, and verve. That is why I suggest that you commence your painting in opaque water-colours, which possess such a high degree of power, and brilliance.

For this reason they are commonly used nowadays in schools, for children also like to express themselves energetically. The fundamental, formative urges, are all emotional; discipline and order, subtlety and finesse, these are conditions which can only evolve, in their best form, from the energetic pursuit of the instincts, and the natural fulfilment of emotional requirements. One cannot build a healthy, balanced system of law and order on the basis of frustration. The foundation of discipline in art, as in life, is the fulfilment of emotional impulses, and urges. The instincts must be gratified before reason takes over. One cannot work things the other way round. That is why many people whose instincts have been thwarted in childhood find it so difficult to loosen up, and express themselves emotionally in adult life. It is the same with pleasure painting. But let me draw some further parallels between aesthetic expression, and life itself.

The child is indeed father to the man, the nature of adult personality being wholly determined by the extent to which the child has been able to gratify and resolve its instinctive needs. I am speaking now, purely of the extent to which *psychological* personality is determined by the child's early environment; heredity of course is a determining *physiological* factor beyond our control. Thus, the child

**BACCARAT: The Fur Cape. (1920)**
**W. R. Sickert (1860–1942)**

A portrait in reverse; yet one that describes the personality of the sitter perhaps more completely than if she faced the spectator.

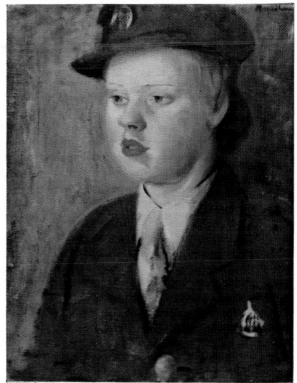

*Above:* **SOMERSET MAUGHAM ESQ.**
**Graham Sutherland (1903–    )**

*Right:* **PTE CLARKE. A.T.S.**
**Rodrigo Moynihan (1910–    )**

Technical style and evocative colour as the basis of psychological portraiture. Compare the sharp, caustic rendering of the Sutherland portrait, with the soft, chubbiness of the Moynihan; the astringent colour of the one, with the voluptuous hues of the other.

**SPANISH LANDSCAPE (1935)**    **Andre Masson (1896–    )**
A combination of colour and poetic imagination (see page 94).

**POOL OF LONDON (1906)**    **Andre Derain (1880–1954)**
The painter as Fauvist ("wild beast"). Fauvism is distinguished by the use of savage and violent colour.

denied the boon of love and affection in its early years may grow into an embittered and resentful adult: a fact which is quite likely to manifest itself in the pictures such an unhappy adult may paint.

Conversely, the lack of the opportunity in childhood to *express* love and affection, as well as to receive it, may produce in the adult a crucial timidity, an inability to express emotion which can prove disastrous, especially in the sexual relationships that are such a vital factor in the pattern of human happiness, or distress. Frigidity, in either sex—although the term is more commonly used in respect of women—may well have its origin in some such infantile frustration. This too can manifest itself aesthetically in the production of timid, non-committal pictures. The need to love, and to be loved, is one of the most fundamental of all human needs, and the pattern of fulfilment or frustration is established in early childhood.

What has all this to do with painting? Well, it is now an accepted fact that the expression of emotion through painting, whether practised by children, or by adults,[1] is a source of deep psychological satisfaction and, in the adult practitioner, often a key to the release of tension. In other words, expressionist pleasure painting is in itself an emotional *milieu*. A unique system of self-expression which has its parallel in the exchange of love and affection in the human situation; the mother and child relationship for instance. It is a system which can also in some measure, even compensate for the lack of emotional fulfilment in human relationships, or for other inadequacies of daily life.

The full significance of painting as a vital form of self-expression can only be understood in relation to the need for emotional expression in the context of life itself. Art, it has been said is not one aspect of life, but the whole of life seen in one aspect.

We frequently use expressions like "blowing off steam", "letting one's hair down", "painting the town red", and so on All these, and similar figures of speech describe the need which all of us must surely feel from time to time, to cut a caper, to kick over the traces and break away from that deadening pattern of conventional behaviour that enslaves, and stifles the spirit—and the flesh.

It was Cyril Connolly who said, that in every fat man, a thin man is wildly signalling to be let out. I would take this attractive idea a stage further and propose that in every tame, conventional man, a savage, and unconventional man is wildly signalling to be let out. Free-expression painting is one such means of

---

[1]There is also of course the additional category of those adults who practise painting primarily for its therapeutic qualities. In the sanatorium, and in cases of convalescence, painting is an acknowledged curative force. As an antidote for neuroses, and as a factor in the diagnosis and treatment of more serious psychotic disorders it occupies a distinct place nowadays in the field of psychological medicine.

painting the town red, so to speak. Children of course are the most instinctive and pure expressionist painters, since they have little inhibition, and blithely distort both form and colour for the sake of the free flow of emotional feeling. Their art is frequently ruthless, and violent, while penetrating with unerring insight to the heart of the matter. Nothing is so devastating as the incisive portraiture of children, for instance. For these reasons there is much that the adult painter can learn from the art of children. Let painting be for you, at the outset, a becoming young and uninhibited again.

Now let me consolidate my point about the importance of childhood environment. Very often, looking at the paintings of adults, I have been able on the one hand to interpret the joyous freedom with which some amateurs express themselves, as indicating an emotionally happy childhood; on the other hand, the tentative, indecisive, and niggardly treatment of others suggests an emotional unhappiness in those early, formative years. However, irrespective of the circumstances of your own childhood, you can at least start painting in the right way: simply try to express your feelings with spontaneity and vigour. You will find opaque water-paints most co-operative.

What happens in one's "aesthetic childhood" can prove just as far reaching an influence on the course of future events in the artistic field, as the effects of domestic environment in determining the shape of adult personality. The true basis of progress is freedom—freedom to progress. Opaque water-colours are the perfect medium in which to indulge this initial freedom, for they can be mixed with water without losing any of their rich, full body, while at the same time they will flow from your brush with the sweetest ease, and fluency.

I mentioned at the beginning of this chapter that opaque water-colours were not perhaps quite so sympathetic as oils, but this is not so much a criticism of one medium as the recommendation of another for different reasons. Oils are more sympathetic in the sense that they can be moulded at leisure into the shape of the artist's conception. This is so because they take some little time to dry, and can be worked on, and into, for a few days if needs be, especially if the colour is kept alive, and fresh, with a little oil[1].

Water paints of any sort dry rapidly, so that the complete picture must be executed with comparative speed. Neither is it advisable to attempt alteration or correction when working in water-colour, since it is impossible to work on a passage of dry colour without raising the underpainting. It is therefore essentially a medium for speedy handling. Once a statement has been made it is virtually irrevocable. Nevertheless, for the spontaneous expression of a subject that has

---

[1] To keep an oil painting thoroughly wet and fresh from one day to the next, simply brush a delicate film of clean linseed oil over those passages that have reached the tacky stage in the process of drying.

stimulated a mood of excitement in the artist, there is no medium to rival opaque water-paints. They demand just that extra ounce of effort and concentration, because the artist realizes he is working against time. In oils, on the other hand, the beginner often fails to work with a maximum of spontaneity. He tends to fiddle, and play around, simply because he knows that the paint will take some while to dry. Oils are the medium for the beginner who has already taken a deep plunge into painting. If they are used too soon, they may create a tentative, non-committal attitude. I would suggest a month or two of lively painting in opaque water-paints before you progress to oils.

So far I have spoken only about the psychology of working in opaque water-paints; now let me tell you what you will need in the way of materials, and how to use them. Opaque water-colours can be obtained in three forms—in powders, pots, or tubes. In their powdered form they are usually known as "powder tempera colours"[1]. The pigment is simply mixed with a little water and is then ready for use. The principle is the same as in the methods employed by the medieval *fresco*, and *tempera* painters, who mixed their pigments with water when working on the fresh wet plaster of wall surfaces, and with water, and the yolk of egg, when painting on wooden panels.

Medieval artists of course, never used fresco, or tempera, with the freedom that modern painters can enjoy when working in a similar medium. To begin with they had to cover extensive wall surfaces with a medium that united almost instantaneously with the wet plaster. This led, not to freedom of handling, or expression, but to the evolution of a pernickety and stylised system of building up the subject in numerous small portions. Tempera painting too was highly formalized; a first rendering of the subject in tempera being completed by the overlay of a series of transparent oil glazes. This was known as the "mixed method", a technique perfected by the Flemish masters, Hubert van Eyck (*c.* 1370–1426?), and his more celebrated brother, Jan van Eyck (*c.* 1380–1441).

Today, powder tempera colours are usually packed in tins. When purchased in pots, or tubes opaque water-paints are known as poster colours. In this form they are commonly used nowadays by all sorts of commercial designers. It is entirely a matter of personal preference in which form you buy your paints. To begin with, small tubes of poster colour are probably the most economical way of purchasing this type of paint. On the other hand, there is a great deal of pleasure to be obtained from the mixing of powdered pigments to the required consistencies.

So far as your range of colours is concerned, it is not necessary to buy a great many different colours: indeed, the beginner should restrict his palette to a mini-

[1] Early painters spoke of "tempering" their pigments with a vehicle—such as water, or egg.

mum, since many colours do not necessarily make for good colour. They are much more likely to produce confusion. Many distinguished, and even great artists, often worked chromatic miracles with few colours. Rembrandt, who worked in a comparatively low key, is a striking example of the beauty that can be achieved with a limited palette. His colour is based substantially on brown, yet it glows and burns with a rich fire.

Every colour, and every shade of every colour in existence can in fact be mixed from the three basic primaries, red, yellow, and blue, with the addition of varying amounts of white. I shall be talking about colour, and colour mixing, in a later chapter. The following basic chromatic range should be sufficient for your immediate purposes:

Red, yellow, blue, green, brown, white, and black.

The actual names of the colours, such as pillar-box red, sky blue, and so on, vary according to the manufacturer, but if you ask for the *bright* variety of red, yellow, blue, and green, your local supplier will be pleased to assist you. It is important to remember that when pigments are mixed with water they are relatively deep in tint; when dry they get very much paler. Allowance must be made for this when opaque water-colour paints are used.

Now for your brushes. Three to six long-handled hog-hair brushes such as children use at school are quite sufficient for a start. The number you buy depends of course on how much money you are prepared to spend. Naturally, the more brushes you possess the better, and it is a good thing to keep adding to your collection. Your brushes should vary in size from fine, to broad, and since I have suggested that you should work with boldness, and breadth, you should aim at building up a stock of the bigger brushes. Here again your supplier will advise you on specific sizes.

When they are not in use, stand them, bristles uppermost in a pot, or jar. In a gay vase, a cluster of brushes make a handsome and inviting spectacle in themselves.

There are many alternatives for the palette. You can, if you wish, buy one of the many sorts and sizes of enamelled palettes that are specially made for water-colour painting, or you can simply use saucers, or shallow dishes. Personally, there is nothing, I think, more serviceable for colour mixing than an ordinary, cheap, kitchen patty-tin, with half a dozen or so pans.

I suggest that you work on reasonably large sheets of paper; if your painting surface is too small, it will tend to cramp your style. An ideal size is *half-imperial* (15″ × 22″). This is one of the most common stock sizes. White cartridge paper is excellent, although you can experiment with the various toned, and coloured papers that are also available. However, to start with, I should work on white cartridge.

36

Your paper will of course have to be pinned to something solid before you can commence your work. As an alternative for the relatively expensive official drawing board—these also are available in such stock sizes as quarter- and half-imperial—you can use a sheet of stout cardboard, or any other suitable surface.

The remainder of your necessities are all minor items. Some pencils for laying in your subject, a box of drawing pins, jam-jars for your water (plenty of clean water is essential, as your brushes will require frequent cleaning while you work), a supply of rag for wiping your brushes and, if you are using powder colours, an old spoon or some other implement for transferring your pigment from the tin, to the palette.

The principle of using your materials is very simple. The painting surface should first be propped up at an angle of 10 to 15 degrees from the horizontal (one or two books will give you this inclination), then the initial, but by no means conclusive layout of the subject should be roughed in with pencil, and the colours made ready in the palette. Now, with the mind fully alerted, and the brush gleaming with rich colour, you are ready to begin. . . .

## CHAPTER 3

# Painting in Oils

### *by Colin Moss*

OIL-PAINTING of a rudimentary kind was in being when the mammoth still roamed the plains of Europe. The first men, creating for their own mysterious, magical purposes their magnificent friezes of animal paintings in the remote depths of primeval caves, made their colours by mixing various earths and soot with animal fat. Broadly, the same process holds good today; oil paint is manufactured by grinding pigments of animal, vegetable, or mineral derivation in oil.

Not, however, until relatively modern times (the fifteenth century in Flanders and Venice) did the medium begin to attain the pre-eminence which it enjoys today. During the last five hundred years or so, it is no exaggeration to say that the vast preponderance of the masterpieces of European painting have been executed in oils. Why have the masters preferred this heavy, viscous substance to the airy, seductive delights of water-colour and pastel, or the crisp brilliance of tempera? There are many reasons: to the contemplative type of mind, which needs long periods of meditation whilst painting a picture, no other medium is so complaisant.

Those who have tried their hands at water-colour, for instance, will know that to break off in the middle of laying a wash usually has fatal results, whereas in oils it is perfectly possible to "break off" for twenty years, should the necessity arise. Again, when creating a major work the artist may, almost assuredly will, at some point, have drastically to re-think and alter some part of his design. To the oil-painter such alterations are a simple matter, as I shall later show, far simpler than, for instance, for the water-colourist, in whose medium any attempt to make major adjustments is courting disaster.

Turning, however, from such obvious practical and technical advantages, there is another less easily apprehended, but nevertheless immensely important factor to be taken into account. It is the mystique which exists between artist and paint. In no other material can the painter enter physically so completely into his painting; the sensuous response of the pigment to the hand is unrivalled. It is impossible to imagine that the tragic grandeur of Rembrandt, the frenzied sun-worship of Van Gogh, the sumptuous opulence of Rubens, could have happened in anything but oils. The flute is a pleasant enough instrument, but it cannot match the organ: to the painter, oil alone can emulate the full, sonorous range of the great cathedral organ. As a teacher, it has been my privilege for some years to encourage and instruct large numbers of amateur painters, and I have constantly found that they have produced more vital, uninhibited paintings, and have enjoyed themselves and expanded their personalities more fully in this rich, big-hearted, pliant medium than any other.

I shall now consider the minimum equipment and materials, in my opinion, necessary to the beginner. In this connexion, I would emphasize the fact that my choice has been influenced by two important factors; first, economy. Painting in oils can be an expensive business, but the following recommendations and suggestions are designed with a view to cutting costs without encouraging the use of bad and unreliable materials. Secondly, I have sought to give information on the preparation of various home-made substitutes for the more expensive require-ments. The chemistry of paint is an esoteric science, upon which a considerable literature exists, written often by professionals for the guidance of their colleagues. Many of these books are admirable for their purpose, and may readily be obtained by those who are interested, but since it is not anticipated that the majority of readers of this book aim particularly to paint pictures which are guaranteed to last for centuries, I have stuck to simple methods which have proved themselves in practice. It may well be that professional purists could find grounds for criticism in the ensuing pages, but for general purposes there is, I hope, little at which to cavil.

Logically, the first consideration would seem to be the type and range of colours required. Most artists' colourmen make oils in two ranges, namely "artists" and "students". The colours in the artists' range are considerably the more expensive, for the good reason that many of them are guaranteed permanent, whereas the students' colours are subject to fading and deterioration in course of time. Charts may be obtained from dealers or manufacturers which show the degree of permanency of the individual colours in the artists' range.

It is assumed that, for the purposes of the amateur at the outset of his career, students' colours will suffice. Later he may reach a degree of proficiency at which he feels that the outlay of money on expensive permanent pigments is justified. Certain useful colours, termed "earth colours", are permanent in either range, and are usually a little cheaper in students' oils, so the latter can safely be used at all times. I recommend, of these earths, Yellow Ochre, Burnt Umber, Burnt

Sienna and Light Red. Lamp Black is another useful standby, which may safely be used in the students' type. Do not buy Ivory Black, which is said to cause cracking when mixed with other colours. It is in the more brilliant colours that the greatest divergence in price between the two ranges occurs, since they have, as previously noted, no guaranteed permanence in the students' type; but some are necessary in order to obtain the full range of colour orchestration, and I have found the following indispensable:

Alizarin Crimson, Cadmium Red, Cadmium Yellow, Ultramarine (sometimes called French Ultramarine) and Viridian. These, together with White, form a basic palette suited to the needs of the beginner. I recommend Titanium White, because it is absolutely "inert", i.e., it does not set up any deleterious chemical action when mixed with any of the other colours. There are two other whites popularly on sale, Flake White and Zinc White. We now have

| | | |
|---|---|---|
| Yellows | — | Yellow Ochre, Cadmium Yellow. |
| Reds | — | Light Red, Alizarin Crimson, Cadmium Red. |
| Blue | — | Ultramarine |
| Browns | — | Burnt Sienna, Burnt Umber. |
| Green | — | Viridian. |
| Black | — | Lamp Black. |
| White | — | Titanium White. |

Thus there are nine colours, plus Black and White, which are perfectly adequate for the needs of the beginner, indeed it is generally conceded by painters and teachers that the fewer the colours used, especially in the early stages, the better. Too wide and exotic a range confuses the student, and often leads to garish and discordant colour. However, with progress, it is possible safely to take into use a few more of the brilliant colours. I suggest

Lemon Yellow.
Cerulean Blue.
Cadmium Orange.
Cobalt Violet.

Cobalt Violet is a poisonous substance, and care should be taken to remove it from the hands after use.

The full range (to be employed only after experience has bred discretion) now totals thirteen colours, plus Black and White, and should be adequate to accomplish the subtlest nuance. I have avoided the mention of certain colours like Chrome Yellow, Chrome Orange and Vermilion, which correspond closely to Cadmium Yellow, Cadmium Orange and Cadmium Red respectively, because they are less permanent. If, however, students' quality colours only are being used, then they may, at a pinch, substitute for the Cadmiums. When working in artists' colours, the Chromes and Vermilion should be avoided. The first thirteen colours listed are all reliable and permanent in the artists' range; I stress this point because there are certain other dangerous colours, e.g. Emerald Green, which turn the Cadmiums, Ultramarine and Vermilion black in a few months if mixed with them in a painting. Whilst the amateur is more probably painting for his own enjoyment than for posterity, it is as well that he should have a basic knowledge of the behaviour of the materials he is using, and it is hoped that the foregoing notes on the properties of the various colours may have supplied that knowledge without seeming too boring and technical.

Paint, like most things sold in tubes, works out cheaper in the larger sizes. When buying White, which is generally needed in much greater quantities than any of the colours, get pound or half-pound tubes. For the rest, the "Studio" tube (a trade name for a fairly large size) is recommended.

Having established an adequate and reliable palette (in this sense "palette" means "range of colours") we shall consider the various substances upon which oil paintings can be executed. There are many of these, ranging from the relatively costly canvas to the sheet of paper with a coat or two of size on it.

*Canvas.* This is a general term applied to various types of strong fabric, such as linen, cotton or hemp covered with some substance or combination of substances, suitable to the application of oil paint, and stretched upon expandable wooden frames known literally as "stretchers". They are the most expensive of all the materials listed in this section, and for that reason are not strongly recommended to the beginner. True, they can be home-made at a relatively small cost, but this is a lengthy and tricky business, and in a note of this nature, addressed to people who have probably neither the time nor inclination for such exercises, I feel it would be superfluous to describe the more involved methods, even if space permitted.

There is, of course, no other surface which has the delightful spring and resilience of canvas, and it can be obtained in a great variety of textures, to suit individual tastes. For those who prefer it to all other materials, here is one suggestion. Old, worthless paintings can often be bought for a song at auctions or from second-hand dealers.

It is bad practice to paint on top of these old canvases, but if one is prepared to rip off the old canvas from its stretcher and then buy a piece of "primed", i.e., prepared, canvas from the local art-shop and fix it to the old stretcher, one has to all intents and purposes, a new canvas for about half the retail price. The piece of canvas purchased should be about three inches longer and three inches wider than the stretcher. Remove the wedges from the inner corners of the stretcher, then

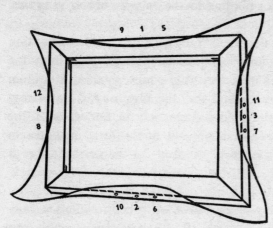

The sequence of tack insertions when
stretching a canvas.

hammer the outer corners together so that the stretcher is its smallest possible size. Then stretch the canvas as tautly as possible over it, securing it to the edges of the stretcher by means of tacks or drawing-pins, at intervals of about four inches. Place your first tack in the middle of one long side, and your second opposite to it, i.e., in the middle of the other long side, stretching the canvas tight between them. Do the same with the two short edges. Then drive tacks outwards towards the corners, working in the same rotation. Now replace the wedges and drive them well home so as to get rid of any rucks in the canvas. Stretchers can, of course, be used repeatedly in this manner.

*Canvas Boards*. These are pieces of primed canvas which have been stretched tightly over, and glued to thick card. They are readily obtainable in various grades and sizes from most dealers, and are fairly inexpensive.

There are also on the market various types of cardboard which have been primed and mechanically stamped so as to give a surface which, to some extent, resembles that of canvas. These are quite cheap and suitable for those who have not time to prepare their own boards.

*Canvas Paper*. Another cheap material, widely on sale. It is ready for use when pinned to a drawing board or other suitable surface. Its chief disadvantages are that it tears rather easily, and has to be fixed in some way to a firm backing before any picture painted on it can be framed.

So much, then, for ready-made goods. The next stage is to consider inexpensive and easy methods whereby panels can be made up at home.

*Hardboard*. This tough and cheap material, easily obtainable from builders' merchants and hardware stores, is the twentieth century's great gift to painters. For small paintings, "off-cuts" can sometimes be had cheaper than the standard rate, but if larger panels are required, a few extra coppers may be charged for cutting them to specific sizes. Or one can buy a biggish piece, and cut panels to size oneself. Hardboard is smooth on one side, and textured on the other. There are at present two types of texture readily available, one of which is rather coarse, and unpleasant to paint on. The other has a much finer grain, closely resembling that of a medium canvas, and takes the paint excellently. Where only the coarser texture

42

is obtainable, it is better to paint on the smooth side, the only drawback being that it is a little slippery.

It must be clearly understood that the board must be sealed before attempting to paint on it, otherwise it will quickly absorb the oil from the pigment, leaving a dull and rather unpleasant surface. The cheapest and easiest method of sealing the surface is to apply three or four coats of size. For this purpose it is reasonably safe to use ordinary packet size of the kind soluble only in hot water. I say "reasonably safe" because manufactured domestic size of this kind may possess certain impurities which could have a deleterious effect on the painting over a very considerable period of time, but for the 'prentice hand it is reliable enough.

I have found that to mix the size in accordance with the directions usually supplied is generally safe enough, but different brands vary slightly in strength, and sometimes one has to arrive at the ideal proportion by trial and error. The golden rule is to add size to water, *not* water to size. Stir it until it is thoroughly mixed and no lumps remain. Now take a fair-sized housepainter's brush and apply the size as thinly and evenly as possible to whichever side, smooth or textured, it is intended to paint on; allow the first coat to dry, then repeat the process until three or four coats have been laid. Once thoroughly dry, the panel is ready for immediate use. A word of warning—do not try to save time and labour by applying one thick coat of size, as this gives a very shiny, slippery surface, and is liable to flake off in course of time. Some artists suggest that the addition of a little finely sifted sand to the size gives a texture or "tooth" if one is obliged to use the smooth side.

To forestall erudite criticism, I will admit that painting on a relatively dark colour like that of hardboard will cause the painting to darken considerably in a century or two. The preparation of white grounds is, however, a complex and exact business, and in any case, most such grounds have to be left to mature for a considerable time before they are safe for use.

*Wood.* Plywood, preferably not less than 4-ply, is quite good, and should be prepared in exactly the same way as hardboard, except that *both* sides of the panel must be sized equally to prevent warping. *Strawboard, Cardboard.* Any thick, strong card may be used. The preparation is the same as for wood. *Paper.* Any strong paper, preferably as roughly surfaced as possible, with a few coats of size on it, will do for practice.

*Metals.* Sheet aluminium is an admirable material, and can be used without any preparation whatever. Authorities recommend that used for car-bodies, but it is possible that the type used in aircraft-construction is unsuitable, owing to the inclusion of other metals in its composition. Copper and zinc have also been extensively used by painters, but require rubbing with coarse sand or emery paper before use as they are very smooth.

Brushes are the next major need. Most painters use hog's-hair brushes for oils. (Sables are also used occasionally, but they are very expensive and not really necessary, so I have ruled them out.) They come usually in three shapes—round, square-ended and filbert-shaped. Preference can be established only by usage, so it is advisable to start with a few of each. Get as many brushes as possible at the outset, and aim to add to them until you possess at least twenty. As to size, the range from size 10 (the largest) to 2 (the smallest) should suffice for most purposes, with a bias in favour of the larger sizes.

Any piece of clean, smooth wood, a sheet of glass or metal, or a large dinner-plate or meat-dish will function quite adequately as a palette. If, however, you can borrow a well-balanced palette, not less than fifteen inches by twelve inches, as a pattern, draw round it on a piece of plywood, and cut out the resulting shape with a fretsaw, taking care to bevel the thumb-hole with a rasp and glass-paper. Rub linseed oil well into it two or three times before use, to prevent absorption. Of course, you may prefer to buy a palette. If so, get one about the size stated above, and rub linseed into it before use.

You will require a palette-knife. Some care is needed here. Get as long and flexible a blade as is available, about ⅜ inch wide at the narrow end, that is, before the rounded tip begins.

Dippers for holding turpentine or linseed oil can be had from dealers, but are not absolutely indispensable, as any small pot or lid will do. Turpentine will be wanted, and should be bought from the chemist, where a purified type may be had at fairly low cost. Do not use crude turpentine or turps-substitute. Linseed oil is hardly ever necessary in my experience, but a little may sometimes be useful. If so, get it from the art-shop. The raw linseed available at hardware and domestic stores can have destructive effects, particularly on the fibre of canvas.

With an easel, our equipment will be complete. This presents a problem, as the better types of easel are expensive. For the smaller paintings usually tackled by beginners, a child's blackboard easel serves very well. Otherwise, with a little ingenuity, a rigid panel such as hardboard or wood can usually be propped upon an old table or chair. Occasionally easels may be had in second-hand shops.

The equipment assembled, the student is ready to do battle. First, the layout of the palette; it is important to have, from the beginning, a permanent orderly system of laying out the colours round the edge of the palette, as one then quickly gets to know the position of each, thus saving time and nervous irritation when working. Opposite are arrangements of colours which I have used for some years.

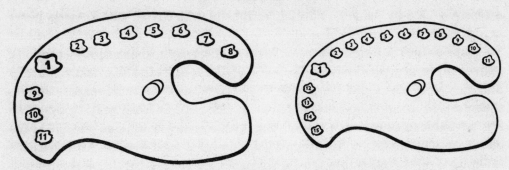

PALETTE LAYOUT: *Left*, Simple; *Right*, Advanced.

*Simple:*—1. Titanium White; 2. Cadmium Yellow; 3. Yellow Ochre; 4. Burnt Umber; 5. Burnt Sienna; 6. Light Red; 7. Cadmium Red; 8. Alizarin Crimson; 9. Lamp Black; 10. French Ultramarine; 11. Viridian.

*Advanced:*—1. Titanium White; 2. Cadmium Orange; 3. Cadmium Yellow; 4. Lemon Yellow; 5. Yellow Ochre; 6. Burnt Umber; 7. Burnt Sienna; 8. Light Red; 9. Cadmium Red; 10. Alizarin Crimson; 11. Cobalt Violet; 12. Lamp Black; 13. French Ultramarine; 14. Cerulean Blue; 15. Viridian.

N.B. In both cases, put out a large amount of White.

In these systems, the yellows, browns, reds, etc., are grouped in orderly fashion, divided into "cold" and "warm" sections, thus defying the pernicious fallacy that painting consists only of a wild orgy of inspiration.

Many people find a dead white ground disconcerting to work on; this trouble can be cured by swilling it over with a very thin wash of Burnt Umber and turps a couple of days before it is taken into use. Most painters make a preliminary drawing on the panel before they actually start painting. One very satisfactory method is to use a small, round brush dipped in a thin mixture of turps and black. Mistakes can be erased by wiping them out with rag and turps. Other artists make their drawing in charcoal, but this must either be "fixed" with charcoal fixative and a spray diffuser or flicked lightly with a rag until all superfluous charcoal is removed. It is possible to draw on white grounds with pencil, but the paint is said to flake off where there is pencil under it in course of time. Whether one should, when using charcoal, or the thinned paint method, make a drawing in full light and shade, or merely in outline is debatable, but I am inclined to favour the former approach, as it develops the sense of the third dimension from the outset. Certainly one should stick to outline only if using pencil, for the reasons stated above.

Having established the drawing, the "moment of truth" is upon us; we commence to paint. In oil-painting, each time a change of colour is necessary, one has to take a fresh, clean brush—hence the plea for a large number of brushes. Should this be impossible, plunge each brush into turps after use, and then wipe it well with rag. Always paint with the largest brush you can control, as this makes for broad painting and lessens the danger of fussy, finicking detail.

It is hardly ever possible to use the "straight" colours as they come from the tubes; they must be mixed together to obtain the desired effects, and avoid glaring crudity. This mixing is done in the middle portion of the palette, and as a general rule it is dangerous to use more than three colours in any one mixture, as promiscuous mingling of many colours inevitably leads to dull, muddy results. Oil paint being a solid, opaque medium, the white is used to lighten the colours as required, hence the larger amount of white usually required. As supplied in tubes, the paint usually contains a great deal of oil, and in my experience, it is never necessary to thin it with turps or linseed; indeed, it is usually very difficult to get the beginner to lay it on with any degree of confidence, the initial tendency being to try to use it as thinly as water-colour. The general rule for the inexperienced is to lay the paint on in a solid layer (this does not mean "thick" in the real sense, as I shall show later), rather than to scrub frantically with the brush, which only produces a thin and feeble stain. Think of the way you like your bread-and-butter, and remember, no "bread-and-scrape". Above all, do not be mean with the paint; put plenty out on the palette at the start.

Some teachers advocate a method of brushing in the whole picture in a thin mixture of turps and colours in the first hour or so to cover up the white ground and establish a unity, but if you have previously stained the canvas with Burnt Umber, this cuts down the glare of the white and automatically creates a certain tonal unity. It is advisable to have your thinnest paint on the dark areas of the picture, and your thickest on the lights. There are excellent reasons for this traditional method, one being that oil-paint tends to lose its opacity with age, and thus the white ground (if you are using one) increasingly glows through the thin darks, making them more luminous. The lights in good painting should, of course, be luminous anyway, and the reason for painting them thickly is to create a rugged surface of many tiny facets, which will reflect light at various angles and give a scintillating, vibrant effect. This procedure of painting the lights thickly is technically known as "impasto", and is nowhere more superbly demonstrated than in the work of Rembrandt. I recommend particularly a study of his small "Bathing Woman" (National Gallery) which illustrates to perfection the magnificent tactile possibilities of the medium in the hands of genius.

Unless the student is going to paint his picture in one layer only (an admirable procedure, but beyond the scope of most), the golden rule is "fat on lean", meaning that the paint should be laid on relatively thinly in the early stages, and gradually built up to the final passages of rich impasto. If at some stage, an alteration has to be made, the safest way is to take the palette-knife, scrape down the paint until the surface of the panel or canvas is reached, and then repaint.

In building up a really heavy impasto, I mean $\frac{1}{8}$ inch or more in thickness, many painters lay the paint on with the palette-knife, in fact whole pictures are sometimes painted with the knife. A good, long, flexible blade, such as previously described, can, with practice, be made to obey the hand as readily as the brush. The method is of particular value to those who find difficulty in achieving sufficient surface richness and variety, or "quality" as painters term it, when using brushes. This does not postulate that, in knife-work, the paint layer must be of an all-over, uniform thickness, which would be monotonous, and is technically frowned upon; but it does mean that both thick and thin areas can be more generously and courageously applied by inexperienced hands than is possible with the parsimonius brush.

When using the knife, it should be wiped clean with rag each time a change of colour is needed, which leads to cleaner and fresher colour than that obtained when using a few brushes, which soon become saturated with paint. Text-books state that Cobalt Violet should never be used with a steel knife, as a chemical action is set up which turns the colour black, but I have never seen this happen; the authorities suggest that a bone or ivory knife be used. Dealers stock special "painting-knives", but I have never found them really necessary.

When using the knife care should be exercised to develop a natural, spontaneous handling. Too many painters fall into a mannered method of coarse, parallel stripes of paint, which gives an unpleasantly crude appearance to the work.

Many beginners have asked me: "which is the best way to put the paint on?" meaning that they want a recipe for some method of spots or squares or parallel lines of paint which will automatically produce good results. The answer is that painting is not cookery, rather it resembles handwriting, and each individual must develop his own style by frequent practice.

Finally, some hints on the care and maintenance of tools. Brushes should be thoroughly cleaned after each session, or they will speedily become hard and useless. First wash them in turps and squeeze out all superfluous paint. Then take a bar of household soap and water, warm if you wish, but not hot, as this loosens the bristles. Rub the brush in the soap and then in the palm of the hand, working up a lather. Repeat the action until the lather comes white, and there is no paint visible on the brush, particularly where it enters the ferrule. If, for some reason, it is impossible to wash brushes immediately after use, stand them head down in a jar of turps, paraffin or water. This will prevent the paint from hardening in them until they can be cleaned.

Palettes should be scraped clean with the knife after use, and thoroughly rubbed with rag and linseed. This produces a splendid polish after a few applications. If the palette is to be used the next day, it is safe and economical to leave the paint on it, cleaning only the mixing area, but never leave it until the paint hardens and cakes. If you do, the palette will become heavy and unbalanced, and the old paint will make for dirty colour-mixing. Unused paint may be preserved for a time by scraping it into a flat tin and covering it with water. When required, pour off the water and replace the paint on the palette. A neglected palette which has become heavily encrusted with old, hard paint may be cleaned by the somewhat drastic-sounding method of pouring turps or paraffin on to it, setting it alight, and then rapidly scraping off the paint with the palette knife. Always clean the dipper thoroughly at the end of the session.

Outdoor sketching in oils, while delightful, presents certain problems. It is difficult to work without some sort of easel if one wishes to do anything on a largish scale. For small work, there are plenty of paint-boxes on sale, the lids of which are fitted to hold panels. These lids have an attachment which fixes them firmly open at a correct angle, and the box is rested on the knees while painting. Of course, this can only be done when seated, and a camp-stool or similar contrivance must be carried. If you wish to stand (and this is always best, indoors or out, since it allows you to step back and see the work from the proper viewing distance) I know of no cheap alternative to an easel.

There are many types of sketching easels on the market, some of which are contraptions so ingenious that they defy attempts to erect them, and frequently close on the fingers with rat-trap ferocity. Choose then, the simplest and strongest looking one you can get, making sure that it will hold securely at top and bottom, a fair-sized panel, and that its legs are fitted with spikes to push into the ground. In high wind, fasten a brick or heavy stone to a piece of strong string and tie the other end to the apex of the easel; this prevents it from becoming airborne.

The transport of wet painting is something of a nightmare if you are dependent on public vehicles (of course, a car, or better still, a shooting-brake, solves all these problems. You can sit inside the latter and paint, defying even English weather). There is, however, a device called a "canvas-pin" which is very useful and ingenious. It is, in effect, a cork with spikes projecting from each end. Two panels or canvases of the same size can be fastened together, face inwards, with four of these pins, one at each corner, thus preventing them from smearing fellow-passengers, and at the same time shielding their author from the gratuitous and often ribald comments of the vulgar.

These notes have been penned expressly to help the embryo painter over technical snags, and may, I fear, make somewhat arid reading—it is difficult to be lyrical about, for instance, the cleaning of brushes. I have hardly touched upon the glorious feeling of satisfaction and fulfilment which, if boldly and generously handled, this wonderful medium can afford to its friends.

**THE ADORATION OF THE SHEPHERDS**    Rembrandt van Rijn (1606–69)

In the art of the Dutch master the technique of oil painting reaches perfection. No other painter has used this rich medium with a more sympathetic feeling for its warm and yielding plasticity. The richness of his *impasto* and the contrast of rough and smooth passages; the dramatic organization of light and dark; the simplicity of his conception and a profound sense of the dignity of humanity, combine to produce a glory without parallel in the history of European painting. In this picture, full of tenderness, the master displays the whole range of his genius.

*Right:* **DYLAN THOMAS**
**Augustus John (born 1878)**

Painted when the poet was a young
man, John's portrait is a magnificent
example of the way in which a subtle
and imaginative portraitist can combine a personal likeness with an
idealized and symbolic conception.
Here is a portrait, not only of Dylan
Thomas, but also of the poet archetype; ethereal, romantic, wild. The
tousled hair and dashing scarf symbolize a Byronic flaunting of the
conventional; the wide eyes, the
faculty of vision; and the long, oval
face, and high brow, the aspiration
to transcend the crudeness of mere
fleshly existence. Yet the full, sensuous
mouth, and bulbous nose, betray the
love of earthly pleasures. Here is the
eternal struggle between the seduc-
tions of the world and the transcendent fires of genius.

**FRANCOISE VAN WASSERHOVEN**
**Rembrandt van Rijn (1606–69)**

Here is a portrait both of a particular
person, and of a universal phenomenon: in this case, the ravages of
old age. The power to penetrate the
mask of personality, and to divine,
beyond the individual, qualities, and
characteristics which are common to
all humanity, has always hall-marked
the great portraitist. In an age when
so much trash flows from the flattering and obsequious brushes of society
and official portrait painters, it is
important that the student should
learn to distinguish between shallow
and transient rubbish, and portrait
painting such as this, which communicates a profound message.

CHAPTER 4

# Choosing a Subject

## *by Colin Moss*

THE late John Minton once confessed that he used to spend hours sitting in his studio, wondering what on earth to paint. If Minton, a professional and prolific painter, suffered from this dilemma, how much more deeply must it affect the beginner, courageously sailing into a completely uncharted sea?

In painting, as in life, success depends very largely upon knowing what you want to do. In the ensuing pages, a variety of suggestions for choice and treatment of subject will be made, in the hope that, from them, the reader will be able to decide what sort of a painter he wants to become. Before commencing there is, however, one word of warning which cannot be stressed too strongly. It is this—don't copy other people's paintings: all too often, I have seen amateurs, with the best of intentions, laboriously making copies of paintings which, in themselves, have already been done once too often. It is true that professional painters often do make copies of the works of the masters, usually for the purpose of learning their technical procedure (See Chapter 14 "Technique and Style") but for the amateur, working without the guidance of an experienced teacher, this is usually a disastrous and stultifying practice.

As a useful jumping-off point I propose to make the generalization that people who paint usually divide themselves into two categories. They are, first, those who like to paint from objects which they have before them at the time—the Realists—and second, those who find that they can express themselves better when dealing with imagined, or remembered things. Like all generalizations, this can, of course, be contradicted in detail, but it will serve well enough for a start.

For Realists, at the outset of their careers, no subject can be more useful than the often despised but, in fact, intensely fascinating, Still Life. I am well aware that these words will conjure up in the minds of many readers a vision of dusty pots and pans, surrounded by decaying fruit and artificial flowers, but a stroll round the National or the Tate Gallery to see what some of the greatest masters have made of such humble bric-à-brac will instantly dispel this melancholy fallacy. I recommend especially Van Gogh's "Chair" and "Sunflowers" (Tate Gallery), the still life in Manet's "Bar aux Folies Bergeres" (Tate Gallery) and Courbet's "Apple and Pomegranates" (National Gallery) in this context. (Facing page 152).

Still life painting presents many advantages, not the least being that, once the group is assembled, it is there for as long as it is required. Decaying fruit, flowers and so forth can easily be replaced, and there is the added priceless boon that this form of painting can be done indoors, in warmth and comfort, during the winter months. However, it is important, at this juncture to plant in the mind of the student that such exotic—and expensive—things as orchids, peaches, cut glass and velvet are not the only possible subjects for the still life painter. Let us poke our noses into the attic, the lumber-room or the tool-shed, and see what treasures we can salvage. Bottles, for instance—wine, beer or spirit—are worth their weight in gold. The tall, slim elegance of the hock bottle; the vital statistics of the Chianti, with its straw skirt; even the honest British take-me-or-leave-me beer bottle, can, to the eye of a painter who loves them, appear as lustrous as the Crown Jewels. The sordid debris of Christmas parties and other celebrations takes on a new significance in the eyes of the still life addict, though let me hasten to add that, if I am offending the susceptibilities of some of my readers, plenty of non-alcoholic beverages are marketed in attractive bottles, and "empties" can usually be had for a song from the wine merchant.

Old, discarded kitchen utensils also take on a new lease of life. Earthenware pots, glazed or unglazed, cracked plates, dishes and other crockery, furnish a selection of shapes and surface textures of endless beauty and variety. Old, tarnished metal objects—lamps, candle-sticks, pewter mugs, anything bronze, brass or copper (but not, please not, chromium-plated) which have long ceased to serve their original purpose—are "musts" for our collection. Worn out gardening boots, the straw hat from that Italian holiday, the canvas from an old deck-chair, all these relics of forgotten summers can again be pressed into service. All old curtains, bedspreads, shirts, skirts and other fabrics must be seen anew, with a sympathetic regard for their colours, patterns and textures. Baskets, hampers and all objects of a like nature that have seen their day are potential still life; the stuffed owl or trout, in their glass prisons, may live again. In short, the still life painter must sedulously cultivate a "magpie" complex.

So far, I have dealt only with inorganic matter, but my study of still life has convinced me that, fascinating as it is, it cannot provide the maximum stimulus unless something which is, or has been alive, is added. This opinion is substantiated in the work of the old Dutch still life painters of the seventeenth and eighteenth centuries, who almost always included fish, fruit, vegetables, flowers, dead game and so forth in their paintings.

Dead fish are not considered beautiful by conventional people. Here I want to lay special emphasis on the suggestion that still life painting offers a splendid opportunity to the painter of originality to unearth the unsuspected loveliness of commonplace or even superficially repulsive things. Anyone who has ever really looked at a fishmonger's slab with a painter's eye, cannot fail to be moved by the sheen on the side of a humble bloater, the rich russet and gold of a kipper. These will provide a splendid centrepiece for your still life if your pocket does not run to the scarlet and silver magnificence of lobster, trout and salmon: and furthermore, if you choose your weather and paint quickly, you can still enjoy them for breakfast the next day.

To carry the analogy still further, I have seen an excellent still life of which the central feature was a pig's head. The greengrocer's or vegetable market is another rich field in our search for still life; better still, your own garden, if you grow vegetables, for you will get them fresher. Cabbages (red or green), cauliflower, leeks, tomatoes, turnips, parsnips, carrots, red and green peppers, maizecobs, onions, will make a superb blaze of colour on a kitchen table—even the potato served Van Gogh. Many vegetables will keep for a long time, which is an added advantage.

Most of us eat poultry and small game from time to time, and since these are none the worse for hanging, a quick painting can often be made. Naturally, birds are best unplucked, and the sheen on the feathers of a good cock pheasant is as appetizing to a painter's eye as is its flesh to his palate. Fruit and flowers are the most usual properties of the still life painter, and I will not dilate upon their obvious charms beyond a warning against the use of artificial flowers and ersatz fruit. (Yes, I know Cézanne used paper flowers, but in this connexion he merely provides the eternal, exasperating exception which proves the rule).

I have occasionally seen provocative subjects like Guy Fawkes masks, dolls and musical instruments used with success and originality, but am chary of recommending them too highly, as they can all too easily give a distasteful flavour of sentimentality and whimsy to the work.

So much for the usual, still life "group" which is normally arranged on a table or sideboard. There are, however, many less conventional ways of treating this subject. The keen amateur of still life should always be keenly watchful for what might be called the "ready-made" subject. John Bratby, the brilliant young social realist painter, has shown great ingenuity in this way; many of his pictures are largely concerned with the seemingly unpremeditated debris which occurs on the breakfast table in his kitchen, when the meal is over. Packets of cereals, teapots, cups, cutlery, loaves of bread, cigarette packages and the like, sprawl across his canvas with an unrivalled effect of vitality and reality. He has gone further and made fascinating still lives from such apparently unpromising material as the interior of the bathroom, the bicycle in the passage, even the dust-bins in the backyard.

I would suggest, that, contrary to the gloomy prognostications of our friends the psychiatrists, the reader goes and sees something *nice* in the woodshed. An old, broken wheelbarrow, a few upturned flowerpots, garden tools, a carpenter's bench, all these undignified trivia, will blossom amazingly on the canvas under the gaze of the sensitive and sympathetic eye.

In my next section I propose to write about the treatment of the human figure (to the exclusion of portraiture, which is covered in Chapter Seven) or Figure Composition, as it is often called by painters. It is sometimes possible to make such a picture quickly from life, e.g., a group of card players will often sit more or less static for several hours and by a synthesis of straight-forward observation and memory lively results may be obtained. Such opportunities are naturally limited, and more usually subjects pertaining to group activities have to be compounded from a combination of sketchbook notes and memory.

Since I am catering here for the type of student who likes to paint what he sees on the spot, and therefore has in all probability, a weak visual memory, I shall furnish a number of hints which I have found useful in tackling figure composition. The use of sketchbooks has been noted elsewhere, and cannot be too strongly stressed; another device which can be of service, if used with discretion, is of course, the camera. It was frequently employed by no less a painter than Sickert, and to a certain degree by Degas, which is a convincing refutation of the idea that to use photographs is cheating. I say "use" advisedly, since the mere slavish *copying* in detail of a photograph with the addition of a little superficial colour is a tedious mechanical operation, which can be much more quickly and easily accomplished by the use of a colour film.

I am suggesting that the photograph may serve as the basic idea and inspiration for a picture; for instance, those holiday "snaps" taken when the subjects are unaware, and are acting spontaneously and unselfconsciously, will often furnish the germs of ideas for the grouping and relationship of figures to each other, and inform us about natural attitudes and gestures, clothing and so forth. Of course, the posed "group" photograph with folded arms and dentifrice smiles, has no value from the painter's standpoint. Many professional painters take photographs of their subjects for future reference, sometimes in conjunction with sketches, at others when the use of a sketchbook is not practicable. Others will draw their inspiration from the thousands of photographs published in newspapers and periodicals. Finally, I would earnestly counsel moderation in the use of the camera—it is a good servant, but a bad master, and should be employed only when other means of gaining information fail.

Another important aspect of the realist or literal-minded painter's attitude towards figure composition is that he should stick to subjects of which he has personal experience. Thus he will enhance the conviction and reality of his work and avoid the pitfall of seeing his subject second-hand, through other people's eyes. The type who works best under the stimulus of imagination may well get results in this way, but not so the out and out realist; for example a city worker, let us say a bank clerk of the realist cast of mind, would experience great difficulty in visualizing convincingly such a subject as agricultural labourers working in a harvest field and would require very extensive and probably unobtainable sketchbook data before he could make any progress, whereas a city street scene or the interior of a restaurant or bus would be within his daily experience, thus giving greater ease of conception and more plausible results.

There is one other aspect of figure work which has been so important an inspiration in Western art that it cannot possibly be ignored in a chapter of this nature: I mean, of course, the nude. The mention of this cabbalistic word is apt to conjure up all kinds of Freudian complexes and taboos, but that is, of course, entirely a matter for the judgment of the reader, and outside of my province. I would, however, draw attention to the masterly essays in this genre by such men as Rubens, Degas, Renoir, and our own Richard Sickert and Matthew Smith. These painters have seen the nude in an entirely robust and healthy way, which is closely allied to the obvious, innocent enjoyment with which they have portrayed a bowl of ripe fruit or a bouquet of fine flowers. Considered in this way, the nude becomes as impersonal a subject as any other still life, and I hold the opinion that groups or clubs of amateurs can derive great benefit from getting together and drawing or painting from a professional model. Wherever possible, I think a nude should be painted in a normal everyday interior, avoiding the artificial "studio pose" flavour which so many professionals give to their paintings of the subject. (See picture facing page 152).

The English have never produced a great interpreter of the nude; but with our notable eccentricity we have displayed commendable enthusiasm and industry in painting horses, dogs, bulls, and other animals in a state of nature. This amiable foible (or ridiculous sentimentalism—according to your personal prejudice) is well worth exploiting in terms of paint. Cats, dogs, rabbits, budgerigars and similar pets kept by townsfolk make excellent subject matter for sketching and painting, provided that you have plenty of time and patience, and above all that they are not prettied-up and sentimentalized until they look like the hackneyed versions of kittens sitting in slippers, dogs with spectacles on, which are the stock-in-trade of vendors of birthday cards and calendars.

Country dwellers have a great advantage here. A fine horse or bull, a turkey or cockerel is a subject fit to arouse any painter's enthusiasm. There is, however, always the valid objection that they will not keep still and a good deal of practice in draughtsmanship is necessary before this difficulty can be overcome. The only alternative for the beginner is the museum. This has its disadvantages in that the moth-eaten and melancholy stuffed beasts, with their glassy stares, too often look embarrassingly dead. Despite this I have seen some very lively interpretations of museum animals by enthusiastic amateurs who have shown great ingenuity in injecting life into their models, and concocting imaginary settings for them.

Landscape painting has been exhaustively dealt with elsewhere in these pages, and requires no further comment so I propose to pass directly to consideration of the problems of those painters who rely chiefly upon their imagination or inner life for their inspiration. Their task is to communicate their daydreams and fantasies, the vision of the inner eye, rather than the physical, tangible subject-matter required by realists. In modern times, painters of the Surrealist school like Dali and Delvaux have explored the possibilities of this sort of painting, as also have Chirico and Chagall. Going further back, we have the Flemings, Bosch, and Brueghel, and the Englishman William Blake, whose famous and extraordinary drawing "The Ghost of a Flea" is a remarkable and extreme example of the power of imaginative vision. It is no mere chance that Blake was also a considerable poet: this is a useful pointer for beginners—those who have a taste for the verses of Blake and the metaphysical poets may well find that their bent in the visual arts is of a parallel kind. (See pictures facing page 80 and between pages 152–153).

There is one obvious practical advantage which immediately presents itself to painters in this category: they have no need always to be planted before a landscape, still life, or model, while at work, although I must hasten to make clear that sketches and observation of physical phenomena may often be required to reinforce the original imaginative idea. The convenience and comfort of just sitting down to paint anything that comes into your head is very tempting and must not, on any account, be allowed to influence the reader in his choice of subject. Only those who have a really powerful urge to paint pictures of a visionary type should attempt them, otherwise failure and disappointment is certain.

I have sought to show that there is a very distinct connexion between painting and literature in the minds of the type of artists now under discussion, and that many of them have drawn their themes from books, plays, poetry and the like. Blake for example, drew extensively upon Dante's *Inferno* for his subject matter and Bosch and Brueghel upon traditional Flemish folk-lore and legends. Delacroix often illustrated the plays of Shakespeare, and the Bible has furnished pictorial matter for endless painters. There is, of course, a vast gulf between such activities and the prolific rash of vulgar illustrations to science-fiction, crime and other horrors prevalent in those contemporary publications paradoxically termed "horror-comics" as my reader will be very well aware. Let us, however, as a beginning, follow the example of Delacroix and con the tragedies of Shakespeare, whose protean imagination furnishes a bottomless supply of stimulating images. I call to mind a passage from "King Lear" (Act III, Scene 2) which goes:

> "Blow, winds and crack your cheeks!
> Rage! Blow!
> You cataracts and hurricanœs, spout
> Till you have drench'd our steeples, drown'd the cocks!
> You sulphurous and thought-executing fires,
> Vaunt-couriers to oak-cleaving thunderbolts,
> Singe my white head! and thou, all-shaking thunder,
> Smite flat the thick rotundity o' the world!
> Crack nature's moulds, all germens spill at once. . . ."

These few lines are so rich with imagery that they could furnish an unlimited variety of interpretation to the painter gifted with a poetic vision. If your taste runs to modern verse, T. S. Eliot's "The Waste Land" will provide splendid material. Virgil, Homer, and other great poets of antiquity will appeal to the classical scholar, while the housewife may find her subject in the nursery rhymes, fairy-tales and traditional songs and legends so dear to her children. It is essential to the "dreamer-painter" that he should, by some means, be transported out of the mundane surroundings of his ordinary, everyday life and move into regions of time and space which he cannot possibly enter physically, and a scene from a play written 2,500 years ago and set in Greece may well give just the necessary stimulus.

The ultimate end of this kind of imaginative quest is, of course, the world of dreams which we all enter in sleep. It is not my purpose here to indulge in speculation upon the psychological implications and interpretations of these dreams, but simply and gratefully to accept them as subject-matter. In dreams, we are able, with consummate ease, to escape from the common sense, material factors, which largely govern our waking lives, into a world created solely by our own imaginations, so that we have, ready-made, passports to Parnassus.

It is often said that one does not dream in colour, but my personal experience, and that of several painters whom I have consulted, is quite in contradiction to this idea. One very important point in connexion with painting dreams is that they must be done as soon as possible after they actually occur, otherwise the first vivid memory is apt to fade. If, for practical reasons, it is impossible to capture your dream in paint during the ensuing day or two, the next best thing is to follow the orthodox psychiatric practice, and to set them down as fully as you can in a notebook kept by the bedside.

So far, we have been dealing with the dyed-in-the-wool Romantic, who feels an ungovernable urge, when painting, to escape from his usual workaday world into the realm of pure imagination. There is, however, an intermediate type of artist, who likes to paint, by a process compounded partly of memory, partly of imagination, subjects and situations of which he has had actual, personal experience.

Samuel Palmer, a follower of Blake, is an excellent example of this type. His lyrical little landscapes, painted in the environment of Shoreham (Kent) strike a beautiful balance between reality and dream. Another such painter is Marc Chagall, who though he has lived nearly all his adult life in Paris, draws largely upon his childhood memories of Czarist Russia for his tender, charming paintings. Looking at it from another angle a painter possessing this kind of compound vision may be able to convey from memory a vividly convincing impression of a moonlit landscape (Palmer often did this), a thunderstorm, or a firework display, which for obvious, practical reasons could not possibly be set down on the spot.

This release from the shackles of realism can be achieved in various ways. Take, for instance, the question of colour; we all know that there is no such thing as a blue horse or cow, but if, for some emotional, symbolic or aesthetic reason your imaginative painter feels a compulsion to have a blue horse in his picture, he should have it without hesitation. The effort of will necessary to make such an unconventional statement in paint is no easy matter for many adults, but it is a commonplace in the art of children.

Today, child art is highly esteemed, and is frequently exhibited. A visit to any such exhibition will open the eyes of the adult beginner setting a course in the direction of imaginative painting, by forcibly demonstrating to him the liberties which can be taken with factual realism. Children are never hindered by such considerations as scale and proportion, and will unhesitatingly make a cat bigger than a house if, by so doing, the message of the picture is more forcefully conveyed. Very often, people who take up painting late in life unconsciously retain this childlike innocence and directness of vision, outstanding examples of recent times being Henri (le Douanier) Rousseau and Grandma Moses. (Facing page 129).

Sometimes, a word, title or phrase will work upon the imagination, and

Let us poke our noses into the attic, the lumber room or the tool shed and see what treasures we can salvage . . .

produce an idea for a picture. Such fragments of speech as "the Jungle", "the Desert" or "Underwater" will immediately conjure up numberless visionary worlds in the minds of romantics who have never visited such places in reality. To push the analogy further, I have seen the most extraordinary and evocative abstract paintings produced under the compulsion of titles like "Toothache" or "Bells Ringing".

It is, as will be readily realized, impossible, in the space available, to list in detail the thousands of subjects and ways of treating them that exist. What is to be hoped is that the foregoing suggestions will set the reader's mind to work. Once that is accomplished, the imagination feeds upon itself, and if kept in motion, will never cease to provide material.

# CHAPTER 5

# How to Paint Landscape in Oils

## by R. O. Dunlop, R.A.

O IL PAINTING is not the most difficult of media, in fact I have always found it much easier than painting in water-colours. It is probably the extra expense involved in oil painting, combined with its messiness and the more cumbersome equipment needed, which makes most beginners prefer the very difficult medium of water-colours. To name but a few of the advantages of using oil paints, first, you do not have to wait for your paint to dry; second, you can put on the full strength of colour and tone immediately—you do not have to work out to a final result from light tints. And third, you can paint out-of-doors under almost any conditions, as your medium can stand up to the weather much better than the more fragile water-colour on paper.

The *materials* of oil painting and their use will be dealt with in a separate chapter and I need not, therefore, dwell on these aspects, but will try to give an idea of the mental outlook that the would-be landscape painter in oils should cultivate.

It is all a question of *seeing*. Seeing life or nature in terms of the medium you are going to use—in this case, oil paint applied to canvas. You have to begin by storing up hundreds of pictorial images, and for this purpose you need constantly with you a small sketchbook or notebook. You have to begin to really *see* things, not for their practical, everyday value or use, but just as shapes of a certain colour, forming patterns and designs.

You often hear people say that they can see things clearly, but cannot put them down. This is rubbish; if you do see clearly a line or a shape, or can register the exact colour of an object, you will be able to express it. If you find you cannot do so, it is because you have not really *seen* it—it is just a vague, muddled impression, not a clear, precise image—in this case, a pictorial image.

So it all comes to this, that the painter must be someone who *sees* life pictorially, rather than through ideas or practical usefulness. It is the clearly realized shape of one thing against another, of their related colour harmony, giving an overall pleasing pattern, which makes the creator of pictures.

Although I am chiefly concerned here with landscape painting, I must say that it is not wise to plunge straight away into landscape painting from scratch, as it were. I strongly advise beginning with still life observations. Take your breakfast table, for instance; observe intensely the exact shape and colour of the egg as it rests in the egg-cup. Relate this shape to the saucer, the spoon, the nearby milk jug, butter dish, teapot and so forth. Get your sketchbook out, outline your picture space (that is the oblong into which you are going to compose your subject) then draw simply, and without hesitation, the various objects in relation. After you have made dozens of these studies, make notes as to the colour schemes involved, noticing the grouping of, say, the whites and off-whites as related to the more positive colours, keeping in mind that you are composing a picture, making a pattern-relationship.

After you have given yourself a fairly intensive course of observation treatment with simple still life objects, then you can take yourself out-of-doors and begin to look at fields, trees, hills, sky, and the buildings, animals and so on related to them. It is not easy to get things into scale at first. Huge groups of trees will only represent a few inches on your canvas, and this reducing of things will involve a certain rough and ready conception of perspective.

Perspective can be resolved into a simple idea. Wherever you are sitting or standing in a landscape, if you look straight in front of you, the level of your eyes will denote what is known as the eye-line. Everything above this eye-line will tend to slant down towards the point where you are looking, and everything beneath the eye-line will slant up towards it. (See Chapter 12).

In order to help the beginner in selecting compositions in nature, it is a good idea to carry with you a view-finder. This can easily be made by cutting a rectangular space from a piece of cardboard, in proportion to the size of your canvas; just a small affair of a few inches that you can carry in your pocket or handbag. You can then put this up to the view you think will make a composition and, by shutting one eye and looking through the aperture, you will see how the various masses of trees or buildings co-ordinate with the land and sky to make a pleasing relationship, and it will help you plan out your masses on the canvas. Remember not to make things too equal—for instance, the amount of sky as opposed to land should not equally divide the canvas, or the foreground be of the exact dimensions of the middle distance. It is the same with tree groupings; one half of the picture space should balance the other half, not by equal spacing, but by one heavy mass balancing a smaller, though perhaps more strongly coloured, shape on the other side.

I am very loath to lay down rules, as I am all too conscious that these are only made to be broken, but there is one thing I do feel rather strongly about, and that is the advantage of standing up when painting landscapes. If you sit down, and it is extraordinary how many people seem to prefer sitting down, you are right on top of your work and cannot get away from it; your nose is on the grindstone, as it were, so that you tend to lose the magnitude of vision and the large sweep of the general rhythm and get niggardly, fussy work. If you are standing up there can be a constant slight movement between yourself and the canvas, you can let your arm move in a bigger sweep, and by stepping back and half closing your eyes you can get the rhythms and masses of opposing shapes and colours in a far more vital way than when sitting down.

I think it is fairly obvious from what I have already said, that in selecting a subject for painting out-of-doors, it is not the actual objects themselves, such as an old bridge, or a picturesque cottage, a church, or a windmill, that should be selected, but a subject where the shapes and colourings go together, form a rhythm and a pattern, in other words, compose themselves into a picture. The first essential is, of course, that you should really love the scene, you should feel *emotional* about it, not just lukewarm; it should give you a pictorial thrill. It does not matter if you have to tramp around for hours looking, and looking, and hoping—at last you will strike a subject that gives you the essential aesthetic thrill, then hold on to that, whatever happens, for then you have really seen something that you feel can be re-expressed in terms of oil paint on canvas. That is your job; it will probably take some little time to gain the necessary experience to be able to translate what you have seen, but it is astonishing how quickly the ability comes once you have started *seeing*.

## TECHNIQUES

As Kipling said, there are a hundred different ways of composing tribal lays, and every single one of them is right. So it is with oil-painting techniques, which range from the Old Master glazing styles, through all the phases of impressionism, pointillism, post-impressionism and so on, down to what is called action-painting at the moment. It is a case of finding the particular technique that expresses your particular personality and pictorial vision. This can only be found by experimenting.

When you begin, try all kinds of methods—paint with hog-hair brushes, then have a go at using sable brushes, or wield the palette knife with thick paint straight from the tube. You will soon discover the particular set of tools and the particular range of colours that seem to fit in with your ideas and visions. As regards the colours, it is as well to keep these to as few in number as possible and avoid such strong fugitive colours as Chrome Yellow or Prussian Blue. But of course, there are some who just adore these two dangerous colours and insist on using them at every opportunity, and finally they master them, or else are mastered by them.

I have found that when using sable brushes, one needs more "medium" with the paint than when using hog-hair; a combination of three parts turpentine to one of mastic varnish is a good mixture for the sable brush technique.

For many years I used to rough in the subject loosely with plenty of artist's rectified turpentine and then, when dry, start repainting from top to bottom entirely with the palette knife, using paint out of the tube without any medium. I found a steel knife, not trowel-shaped, about eight inches long, with a rounded end, the best type, and I also learned that it was a good idea to allow a certain amount of paint to accumulate towards the handle of the knife, only cleaning off down to the steel about two inches from the top. This seems to give a weight and balance which keeps the tool from being *too* pliable and if any incisive drawing is needed, it can be done by using the tip of the knife only. There is no doubt that, for certain brilliant effects, where clean, sharp, impressionist colour is needed, the palette knife is an excellent instrument, but where flowing or calligraphic effects are required, a sable brush cannot be beaten.

As I have said, it is all a question of finding out by trial and error which tools and techniques are the right ones for expressing your own particular outlook. Nowadays there are no hard and fast rules, a fact which gives great joy to the beginner, since he can splash about to his heart's content without feeling any inhibitions; after all, the quality needed most for those who wish to gain the enjoyment of self-expression through painting, is *courage*. Courage not only to *see* for yourself, but to take no notice of what anybody else says and to just get on with it in your own way.

Colour is one of the aspects of painting that is entirely personal and really cannot be taught. One can teach drawing in the sense of indicating the actual delineation of things, but colour is so much a question of emotion and eyesight, which is wrapped up so intimately with the psychology of the individual, that very little can be said about it by the teacher.

Nowadays colour is often divided into realistic colour and symbolic colour. Van Gogh and Gauguin come to mind as examples of artists who were often inclined to use colour symbolically rather than realistically. There is, of course, no reason on earth why the artist should not paint trees scarlet or horses blue if he feels them that way. The delightful animal paintings of Franz Marc come to mind in this connexion, as also the tremulous, delightful colour schemes of Chagall. So do not think it necessary always to paint your grass green or your sky blue. As a matter of fact, in nature one gets such a variety that even the inventions of the symbolists are dwarfed. (See Chapter 17—Modern Art: Synthétism).

In arranging your colours on the palette, it is wise to treat them in a very definite order, starting, say, on the left hand side with your white (by the way, Titanium White is nowadays the best white oil colour to use) then going through your light yellows and browns until you come to the darkest colours on the right hand side. If you keep these in the same order, you will instinctively know where to put your brushes and will avoid that terrible anathema—a muddled palette.

It is wise to squeeze out far more paint than you *think* you will need. It pays to be generous with your colour, a stingy palette has been responsible for thousands of bad paintings.

### DIVIDING THE PICTURE SPACE

In landscapes, the earth part of the picture can be divided into three parts, namely foreground, middle distance and background. In the foreground, the shapes and the colours are more clearly defined as a rule, and put in with the greatest degree of assertiveness. The foreground colours, for instance, are the nearest to what are known as "local" colours, that is red, yellow and blue, as seen without any admixture of tonality or grey. As you proceed into the landscape, the air and atmosphere pervading everything gives what is known as an "aerial" perspective to the scene—in other words, the colours become more subtle and have varying degrees of grey (warm grey or cool grey) intermixed with them, as you proceed to the distance. Dramatic instances of this aerial perspective are the violets, purples and blues of hills near the horizon.

Just as the land is more pronounced in colour and form in the foreground, so when it comes to the sky, the reverse holds good. The colours at the horizon are usually more delicate and subtle while as the sky comes forward—that is, up to the top of your picture—the colours become stronger and more pronounced; you get the inverted bowl effect.

Of course, in this limited space, one cannot be expected to give more than a very brief outline as to how to paint landscapes. The chief things to remember are to keep constant observations, written notes and sketches in your books, to take courage, to stand up to your work, to have faith in your own individual vision, not to be put off by criticism and not to be easily downhearted.

## CHAPTER 6

# How to Paint Landscape in Water-colours

### by R. O. Dunlop, R.A.

WATER-COLOUR painting has been considered in this country, for a very long time, as being the proper medium with which to commence, if you intend to paint. It is hard to find the reasons which started this idea, but they were probably based on such considerations as cost of materials and their capacity to be easily handled and carried—that is to say, a box of water-colour paints, brushes and other equipment, all of which weighs very little and can be easily taken with you into the country.

As regards the actual technique of handling these light, inexpensive materials, that is an entirely different matter. Water-colours are not at all easy to manage, they can so easily become messy and there is practically no way of altering a mistake. Once a blob of colour is put down in water-colour, it more or less has to remain there for ever. Efforts at sponging and scraping more often than not lead to a more messy result, so that in putting down a brush stroke in water-colours, you have to be quite sure in advance exactly where it should go, what shape it should be, and try and get as near as possible to the colour you intend.

There is another thing about water-colour painting—the actual tints you put on, dry out lighter in tone than you expect; therefore, you find yourself adding further layers of colour (when the underneath ones are dry, of course) in order to deepen the tonal effect, so that you are always working up from a light beginning to your finished work. This naturally takes time and in our climate, with its periods of moist, damp air, it may be a very slow process indeed.

I once knew a man—an indefatigable water-colour painter—who painted water-colour landscapes all through the winter in the north of England, and always took with him on his expeditions bundles of old newspapers and boxes of matches, in order that he might be able to light fires near where he was working. He was then able to rush over and dry off the wet washes of colour by the heat from his fires, before proceeding to the next lay on of colour. He was, as you can imagine,

*Below:* **SELF-PORTRAIT**
**Rembrandt van Rijn (1606–69)**

Throughout his life Rembrandt conducted an intensive exploration of his appearance. His remarkable series of self-portraits cover the period from young manhood to the last year of his life. Relentlessly they probe the depths of the artist's personality from the years of material success to the bankruptcy and ruin which impoverished his later life. Here, the painter, undaunted by sorrow and failure, looks out serenely upon a world where all the slings and arrows are spent, and only peace remains.

**ELIZABETH BRANDT**
**Peter Paul Rubens (1577–1640)**

Note the simplicity of conception, and the fresh, economical technique in this portrait of the artist's first wife.

*Right:* **SELF-PORTRAIT**
**Henry Fuseli (1741–1825)**

The Swiss-born artist who became Keeper of The Royal Academy and a close friend of the mystic, William Blake, is famed for his fantasy. A painter of dreams and hauntings, Fuseli has been rightly claimed as a precurser of Surrealism. This compelling portrait affords a unique glimpse of the artist. It is not difficult to see why Fuseli and Blake should have been drawn to each other; at a time when Sir Joshua Reynolds was promoting the "classical tradition", the wave of romanticism then developing in British writing was to find a counterpart in the art of Blake and Fuseli.

*Right:* **THE CRUCIFIXION**
**Matthias Grünewald (c. 1475/80–1528)**
The agitation of drawing and the distortions of form so often employed by Grünewald mark him as one of the great precursors of modern Expressionism.

*Below:*
**THE DELPHIC SYBIL** (Detail)
  **Michelangelo (1475–1564)**
Michelangelo's deep preoccupation with anatomy is clearly illustrated in this detail from his series of Prophets and Sybils in the Sistine Chapel. Like Leonardo, he sought an idealized type, and his distillation, less enigmatic than that of his great contemporary, is seen here as a wide-eyed and lofty archangel, omnipotent, yet devoid of the mystery which distinguishes the subtle ideations of Leonardo.

*Below:* **ST FRANCIS IN ECSTASY**
  **El Greco (1541–1614)**
El Greco's distortions are less brutal than Grünewald's, yet they help to create a mood of mystical exaltation.

an exception—most painters in water-colour find it very difficult to work out-of-doors painting landscapes during our winters, which nowadays seem to take up practically half the year.

Now that I have let you know how difficult I think this lovely medium is, perhaps we can get down to discussing some of the nicer aspects of the subject.

English water-colour painting has always been a thing apart in the world of art. No other country seems to have produced a school of water-colourists with anything like the range and genius of our British masters. Why this should be so is not very easy to define. The traditions of English water-colour painters seem to lie in the region of the topographical artists who were asked to paint a certain scene, a particular country mansion or old ruined castle, for the aristocracy, much in the same way as nowadays a photographer would be brought in to supply records for the albums of those who own stately mansions, or widespreading domains. But naturally, being artists and not photographers, these young water-colour painters —some of them exceedingly gifted—would select and arrange and even alter their scenes in order to compose good pictures. This type of work naturally suffered from the necessity to give accuracy of detail, especially where buildings or definite objects had to be portrayed. There was much more latitude granted, of course, to the pure landscape parts of the pictures, and here the artists could let themselves go.

As everyone knows, the great Joseph William Mallord Turner started his life as an artist painting these topographical water-colours when he was in his teens, and learned many a lesson from his only slightly older companion, Thomas Girtin, who unfortunately died when young. Turner's self-revealing remark on hearing of Girtin's early death: "If he had lived, I would have found it hard to survive," although very competitive in spirit, showed what the great painter thought of the early work of Girtin.

These young topographers, as they were called, used to travel extensively over the British Isles making their notes and sketches and then working these up into their final pictures for the portfolios of their wealthy clients. It was out of this beginning that the English school of water-colourists arose.

Simplicity of handling, broad washes of colour, rather light in tone, dignity of composition and a certain clean use of limpid washes, seemed to typify the technique that was handed on from generation to generation down to the present day. If you examine the water-colour section of any of our big exhibitions held in London at the present time, you will at once be conscious of this tradition of the clear, limpid English water-colour, which is on a far higher level, technically, than the oil paintings in the adjoining rooms. There is, of course, going along with this tradition, a tendency to favour certain hackneyed subjects and a corresponding lack of individuality of vision, but there is usually a very high standard of accomplishment.

Perhaps another reason for the supremacy of the English water-colour painters is the climate of these islands. Water-colours are essentially the medium for atmospheric effects, quickly passing clouds, saturated atmospheric distances— all the swiftly moving panorama of nature in a fickle climate. So, although it is a hard medium to master, it is the perfect medium for the climatic conditions of our native landscape.

## TECHNIQUES

In talking about the actual technical handling of water-colours and the equipment necessary, I can only give my own opinions based on my experience in this subtle, fascinating, but difficult medium.

First, I advise using *tubes* of paint, rather than pans; the colour seems to remain moister, more intense and fresher when squeezed from a tube (always remember to replace the top immediately you have squeezed out a small amount). I, therefore, am not a believer in the ordinary water-colour paint box with its white japanned lid, supposed to be for mixing the colours—no one can mix colours in which water is the medium in those horrible glossy recesses. How they ever came to be invented and sold, God alone knows. You need a china palette, or preferably a plain white soup dish, on the rim of which you can squeeze out your colours, always in the same rotation, starting on the left with your light colours and going through to the right with your deepest.

As regards colours, I advocate keeping them down to the minimum, at any rate for the first few months. My palette would probably be Yellow Ochre, Naples Yellow (for very occasional use) Raw Sienna, Burnt Sienna, Cadmium Yellow, Rose Madder, Light Red, Burnt Umber, Cobalt Blue, Ultramarine Blue, and Sepia or Vandyke Brown. It is wise to arrange your colours as you squeeze them out, always in the same order, as you then get to know instinctively where they are placed.

You need plenty of rags—and when I say plenty, I mean plenty. That centre of your soup dish will need constant cleaning. The rags should be soft and absorbent. And also you need *plenty* of *Water*—you want at least a pint bottle of water with you, which can be poured into smaller containers tied to your easel. The great thing about water-colour painting is to *keep it clean*, therefore everything which will enable you to keep it clean, a clean palette, brushes, and water, you must regard as the first essential.

Another fundamental principle lying behind water-colour painting is that *water runs downhill*. Therefore, your job is really guiding liquid of a certain colour as it runs downhill into a definite shape. For this, naturally, you will require a sloping surface, slightly more sloping than with other media, because you do not want your liquid to run down too fast, or you will not be able to control it properly. Therefore, you want your board sloping at a good angle, so that the colour will run gradually and can be guided easily into position. Again, I am a great believer in standing up when painting, even with water-colours; and although I know that most water-colour painters are in the habit of sitting, I think this is a decided mistake. The freedom of action, the greater breadth of vision and the wider sweep of the arm which you get from standing and moving backwards and forwards, are very necessary to avoid niggardly, close-fisted work.

### PREPARING THE PAPER

It is most important to take plenty of time in preparing your paper. I know there are lots of different types of painting "blocks" made up ready to take out. Whilst these are satisfactory for small studies, they are not really adequate for the larger, more important water-colours which you will soon wish to embark upon. White paper—a good quality cartridge, for instance—is probably the best to commence with. Tinted papers and certain specialized papers, such as the thick grey David Cox paper and the sugar-bag paper, can be used when you have become thoroughly experienced with the white paper. Tinted papers tend to flatter your efforts and should be avoided until you have attained a mastery of your technique.

Now your sheet of white cartridge can be cut into the size you like working on—say twenty inches by sixteen—and it must be well and truly laid upon a light drawing board, which can be a piece of three-ply wood, a little larger than your paper size. With a sponge and a little water, thoroughly damp the back of the paper, place it on your board and then fix it with a length of brown gummed strip paper all round, which not only makes a nice frame for your picture, but when the paper dries, you will find it taut, and ready to work on. There is nothing worse than having pieces of paper wobbling about and curling up on boards where you have tried to hold them down with drawing pins. So don't try to use pins; damp your paper and fix it with the strips of gummed paper.

### BRUSHES

The worst of water-colour brushes is that you cannot get them large enough. This old tradition of the meticulous, finicky water-colour seems to still hold good in the minds of the brush manufacturers. So get the *largest* brushes you can lay your hands on, sables, preferably, if you can afford them—a good sable is well worth the money and will last for ages if well looked after.

Carry your brushes in a long metal brush container, wrap them up well with soft rags at the tops, and really look after them with loving care. They are the most important items of your equipment. If you have plenty of water always with you to keep them clean, you will probably need only about four good brushes.

## LAYING ON OF WASHES

Always be bold in mixing up your colour tints on the plate; mix about three times what you think you will need, using plenty of water, and with your large brushes courageously put on your washes, letting the water run, wiping your brush quickly if there is too much fluid, and draining it off with the dry brush where you wish it to end. Never, on any account, put one wash on top of another until the underneath one is dry. So in the winter you will have to light up those fires.

The general idea behind the English water-colour technique has been to use only transparent colour washes, leaving the paper to play its own important part in the picture. In other words, the use of opaque colour, i.e., mixing white with the colours, making them dense instead of transparent, is usually frowned upon as not being in keeping with the true traditional use of water-colour as practised by the masters. In Paris, and on the Continent generally, water-colour painting is not treated with this puritanical respect; opaque colour is mixed with transparent colour and pen and ink, chalk, pastels, all sorts of things, utilized to gain effects.

While I respect the rather austere English tradition and practice in water-colours, I am not at all against experimenting in any sort of mixed medium if this proves better for the expression of the vision of the individual. What I *am* against, more than anything, is the namby-pamby, weak toned, wishy-washy efforts.

As I have intimated, water-colours are not for the solid, full-toned rendering of a landscape, but more for the delightful, accidental effects, the great sweeping, billowing clouds, the oncoming storm, the slashing effect of evening light—subjects where the white glistening of the paper through the colour can play its part, the placing and spacing of objects being more important, probably, than the detailed shapes.

CHAPTER 7

# Portrait Painting

## by Stephen Bone

THE subject seems to fall naturally into three parts; first, The Human Face and its Peculiarities; second, How to paint a Likeness of It; third, How to turn that Likeness into a Picture. I am however a little uncertain if this is the best order in which to consider them, logical though it seems, for the artist in his studio finds that his first problem, the one that must be solved before he can begin to consider the others, is just this one which I have left to the last, the problem of how to plan not merely a portrait but also a picture. The arrangement of the composition, the pose, the lighting, even the choice of clothes and the background, will have to be settled before the artist begins to grapple with the problems of face-painting. If you have a sitter coming to be painted in an hour or two you would probably be well advised to read this short essay backwards.

Let us assume, however, that you have a few minutes to spare before the sitter comes knocking on the door, to consider at leisure the raw material of portrait painting—the human face.

"Your face is the same as everybody has," said Humpty Dumpty to Alice, "the two eyes, so . . . nose in the middle, mouth under. It's always the same. Now if you had the two eyes on the same side of the nose, for instance—or the mouth at the top—that would be some help."

"It wouldn't look nice," Alice objected. But Humpty Dumpty only shut his eyes and said, "Wait till you've tried."

Well, now we have tried—or Picasso has tried for us—and we have learnt some strange things, but, for the present, let us confine ourselves to those faces that are constructed in the way that Humpty Dumpty found so monotonous.

Humpty Dumpty was of course quite right: in many ways all faces *are* much alike; in order to recognize our friends we have to observe very minute differences. Before considering these differences it is as well to be familiar with the similarities, which go far beyond the obvious ones that he enumerated. For the painter one of

69

the most important things about a face is that it is the front part of a head. This the portrait painter must convey. He may be painting a most impressive man or a ravishingly lovely girl but he is also painting the front or side view of a solid object that is about eight inches high, eight inches deep and five inches across.

The face is a part of the head. The importance of this cannot be exaggerated. The great masterpieces of portraiture achieve much of their almost supernatural effect of actuality, of appearing to place us in the very presence of the sitter, by the apparently obvious and prosaic method of setting down with unerring accuracy and extraordinary force the solid shape of the man or woman in front of them. A smile or a frown may be a fascinating expression of character but it also is a physical fact—a slight change in the shape of a solid object—and this the great portrait painters never lost sight of for one moment.

Just as the face is a part of the head, so the features are parts of the face. The eyes, nose, and mouth are, as any sculptor knows, a series of complicated hollows or bulges on the surface of the face and the portrait painter must always think of them in this way. He has one problem that the sculptor does not know: he must draw these complicated shapes in perspective on a flat surface, foreshortening some —often all of them—and making each foreshortened shape play its due part in the building up of a solid looking face, which is a part of an equally solid head.

The most obvious characteristics of a face are the features—the nose, mouth, and eyes—but the width and length of the face as a whole are of the greatest importance to the portrait painter and unless these are correctly established no pretty drawing of the separate features will ever produce a satisfactory likeness. Anatomists attach a great deal of importance to something called the "facial angle". (See pictures on pages 76-8). It is worth pointing out that, even if you are painting a full-face portrait, the facial angle of your sitter is important because it will determine the amount of the foreshortening of the mouth and chin and forehead. The width of the face is also of great importance and even a profile portrait should make it clear if the sitter has the wide, flat face of a Chinese or the narrow, "hatchet face" of Uncle Sam.

Of the various features of the face the one which has the first claim on our attention is the eyes. When we meet a friend or a stranger the eyes are the first thing we look at; they are supposed to be the most expressive part of the whole face. This is partly because from the direction of the glance one can deduce a good deal about anyone's thoughts, but expressiveness of the eye itself has been much exaggerated. It may seem surprising, but, when one begins to examine the matter, it becomes apparent that the only change in expression of which the eye itself is capable, apart from the production of tears, is a change in the size of the pupil— a trifling alteration from the point of view of the painter and one which depends on the intensity of the light and has no emotional or psychological significance at all.

It is not the eye but the eyelids and eyebrows that are so extraordinarily significant and which we all watch so keenly, though usually unconsciously, when we meet another man or woman. Anyone who doubts this should look at one of those portrait busts in marble with the eyes left completely blank, without even an indication of the position of the pupils; it will be found that if one draws pupil and iris on the blank marble this does little or nothing to increase the force or vividness of the expression.

The visible part of the eye is of course only a small part of the eyeball. It is important to remember, or perhaps one should say it is important never to forget, that the eye appearing between the lids is a part of a large spherical object and that this is shown by the lids as well as by the eye itself. The upper lid is much more movable than the lower one; the eye is shut mainly by the movement of the upper lid. When the eye is open the upper lid is drawn back and there is a strongly marked fold that runs in a curve above the eye.

Above the eyes there is a projecting ridge of bone on which the eyebrows grow. The ridge is a part of the skull and does not move, but the eyebrows can be pulled upwards or pushed down or drawn together. Here as in other parts of the face a good painting should convey the effect of a solid structure, the skull, covered by a layer which, within limits, is movable.

The portrait painter is seldom called upon to paint the eyes shut. Nor does he often have to paint the mouth open. This is perhaps just as well for its shape when closed is quite complicated enough. It was pointed out that the shape of the eyelids was largely due to the spherical shape of the eyeball underneath them. In the same way, but less obviously, the shape of the lips is largely due to the horse-shoe shaped rows of teeth which they hide. The lips do not take the shape of the teeth as clearly as the eyelids take the shape of the eyeball however, for the lips are thicker and more muscular and have a good deal more shape of their own. Their shape should be studied with great care.

Between the eyes and above the mouth comes the longest feature of the face, the nose. Its length is, however, a little misleading because, when you are looking straight into the eyes of anyone whose head is on the same level as your own, you will see the nose strongly foreshortened. Its true length, which of course you know quite well, is a good deal longer than what you actually see, and it is fatally easy to allow your knowledge of its true length to influence you when you come to set down a face on canvas.

The aspect of the face that is usually chosen by portrait painters, for reasons that will be considered later, is what is called the three-quarter view. In this aspect the nose is particularly difficult to draw since one side of it is foreshortened very

71

strongly, or may be completely hidden, while the other side, the near one, may be foreshortened hardly at all. It is by no means easy to suggest that the two sides are really the same size and shape and that it is merely the different point of view that makes them seem so unlike each other.

Below the mouth comes the chin. Here, as with most of the other features, one can be misled by the sort of terms usually applied to the face. "A prominent chin" and "a receding chin" should be plain enough, but in fact one sometimes finds that the first is assumed to be a large one and the second small, which is often not the case at all. A receding chin can be a very long one. The superficial modelling of the chin is of course of great interest, but before giving yourself up to this it is important to be sure that you have correctly estimated its length, width, and prominence (or recession).

Finally, the cheeks and that often ignored feature, the ears. The width of the face is one thing; the plumpness of the cheeks is another. It is possible for a thin man to have a very wide face. The upper part of the cheeks has a solid substructure of bone; the lower part is soft; a fact that is often very evident when the cheeks sag in age. A thin cheek will result in a prominent "cheek bone". The way in which a smile affects the cheeks is obvious; it lifts them and narrows the outer corners of the eyes—one can tell a man is smiling even if one is standing behind him and can see only the curve of his cheek.

The ear, or rather the placing of the ear, tests severely the artist's sense of construction. If he has really been considering the face as a part of the head, never for a moment losing sight of its solid shape, then he will not have much difficulty in placing the ears correctly. If he has been merely copying features he will find it extremely difficult to put in its correct place an outlying feature like the ear.

There are various rules of proportion that have been found quite useful by many generations of artists. The face below the hair-line is supposed to be divisible into three equal parts, the upper one consisting of forehead, the middle one of nose and cheeks, the lower one of lips and chin. The eyes are supposed to be separated by a space the same length as one of them. The ear is supposed to be the same length as the nose. The distance from ear to nose tip is about the same as that from eye brow to chin. Do not forget that these rough and ready rules are meant only to apply to *adult* heads. The proportions of a child are quite different; the face is relatively much smaller when compared with the head as a whole; the nose is relatively much smaller when compared with the total size of the face.

The chief use of such measurements is that they supply a standard of comparison. They fit no one exactly but they do help the artist to determine whether the sitter has eyes close or widely set or has a short or a long nose. They are however very dangerous if they are taken too literally. The human face, like the head of which it forms a part, is a solid object, and so is subject to the rules of perspective and foreshortening; the painter is not really concerned with the actual measurements of the features, what concerns him is the size they appear to be when seen from one definite point of view, and the one thing of which he can be sure is that whatever point of view he chooses, it is certain that most—or all—of the features will be strongly foreshortened.

When trying to depict accurately such a subtly-shaped and complex object as the human face, powers of precise observation and an ability to see every detail as a part of the whole are of far greater importance than any skilful technical tricks with a paint-brush; indeed brilliant tricks which we may enjoy when they occur as a sort of ornament in the work of a master like Frans Hals are positively repulsive when encountered in a picture that is uncertain or weak in construction. Portrait painting is not a matter of learning technical tricks, it is chiefly a matter of seeing correctly, and whole. Nevertheless there are one or two observations that may usefully be made about procedure, and there are one or two simple traps that the beginner can be warned against.

The first of these traps is one into which a surprising number of beginners fall although nothing is easier than to avoid it. It concerns the question of scale. The artist is sitting at his easel; the distance from his eyes to his canvas is about a yard. He looks at his model who is three yards away. To try to paint a life-size head in these circumstances is absurd; the head he paints on his canvas will look like a head that is only a yard from his eyes; the model whom he is supposed to be painting will look like what she is—a person three yards away and of course very much smaller. Every time the artist looks from the model to his canvas in order to compare one with the other, he will be comparing two things of different sizes. He should avoid handicapping himself in this severe and unnecessary manner either by painting a *small* portrait; by bringing the model as near to him as his canvas is (probably impractical); or by wheeling the easel with the canvas on it close beside the model and stepping back from it so that his life-size picture of the model's head looks the same size as the original.

If he does the last he will of course find that the change from a sitting position to a standing one will mean raising the picture for the convenience of working on it, and this will mean, that if the model is sitting, it will be convenient to raise her up also. (One can place her chair on a "models' throne" which is merely a low platform made for the purpose, or one can get her to sit on a table—with suitable support for the feet).

Before leaving this question of scale there is one point that should be made. The portrait painters of the past arranged their pictures to suggest that the spectator was looking *through* the surface of the canvas ("the picture plane") to observe something that was taking place behind it; as if the picture frame enclosed a sheet of glass through which one could see the sitter. This of course means that, in what is called a life-size portrait, the actual measurements of the sitter's own face were rather larger than those of the painted face as this was supposed to be a little way behind the picture plane. Today this is sometimes ignored and the painted face is as large as the flesh and blood one or even larger, and seems not to lie behind the canvas at all but to thrust forward into the room. This often produces a striking and powerful effect but is disturbing and not really consistent with an attempt at "illusionist" painting.

If you are standing to paint, and are stepping back each time you want to get a good look at the model and compare what you see with the progress of your picture, then it is essential only to look at her when you have stepped back the regular four paces or whatever it is; otherwise you will be in danger of doing what is fatal to the success of any portrait—you will be confusing two different points of view. Much the same effect is produced when the tired sitter moves her position; this the artist cannot always control, so it makes it even more important that he should not add to the confusion by shifting his own point of view.

The actual process of painting a portrait does not differ in essentials from that of painting a still-life or even a landscape. You should avoid much preliminary drawing with charcoal or pencil as this will tend to dirty the paint put over it (perhaps it is best to do this preliminary drawing with thin, turpentiny oil paint which will disappear naturally as the painting proceeds); you should cover up the white canvas as quickly as possible with thin paint of some neutral colour or the shining white canvas will have a dazzling effect and will make it difficult to estimate correctly the subtle tones of the face; you should start by painting thinly, and with rather vague edges, patches of tone and colour; you should begin with the middle tones and leave out both the darkest shadows and the lightest lights—plenty of time for those later on.

At the end of the first sitting your canvas should look rather dim and vague and grey but as accurate as you can possibly get it in the construction and proportions of the face; the later sittings will be occupied with making your picture stronger, more precise, and more brightly coloured—though regarding this last point there is a warning that should perhaps be given. European faces are pink, more or less, all over; it is far easier to increase the pinkness of a painted face than it is to reduce it, and the prudent artist will keep his portrait on the pale, even the sallow, side rather than the highly coloured or rubicund one—at least until he is in sight of the end.

It is essential that the portrait painter should be warned of one very serious danger that threatens him: the danger of finishing too early. It is fatal to start drawing details of the eyes before you are certain that you have placed them correctly in the face and it is always a great temptation to draw the significant line where the two lips meet before you have properly modelled the areas round about. The details of the face must be added only to a thoroughly sound substructure and, even then, only if they really add to the effectiveness of the whole.

Portrait painting is an art, a craft—and a trade. So far we have been considering it as a craft—the accurate observation and the accurate setting down on canvas of what has been observed. It is high time to start considering it as an art—the art of making good pictures, not merely good likenesses.

The first and most obvious reflection is that, so far, this account of portrait painting has been confined to the face. As a matter of fact it would be a good thing if a great many of the artists who paint portraits today would do the same. One constantly sees in exhibitions large portraits in which the head is quite well painted and quite interesting but the rest of the picture could hardly be duller—this is of course particularly noticeable in portraits of men in business suits, but it is not confined to them. This shortcoming is much less frequent in seventeenth- or eighteenth-century pictures; even the weaker and duller of these pictures are, as a rule, equally interesting all over. This is partly due to the much greater decorative possibilities of the costume, particularly the male costume, but a more important reason is that the artists regarded it as an essential part of their job to produce a striking and interesting design, even if it meant placing the sitter (usually, of course, the hired model who was standing in for him) in an affected or theatrical pose. Today most artists merely ask the sitter to sit down; the sitter clasps his hands in front of him; the artist starts to paint yet another dark blue business suit.

In this matter of how to turn a portrait into a picture there is a great deal to be learnt from a visit to the National Gallery or even from good books of reproductions. After all the problems that confront the portrait painter today are very like those that confronted Holbein or Reynolds; the human face is still the same size and shape; human hands take up the same positions; and it is most instructive to see how these and other great masters solved much the same difficulties that you will encounter. There is, in fact, a great deal to be said for the practice of boldly "lifting" some idea for an interesting pose and using it for your own purposes— Reynolds was particularly fond of doing this and his own pictures always show a remarkable variety in composition which will repay a lot of study.

Although there exist a certain number of highly successful profile portraits (they were popular in the early days of the Italian Renaissance and the fashion might well be revived), the face is as a rule much more expressive when both eyes are shown. A completely full-face portrait, however, does not enable one to see very clearly the shape of the nose and the most usual view of the face is therefore

*Left:* The three-quarter position is the most frequent of all arrangements for a portrait; the light falls on the right cheek and the shadow of the nose helps to outline its shape. *Centre:* Here diffused light comes from well above the sitter's head (note the shadow under the nose) the sitter is gazing directly at the artist and sharply defined shadows are not cast. *Right:* A strong top light is usually considered unflattering as it tends to emphasize the signs of age in a face. It can emphasize in a way that is almost arrogant the perfection of flawless beauty.

what is called the "three-quarter" one. In this view the direction of the gaze is of the greatest importance. The head can be turned to one side and the eyes can look in the same direction, or the head can be turned to one side and the eyes can look in the opposite direction, or the eyes can look straight out of the picture at the spectator. The eyes can look slightly upwards as if gazing at some distant object, or downwards in thought.

Equally important is the lighting. The light can fall so that the head is turned away from it or towards it, it can fall from above or rise from below, or it is possible to have the head illuminated by two lights, one on either side of the face. The light may be sharp as if from a small window or very diffused as if in the open air on a grey day. The shadows may be very dark and heavy or they may be greatly lightened by strong reflected light. (If you want more reflected light hang up white sheets in the room; if you want a more diffused light try the effect of a white muslin curtain over the window.)

For the pose of the figure as a whole, you will want to think out (or discover) something that is interesting in itself, characteristic of the sitter, and not too tiring to maintain. This is no easy task. Study of the famous portraits of the past will help to provide suggestions and you must at all times be ready to take advantage of the lucky accident, the unexpected pose that the sitter may take up when he becomes interested in something and forgets that he has come to get his portrait painted. Do not lose sight of how much success in composing any sort of picture

*Left:* It is possible to paint the face almost without shadows. Here the light is nearly directly behind the artist's head. The only real shadows are the tiny but important ones that emphasize the corners of the nose and mouth. *Centre:* This shows the other method of avoiding shadows— using a very diffused light. The light seems to be coming from all sides but, since there is no shadow under the nose, emanates mostly from a little below the sitter's face. *Right:* This is a head lit from below. Direct sunlight is cut off by the large hat but there is a great deal of reflected light from the ground and from the dress. This is a true full-face portrait, not very common.

depends on apparently small matters—in a portrait, the exact amount of space above the head for instance, or the exact shape of that important triangle that is made up of lefthand-righthand-face. Try what different clothes will do and different backgrounds; try experiments like painting a soldier on parade, a lady arranging flowers, a boy playing cricket, a small girl tidying her doll's house, a business man consulting his works manager, a keen gardener potting plants; do not forget the many possibilities of making interesting compositions with the help of stairs, doorways, open windows, garden seats, couches, even motor-cars and boats. One can get welcome assistance from pet animals. If the sitter wants to read a book try to persuade him to put it on one side and listen to the radio—or even watch television, since the downward-gazing face of a reader is not, as a rule, very expressive. Try to persuade the male sitter to wear a muffler or a high-necked sweater or overalls or uniform if you feel that you cannot bear to paint yet another neat lounge suit. Try to persuade the female sitter to dress "up to the nines" but to go easy on lipstick—that bane of the twentieth-century artist. Try painting someone in a hat. Try making someone sit on the floor.

There are several aspects of portrait painting that cannot even be mentioned in an article as short as this but there is one that cannot be altogether omitted: the use of photography. The short answer to this very difficult problem seems to be that the painter who can do without the camera altogether is the only one who

*Left:* This head is turned in much the same way as the first two (on page 76) but it is lit from the opposite side. It is rather difficult to make this arrangement satisfactory as the lit edge of the nose comes against the lit cheek. *Centre:* Other three-quarter face portraits in this series show the whole outline of the far cheek but in this, part of it is hidden by the nose. It is important to decide whether the nose is to appear in silhouette as it is unsatisfactory to let its tip touch the outline of the distant cheek. *Right:* The use of two sources of light, as here, is a modern device that can easily become rather tedious. On the whole it is much easier to give unity to a head if one source of light is obviously the principal.

can use it without too great a risk of being seduced into producing empty, badly constructed, uninteresting work. An artist who knows exactly what information he wants from a photograph before he looks at it and takes just that information and no more, may perhaps take up a photograph without endangering his picture— or without endangering it much.

Another subject that it would have been pleasant to have discussed at length is that of the group portrait, the conversation piece. The chief difficulty here is to give sufficient unity to a number of figures, none of which can be subordinated to the others. The problem at its worst is that of depicting a board of directors; it is much easier to paint a family where there will be both sexes and several different ages to give variety to the composition. The secret is of course to give the group as far as possible an interest in common.

That knock on the door must be your sitter at last. Go and let him in (or is it her?). Don't let yourself be bullied, remember that he (even she) is just your raw material. You are not a mere face painter; you are a picture maker. Remember that.

NOTE: Of the series of heads shown on pages 76, 77 and 78, the first is based on a painting by Titian, the second on one by Reynolds, the third and fourth on pictures by Ingres, the fifth on one by Renoir, the sixth on one by Reynolds, the seventh on one by Hals; the eighth and ninth are drawings by Stephen Bone, the author of this chapter.

# CHAPTER 8

# Drawing Portraits

IN HIS chapter on portrait painting, Stephen Bone describes the subject as falling into three parts: (a) The human face and its peculiarities; (b) How to paint a likeness of it; (c) How to turn that likeness into a picture. These conditions can, and often do of course, apply equally to the art of portrait drawing, although the portrait draughtsman frequently puts all his eggs into one basket; the face and its peculiarities. In this event, everything is concentrated upon the face in isolation, the artist being less concerned with composition, and picture making, than with the desire to distil the pure alcohol of personality. You might say that the portrait draughtsman takes his faces neat, whereas the portrait painter takes them with a splash of composition. This difference in approach, where it exists, does not of course indicate that the method of the draughtsman is necessarily superior, or more revealing than that of the painter; it is simply that the tools of drawing—pen and pencil especially—lend themselves more naturally to a compactness of technical style, rather than a diffusion. The brush can sweep the canvas with comparative breadth, but the point, of pen or pencil, is of course a medium of concentration.

This does not mean that a drawing cannot be bold, and free: it most certainly can. What in the circumstances is usually a waste of time and effort, is the construction of detailed or complex backgrounds in mediums that do not naturally lend themselves to this end. Indeed, probably the greatest portraitist of all time—Rembrandt—treated his portrait painting with the single-mindedness of the draughtsman. He was singularly disinterested in the paraphernalia of backgrounds, preferring to lose their incidental detail in pools of shadow, and to concentrate everything upon the features.

I am concerned therefore in this chapter with portrait drawing as a means of portraying personality, in detachment: in isolation from the clamour of a specific setting, however relevant, so that the maximum attention may be focused upon a solitary consideration—that of character.

Self-portrait: John Vanderbank.

Personally I am inclined to feel that the most revealing form of portraiture is indeed that of the portrait draughtsman. In itself, the incisive character of line is revelatory, cutting to the bone of personality like a scalpel, while the isolation of the portrait drawing, adrift in the empty paper, ensures the maximum attentions of artist, and the spectator. The self-portrait of John Vanderbank (1694–1739), an English eighteenth-century illustrator, is a fine example of the incision and concentration which the draughtsman can achieve in line. Here is a spirited, spontaneous drawing, surging with vitality, and executed with a crystal clarity.

More psychologically penetrating is the superb self-portrait by Henry Fuseli (1741–1825), the Swiss born British painter, celebrated for his fantastic and macabre subject matter. The artist, haunted by visions of romantic terror, and erotic fantasy,[1] has expressed in this most searching study, the very essence of his tortured introspection. Fuseli is one of the greatest of British draughtsmen, and his drawings should be sought out by every devoted student of the pen and pencil[2].

I have often been asked by students how best to begin a portrait drawing? Should one begin with a basic egg shape, and then start to carve from this generic form the peculiarities of individual personality? Or should one start from some specific feature, such as the hair, the nose, or the contour of the cheek? While I am always loathe to lay down any law in such matters, I find personally that it is best to start with the eyes. Certainly one must bear in mind that every head, irrespective of its individual characteristics, conforms in a number of general respects. Yet this basic conformity need not obtrude, and I think it is better to start with a feature such as the eyes, which you can relate, in your mind, to those impersonal factors which govern the construction of heads in general. The fact that all heads are basically ovoids, halved by the line of the eyes, is a matter of structure, and not of personality. One may learn how to draw the head as an impersonal generic fact by dividing an ovoid horizontally, and vertically, and placing the features accordingly (see facing page): but in drawing a specific portrait these structural facts must underlay personality.

[1] A whole section of Fuseli's drawings is unpublishable because of their obscene nature. This aspect of the artist's work is brilliantly dealt with by Mr. Ruthven Todd in his book, *Tracks in the Snow*.
[2] *The Drawings of Fuseli*, Paul Ganz.

**THE GARDEN OF DELIGHTS (Centre Panel)      Hieronymus Bosch (c. 1450/60–1516)**

The symbolism and allegory peculiar to this superbly imaginative painter, who was born at Hertogen-bosch in Holland, can only be understood when considered in relation to medieval Christian mythology with its hard core of heaven, sin, and damnation. Bosch drew freely upon the extensive iconography of medieval symbolism. The toad and the jug, for instance, represented the devil; fruits were sexual symbols; egg shapes and forms, symbols of fertility; oysters and clams, symbols of the female. The centre panel above is from a triptych which depicts also the presentation of Eve to Adam in Eden, and the torments of hell. The centrepiece has two possible interpretations. To some authorities it represents, symbolically, the sinful pleasures of the flesh: to others, it portrays the return of mankind to the paradise it lost while passing through the hell of the world—a paradise regained, wherein the whole of creation partakes of an ecstatic celebration. Either way the symbolism is appropriate.

*Above:* **THE AVENUE**
**Meindert Hobbema (1638–1709)**
Parallel lines converge to meet at
vanishing points on the eye level, or
horizon line. The basic principle of
*linear perspective* is demonstrated.

*Left:* **THE RETURN OF THE
PRODIGAL**
**Rembrandt van Rijn (1606–69)**
Rembrandt's power to inspire in the
spectator a sense of identification
with the subject is nowhere more
keenly felt than here. We can feel
ourselves the weariness of the prodigal, and even the physical sensation
of kneeling is communicated; while
the hands of the father warm us with
their tender compassion.

I think it is best to start with the eyes because here is the main focus of personality. The mouth may tell a great deal, but the eyes are the key to the mystery of character. If you can fix something of this revelation of the inner meaning of your subject in the early stages of a sitting, when the subject is fresh, and alert, you will have accomplished much. But to leave the eyes, the very threshold of personality, until some later stage in a drawing, when your subject will have grown tired, and even a little irritable, is to miss the chance of capturing, perhaps a supreme moment of revelation.

Draw the eyes first, not necessarily in detail, but rather more from the psychological point of view; then start building around them, delineating the contour of a cheek, the form of the nose, and so on, moving rapidly over the whole area of the head, and constructing each element in relation to everything else, so far as possible, simultaneously. It is important to construct the head as a unity, yet without completing any single detail until the separate parts have been soundly related to each other. This means drawing both the particular, and the general, at one and the same time. Keep your drawing very fluid in the initial stages; you may indeed feel eventually that much of it can be left in a relatively mobile condition, and that only certain features will need emphasis beyond your original statement.

Often my procedure is to take a drawing so far in conjunction with the sitter, and then, when I feel that I am approaching a stalemate, I put the drawing away and forget about it for a few hours: or even until the following day. Then, minus the sitter, I return to the drawing and consider it very carefully. That is to say, I sit and look at it for some time. In such reflective circumstances one frequently notices a fault, or weakness, that escaped attention when tussling with the subject in person: the need of a strengthening line perhaps, or the elimination of a superfluity. Considered in tranquillity, the drawing clears itself up, so to speak, and I strongly recommend the reflective method to the portrait draughtsman who wishes to take his study a stage beyond the spontaneous sketch, which form of drawing ought not of course to be tampered with after its completion. John Vanderbank's self-portrait is such an instance.

On the other hand, my drawing of Dame Edith Sitwell, drawn in part while she was rehearsing the reading of a poem in a television studio, was completed a few days after my first encounter with this extraordinary personality. Hers is a most deceptive face, for although at first the forms seem obvious, and clean cut, they are continuously invaded by the surge and swell of a dynamic undercurrent which transforms the static into the subtly mobile. The curious blend of the fixed, and the moving, the sense of a vigorous, sharply glinting river flowing among implacable and changeless rocks, was quite unobtainable at a first brush. Here was a personality that openly defied imprisonment in pencil and paper; a stimulating, challenging character that yielded its secrets only to the reflective approach. Over a period of a week, or more, I pursued a slow process of sharpening, and softening, working from recollection, from my *intuitive* sense of the sitter, checking up occasionally on some detail by reference to photographs, and finally, from a second, brief encounter with the subject herself. (See between pages 136-7).

One of the most important aspects of portrait drawing is I feel the nature of the working relationship between the artist and the sitter. Many portraits fail because the subject is gradually transformed from a living force into an expressionless, helplessly bored dummy. The relationship should be much more relaxed than this. Frequent breaks are important, and I see no reason why now and then during the process of drawing, a dash of characteristic animation should not be ferreted out, by getting the sitter to engage in conversation. This often brings the whole face into life, and kills the negative, suspended animation appearance of the over posed, over self-conscious sitter.

There is no reason why talking with, or just to your subject, should interfere with your drawing, or diminish its potency. It is vitally important that the portraitist should keep the flame of interest and expression alive in the subject, and whenever this appears to be flagging, a few words of conversation can prove most reviving. The fires of personality will burn up brightly in response to a well timed question, or an observation that provoked some subtle or telling physical reaction: the lift of an eyebrow, the curl of a lip, or the puckering of the mouth, these are the sort of characteristic responses that unmask personality. The eyes and mouth are particularly susceptible to the stimulus of ideas, and condition the most typical expressions of the subject. Try talking to your subject when drawing the mouth, and note with care what form it assumes in response to your words. This of course is a case where you would be talking to, and not with the subject. When delineating the contours of the face, and other features, silence may well prevail. When drawing the hair, on the other hand, its representation may benefit from a real burst of friendly chatter. You may of course prefer to work in complete silence, but it is I think, important to dispel the notion that the sitter must of necessity lapse into a temporary death while having a portrait drawn, because silence, and stillness are imperative to the artist. Far more important is the degree of concentration which the portraitist can focus on a moment of fleeting revelation.

*     *     *

There are many materials that lend themselves, with their own peculiar characteristics, to the portrait draughtsman, and among the most sympathetic I would list the following: (a) Pen and ink, (b) pen and wash, (c) brush and wash, (d) pencil, and pencil and wash, (e) chalks, (f) charcoal.

The type of pen you use is entirely a matter of discovering through the normal process of trial and error, which particular sort of nib best suits your own requirements. Usually a pennyworth of nib in the humblest penholder proves completely adequate, although some artists may find that a fountain-pen suits them best. The choice of pen, and nib, is a personal matter. For the application of ink, and water-colour washes, a good quality sable is unquestionably the best sort of brush to use. You should build up a selection of these, varying in size, and possessing plenty of spring and resilience since the personality of the brush itself plays an important part in shaping the character, and the spirit of a drawing. A lively and resilient brush will go a long way towards the production of a robust and energetic drawing. A limp, and lifeless brush, on the other hand, will inevitably produce a feeble drawing no matter how bold the intention of the artist. It is important therefore to equip yourself with a range of good quality sables.

Pencils also are a matter of trial and error, although whatever sort of pencil you use, it should I think combine the qualities of *hard*, and *soft*, in just the right degree. It should for instance be possible, with the same pencil, to delineate a clean, sharp, incisive line on the one hand, and to lay in a broad area of soft, flooding shadow, on the other. Pencils in the range, 2B to 4B, are usually the most yielding, and sympathetic, in this respect. There are so many excellent pencils on the market today that it is most difficult to prescribe any hard and fast rules about the type, or the degree.

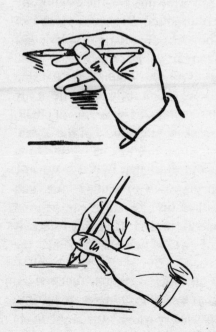

Now it might be helpful at this point to say something about the physical handling of a pencil since the key to dexterity and control depends in particular upon one important factor—the use of the third, and especially the little finger, as a sort of moving platform, constantly in touch with the surface of the paper during the process of drawing. (See top sketch). These fingers should ride smoothly over the surface, acting as a stabilizing base, or pivot, for the manipulation of the pencil by the thumb, and the first and second fingers. For delineating the incisive, sharp lines of contours, the pencil is best held at an angle of about 45° with the plane of the paper. (See lower sketch). This angle can even be as wide as 90°. For laying in broad areas, or passages of tone, the angle is considerably decreased, and the pencil is best

held as shown in the sketch on this page, the side of the pencil making contact with the paper. The tone is applied in a series of swift strokes, and the pencil subjected to such variations of pressure as will provide the required degrees of light and dark.

Practise using the pencil, not in relation to any particular subject, but purely as a mechanical exercise; as a pianist practises the scales. Draw a series of clean, sharp contours, varying the angle of your pencil from 45° to 90°. Apply areas of tone to a sheet of paper. You will soon develop a control and dexterity that will stand you in excellent stead when you start your portrait drawing. You should also practice the free-hand drawing of straight lines. It is possible with a little practise to draw a straight line that would be hard to improve upon with a ruler. The method is as follows. With the pencil at an angle of 45° draw a swift line across the paper. It can be diagonal, horizontal, or vertical. You will be astonished at the degree of control which the third and fourth fingers provide in this particular exercise. As such, it is of course unlikely to possess any practical application in portrait drawing. Its value lies in developing a mastery of the pencil, and a satisfying self-confidence, when you find that you can draw a tolerably straight line without having to use a ruler. The most suitable chalks for portrait drawing are the beautifully sympathetic sticks of red and black *conté à paris* (a product of France) which can be obtained either singly, or in neat little boxes. The sticks are square in shape, and about two and a half inches in length. When you require a fine, clean line, you use one of the points of the square; for putting in areas of tone, or shadow, the flat side of the chalk is brought into play. Although these sticks tend to break quite easily it is surprising how comfortably you can draw with an inch, or even less, of chalk.

It is a medium which can give you the most subtle combinations of the crystal clear, and the soft and melting. The clean, astringent outline of a taut, searching contour; the gentle flood of a liquid shadow. It is a medium that responds warmly to a spot of finger rubbing, a method of producing areas of unified tone, and particularly effective when *conté* is used. The chalked tip of a finger can be used to effect the most subtle and telling shadows, the merest touch often being sufficient for a particularly delicate piece of tone: perhaps a breath of pale shadow under the eyes?

Charcoal is also quite suitable for portrait drawing, although much more difficult to control than the other mediums I have so far mentioned. It brushes away very easily, and tends to get dirty unless it is used sparingly. It is a relatively clumsy medium, but can be used to obtain bold, and yet subtle results, if it is used with care, and with restraint. It is best used I would suggest for the fleeting, spontaneous sketch, rather than for the more detailed forms of drawing, since it is extremely difficult to correct. It cannot easily be drawn over, or into, without its degeneration into mess, and confusion. Nevertheless, charcoal is a medium of considerable character, and once you have appreciated its peculiar limitations—it must be used with a fresh, irrevocable directness—you should be in a position to achieve the most satisfying results.

Finally, two important practical points. Pencils are best sharpened with an ordinary razor blade. No other sharpening tool will give you the same degree of control over the cutting of the wood, and the shaping of your point. Cutting should commence about three-quarters of an inch from the end opposite to the letters denoting the pencil's degree, the wood being gradually tapered to bare about a quarter of an inch of graphite which should not be sharpened into too fine a point.

All drawings in pencil, chalk, or charcoal, should be "fixed" to prevent damage. It is quite a simple procedure. The drawing should be pinned to a board and laid on the table at a slight incline with its surface. The support of a single book at the top end of the board will give you the right inclination. The drawing is then sprayed with a fixative, the artist using a small mouth diffuser, or fixative spray, as it is commonly called. The drawing should then be left for a half-hour or so, by which time it should have dried thoroughly. Portrait drawings are particularly in need of this protective coating, since whereas a landscape sketch might not suffer any great harm from a spot of inadvertent rubbing, a portrait, in which every mark should be indispensable, could suffer only damage.

You need never of course be at a loss for a portrait subject; you can always draw, or for that matter, paint yourself. Many artists have found in their own faces a source of refreshing interest, for who do we know less well than ourselves? The study of one's own countenance is therefore something of a revelation. Indeed, to most people studying it carefully for the first time it is virtually the face of a stranger. A man of course knows his face less well than a woman hers, for he does not really *see* himself when shaving, or combing his hair. Indeed, if I know most men, they will think it even slightly eccentric for a man to pay more than the absolute minimum of attention to his reflection in the mirror. Self-portraiture therefore (particularly for a man) will reveal a number of unfamiliar peculiarities to people scrutinizing their faces intently for the first time. "Is my nose *really* crooked?" "Good heavens! one eyelid droops more than the other!" "Well, I never knew my mouth was twisted like that!" These are the kind of discoveries the keen observer will soon disclose with the aid of the mirror.

A face, while based in general upon certain symmetrical principles, is frequently strikingly *asymmetrical* in its particulars, and their relationship to one another. This is what imparts character to a face. A face which is too symmetrical in the classical sense, however beautiful, is fundamentally a lifeless face. An *asymmetrical*, uglyish face—which is the average—is at least full of interest, and vitality. Have you never noticed how dead are the faces of very pretty girls? How alive, those of ugly people? Scrutinize your face ruthlessly, and represent it honestly. Self-portraiture relieves the artist of the intolerable burden carried by the professional portraitist—the need to flatter.

No artist in history has left a more complete, and frank record of his facial appearance than Rembrandt. With a shrewd, completely unbiased eye, he has left a remarkable record of the seasons of his life, and his self-portraiture should be carefully studied as a supplement to your own self-analysis.

The method of making a self-portrait is really quite simple. It is necessary only to arrange a good sized mirror at right angles to your working surface, and look from one to the other while you draw or paint.

# CHAPTER 9

# Colour

IT IS often argued that whereas you can teach a student to draw, you cannot teach him how to become a good colourist. The idea is based on the fact that drawing is dependent upon such calculable elements as anatomy, and proportion, whereas a sense of colour is evidently a much more personal, and indefinable matter. Either a painter is by instinct a good colourist, or he is a bad one—always. At first there would seem to be good reason for this argument, since it is obvious that the one element which any group of masters may possess in common, is the quality of pure draughtsmanship. Consider for instance the figure-work of Leonardo, Titian, Rubens, Rembrandt, and Manet. However different the conception and technical style of these masters may be, their draughtsmanship conforms equally to scientific principle. But their sense of colour? How they differ from each other in this respect.

Yet even these chromatic dissimilarities are based on certain invariable colour principles. But they are principles sufficiently flexible to permit of considerable extension, or modification, by the artist himself. Thus, for all their apparent differences, the softly burning, low tones, of Titian's colour, and the flaming, high pitched brilliance of Van Gogh's palette, conform in principle to certain fundamentals.

> "The colour of the object illuminated partakes of the colour of that which illuminated it . . . the surface of every opaque body shares in the colour of the surrounding objects."

Here, in the words of Leonardo, is one of the most fundamental aspects of colour theory.

The sooner the student painter appreciates that there is really no such thing as a colour in isolation, the sooner he will find it possible to compose in terms of integrated colour. The sooner he will be able to *orchestrate* colour, so to speak; to blend the elements into a whole—a unity. Many artists, particularly beginners, make the crucial mistake of painting, let us say the "local" colour of an orange in a still-life group, independently of the extent to which it is affected by the other "colours" in proximity, or by the prevailing conditions of light and atmosphere. Colour is a unity, and individual colours can be assessed only in relation to a number of other factors. Strictly speaking, local colour—that is the alleged colour of an object uninfluenced by those other considerations I have mentioned—has no exact existence, since all things are subject, from the point of view of colour, to the special circumstances in which they are seen. In any given subject therefore, colour must be realized as a unity, rather than as an insoluble jigsaw of disorientated fragments of local colour.

Here is a simple exercise that will clearly illustrate the points I have made so far. Place an orange, an apple, and perhaps a grapefruit, close to each other on a table-cloth—any sort, any colour. Now if you really look at this little group analytically, you will observe an interesting fact. The fruits will almost certainly pick up colour from a variety of sources apart from one another, and I suggest you work these out purely as an exercise in colour analysis. Then arrange the same objects in a few different lights; close to a window, in shadow, under an artificial light, and so on. The colours will change with each fresh set of circumstances, thus proving that there is nothing constant about colour, which is an infinitely variable phenomenon.

Before considering any further practical aspects of colour theory, it might be helpful to take a look at colour purely from the scientific point of view since in the final outcome, aesthetics are inevitably a compromise between the subjectivity of the artist's conception, and the objectivity of the means he must of necessity employ to express his vision. Colour in painting, however modified or extended by the artist's personality, is dependent for its success upon certain invariables. Even imaginative colour such as the expressionist, or the symbolist may use, must, if it is to evoke a pleasurable aesthetic response, conform to these considerations. What *is* colour? It is in fact, simply the decomposition of white light, which is composed of the seven spectrum colours, red, orange, yellow, green, blue, indigo and violet. When we pass a ray of light through a glass prism, it breaks into the six primary colours (the three key primaries are red, yellow, and blue), which are known as *the spectrum of white light*.

The colour of an object is determined by the way in which it either absorbs, or reflects, the rays—or waves if you like—of these spectrum colours. Thus an object that *reflects* all the colours of the spectrum will appear as white, whereas one that *absorbs* them all, will appear as black. Other objects and substances absorb only certain of these spectrum colours, and reflect others. Accordingly, they appear as red, yellow, green, blue, violet, and so on. As you can see then, the hue of an object depends on the wavelength of the colour, or colours, it does *not* absorb. A blue object for instance will absorb all the colours of the spectrum except the wave length of blue, which it will reflect. Here then is the raw material from which the painter must compose his orchestrations of colour. The spectrum of white light is the basis of all aesthetic colour, whether that be the low key harmonies of Rembrandt, or the shrill, high pitched contrasts of El Greco.

A good analogy is to think of painting as colour cookery. Just as the skilful chef does not simply fling all the available ingredients higgledy-piggledy into the pot without selection, and further, without having worked out certain harmonies, proportions, and spicings, so the painter, using the ingredients of the spectrum, must concoct an appetizing, and satisfying feast for the eye—and the emotions.

Colour then, is simply *light*. The French Impressionists applied this fact scientifically in their painting, which consequently, overflows with light, and atmosphere. It follows quite logically, that if you restrict your palette to the spectrum of white light, your painting is bound to be luminous, and bright.

Colour theory is something additional to this fundamental fact; it is concerned with the laws that govern the controlled use of this raw material—the seven colours of the solar spectrum.

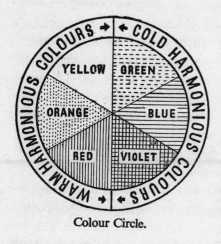

Colour Circle.

For our purposes, these are best considered in the form of a *colour circle*[1]. As you will see from my diagram, one half contains the *warm*, and the other, the *cool* colours of the spectrum. Warm harmonious colours, and cool harmonious colours. The colours which appear directly opposite one another—such as red and green, orange and blue—are known as *complementary*, or *contrasting* colours. Aesthetically, a picture painted either wholly in warm, or cool colours, would be extremely dull and uninspiring to look at, since the physiological construction of the eye craves colour contrast. This is quite simple to prove by a little experiment. Lay a square of bright green material—a piece of coloured paper, card, or something similar—over a sheet of white paper, and gaze intently at the coloured area for about twenty-five seconds. Then remove the green square and concentrate on the white surface underneath. Your eye, fatigued by the green, will automatically superimpose a complementary tint on the white surface so that you will see a

[1] If a colour circle is revolved rapidly, the individual colours will reintegrate and the spinning disk will appear as white. That shown above is divided into only six segments since for immediate purposes violet and indigo are synonymous.

pinkish colour. Concentrate on the white surface for a few seconds until this appears.

Landscape painters—Constable is a notable example—frequently apply this principle by introducing a spot of bright red among the masses of green; a dash of exhilarating contrast to stimulate, and excite the eye. When looking at a landscape in which the artist has employed the principle of contrast effect—you can do this quite well with a reproduction—blot out the red by holding your thumb in front of you and closing one eye, and at once the painting will lose a great deal of its life—it will, so to speak, "die".

This leads us to another important consideration. Apart from the introduction of a spot or two of the complementary of green to enliven a landscape, contrasting colours when used together more generally, possess the power of intensifying each other[1]. The way to make the most of the yellows in a painting for instance, is to bring something from the violet range into close, or near relationship. Combinations of complementary, or near complementary colours are considered to produce more satisfying colour schemes than the relationship of hues that appear next to one another on the colour circle. These tend to clash, and in a sense, to neutralize each other. Green and blue for example are notoriously difficult to relate.

Here again is a simple experiment which will illustrate the principle of intensification effect, and of colour neutralization. For this you will need some small squares of brightly coloured paper; four by four inch squares of orange and blue, and a two-inch square of green. From the centre of the blue paper, cut a square two inches by two. Place the blue paper over the orange square so that you can study the two complementary colours in close relationship. You will see quite clearly how they enliven and intensify each other. Next place the green square over the orange inset and observe how, immediately, the blue appears to lose much of its "life", and how the two colours enter into conflict, and "kill" one another.

Make these comparisons a few times until the principle has been thoroughly appreciated. The principle of contrast—or intensification—effect, has been employed in a variety of ways by every great colourist from Titian to Van Gogh. Although the contrast effects of Titian are comparatively low in key, and those of Van Gogh are pitched much higher, the principle is identical.

You should get into the habit of drawing comparisons between the colour of widely divergent painters, and schools of painting, in a search for those immutable standards which underlay their superficial dissimilarities. You can do this by visits to galleries, but more expediently, by building up a comprehensive collection of coloured postcards. These will of course only provide a rude substitute for the originals, but they are nevertheless the most convenient way of making com-

[1]Consider the striking use of contrasting colours in André Derain's "Pool of London" (Facing page 33).

parisons at your leisure. There are hundreds of excellent post-cards available, and I would suggest in the light of our consideration of colour so far, a comparison between the painting of the Venetians, and that of the Impressionists, and the Post-Impressionists, notably Van Gogh, and Gauguin. Differences in the colour tone scale of these three groups—low in the case of the Venetian painters—are supported at many points by the common use of certain immutable principles which form the fundamental bases of all great chromatic orchestration.

Apart from comparatively bold contrasts in colour itself, the subtle contrast of warm and cool shades is another important aspect of colour theory. In painting —as in nature—the alternation of warm and cool colour tones is vital to the creation of satisfying colour compositions. Broadly speaking, the principle is demonstrated by the use of warm light tones, cool middle tones, and warm shadows. On the other hand the Impressionists used *cool* shadows as a foil for their warm, sun-drenched lights. See Monet's "Bassin aux Nympheas" facing page 192. The principle can be studied for instance when portrait painting, where the cool middle tones of the face frequently contain flashes of blue, green, violet, and kindred tints. Such hues are not usually associated with the colour of the face—until you start portrait painting yourself, and to study the portraiture of the masters. Flesh is not just a uniform *pink*; it presents one of the most complex chromatic problems with which the painter has to deal: for even if, superficially, you can say that the local colour of an orange, is "orange"—what is the approximate local colour of a face? So look for the cool middle tones in your subject, and especially in faces, for it is these subtle, delicate nuances in the cool range, that hold such a delicious, and refreshing balance, between the warm lights and darks.

Colour possesses three characteristics:

(a) HUE—The colour itself, e.g. red, yellow, blue.

(b) CHROMA—The relative purity, or brilliance of the colour, e.g. *bright* red, or *dull* green.

(c) VALUE—The degree of its modification by such factors as the prevailing conditions of light, air and distance. [See Ivon Hitchens' "Damp Autumn" facing page 16.] Theoretically, colours tend to become paler and cooler (bluer), as they become more distant. Thus a range of distant hills are modified by light, air and distance, and appear as bluish in colour. [See Richard Wilson's "Landscape With Bathers" facing page 16.]

From the point of view of the practice of painting, *chroma* and *value* are the operative considerations to be borne in mind, especially the question of colour values. Pure colour, as I pointed out earlier is a scientific, rather than an aesthetic fact, and seldom presents itself other than in modified circumstances to the eye of the painter. Therefore unless he is using colour two-dimensionally, in pure, flat areas, for some Expressionist, or imaginative purpose, the painter working in terms of three-dimensional space and form must of necessity deal with *colour values*.

Colour can also be considered—and this applies particularly to landscape— in terms of *advancing*, and *retreating*, colour. Warm colours, such as the reds and browns, appear to advance to the forefront of a picture and should therefore be used in the foreground. Cool, or cold colours on the other hand, such as the blues and violets, appear to retreat into the distance and should be used in the background.

So much then for certain functional aspects of colour theory in their relation to the science of painting. I stress the purely technical side of painting by using the term "science" since it is, after all, vitally important that the artist should appreciate the place of an objective system in the hierarchy of creative expression. Inspiration there must be of course, at the outset, and the exercise of aesthetic sensibility during the process of creation, but unless these are harnessed to certain immutable laws there is little likelihood that inspiration will ever be in a position to assume a coherent, and communicable form. You may apply the principle of contrast effect in colours of a high, or of a low key, according to your own feelings in this matter: but either way you will conform to a pre-ordained law.

Reaching a compromise between yourself and the incommutable system of natural order in which you are set, is a vital factor in the art, and science of painting. Now for a word about another aspect of colour theory. . . .

## COLOUR MIXING

From the three key primaries, red, yellow, and blue, you can, with the addition of varying amounts of white, mix every colour, and every shade and tint of every colour in existence. Theoretically then, you do not need a great many different colours on your palette in order to paint a colourful picture. Titian is reputed to have said that an artist needs only three colours, and he himself used a restricted range. The basis of his palette was red, yellow, and blue, plus white and black. These are the colours Titian used:

| | |
|---|---|
| Lead White (Flake White) | Malachite Green. (Hydrous carbonate |
| Ultramarine | of copper: a green mineral.) |
| Madder Lake | Yellow Ochre |
| Burnt Sienna | Red Ochre |
| | Ivory Black |

You will appreciate that this is not only a restricted palette, but one also which is set in a low key: a characteristic typical of the Venetian School as a whole.

By contrast, the palette of the French master François Boucher (1703–1770), though pitched in a higher key, is equally restricted. Boucher used the following range of colours:

| | |
|---|---|
| White | Rose Madder |
| Light Ochre | Crimson Lake |
| Brown Ochre | Burnt Sienna |
| Vermilion | Cobalt Blue |

This is a palette that contains no black, thus providing, for its time, a remarkable precedent for the Impressionist's rejection of black on scientific grounds. This omission, in Boucher, accounts no doubt, for the extremely delicate, clear, porcelain-like quality of his colour.

It would seem therefore that the first requirement of painting is a relatively simple, basic palette, from which the artist can comfortably mix the widest possible range of additional colours, and tints.

In his chapter on "Painting in Oils" Colin Moss discusses the question of just what colours ought, in his opinion, to form the basis of the beginner's palette, so this is a consideration with which I shall not concern myself here. At some point however, you might find it interesting to experiment yourself with the palettes of Titian, and Boucher, although Malachite Green as such, is no longer in production today. What I would like to consider next is the place of black as a factor in the art of colour mixing. Either black is rejected out of hand, as in Impressionism, or it is retained, if only for the purposes of colour mixing. Unless you are painting in a black and neutral grey monochrome, black should never be used in itself, but only as an element in the production of modified colours, such as a *lowered* red, or blue. As a means of lowering the *tone* of a colour, black can play an important part. It is also of value in the mixing of *coloured greys*. These must be clearly distinguished from *neutral greys*, since the real greys in nature are inevitably coloured greys. Neutral grey is an artificial and colourless element, produced by mixing black and white. Coloured greys—grey-blues, grey-greens, grey-browns, and so on—are obtainable in two ways. We can either mix the grey produced from black and white with a proportion of the colour which is to form the basis of the particular coloured grey we require; or we can produce coloured greys by mixing the appropriate complementaries since complementary colours when mixed, tend towards greyness. The greys produced from the mixing of complementaries will naturally be cleaner than the relatively dirty greys which result from the use of black. The process of trial and error is the only real way of finding out what happens when you mix colours, and I would suggest that at first you experiment with both methods of making coloured greys, not while painting a picture, but simply by mixing colours and laying them one against the other in broad bands on a painting surface. In this way you will be able to make a series of interesting and revealing comparisons.

The danger in using black either as a separate element, or as an ingredient in colour mixing, is just that it can so easily make for dirty painting. This is a very real danger, and one which you are better able to face and deal with for the knowledge that it exists.

White is of course essential in colour mixing, but black is not an indispensable ingredient, although when carefully controlled it can play an important part. The addition of white to a colour reduces its brilliance: the addition of black both reduces its intensity and lowers its tone, making it darker. You can, if you wish to dispense with black, produce rich, and beautiful darks by mixing pure colours with the addition of little, or no white. For instance, pure red and blue will give you a deep purple that is extremely useful for the darkest shadows in a sunny landscape. A deep, cool shadow, as the Impressionists found, is the perfect foil for the brilliance of sun-drenched lights, and warm half-tones. In such circumstances cool shadows are a vital contrast.

Of course neither black nor white is in itself, colour. Their main function, apart from the reduction of brilliance, is to assist in the production of *tones*, so that the painter can create his lights and darks. *Chiaroscuro*[1]—witness Rembrandt— is an element of great importance in the art of painting.

There is little more, if anything, from the theoretical point of view that the painter needs to know about colour mixing. Inevitably, success must depend upon your own personal experiments, and how you, as a unique individual, see, and conceive colour, for your own particular purposes. Yet whether you use colour *realistically*, as the Impressionists did, *emotionally*, as El Greco and the modern Expressionists have done or *imaginatively*, as André Masson (born 1896) has done in his fiery "Spanish Landscape" facing page 33, you will need to bear in mind the few, unassailable laws, that have always provided the basis of good colour.

Masson, who joined the Surrealists in 1924, has intensified the colours in the landscape I reproduce, not so much as a means of heightening the emotional significance of his subject (an objective which is closer to Expressionism), but as the means of investing the shapes and rhythms of the subject with a pure, and glowing lyricism. This is the poetic imagination in full bloom. The painter juxtaposes his colours with the unique, and startling unusualness one may expect from a poet who transforms the ordinariness of words by similar juxtapositions. If Dylan Thomas had written his superb poem "Fern Hill" around the nucleus of a Spanish, instead of a Welsh setting, Masson's "Spanish Landscape" might well have illustrated a portion of the poem in which Thomas orientates his word imagery with the

[1] *Chiaroscuro*: The organization of light and shade in painting.

same magic, imaginative uniqueness that exemplifies the painter's orientation of chromatic imagery. Consider the juxtaposition of the scarlet cocks' combs against the rich greens, and the background of lilac, salmon, and golden yellow; or the singing beauty of the distant hills, with the shrill voices of pure red and blue, struck like a piercing violin note against the lemon sky. This is the substance of the poetic imagination. Now contrast the *poetry* of Masson's colour orientations with a similar quality in this verse from "Fern Hill". . . .

> "And then to awake, and the farm, like a wanderer white
> With the dew, come back, the cock on his shoulder; it was all
>     Shining, it was Adam and maiden,
>         The sky gathered again
>     And the sun grew round that very day.
> So it must have been after the birth of the simple light
> In the first, spinning place, the spellbound horses walking warm
>     Out of the whinnying green stable
>         On to the fields of praise."
>
> (From: *Deaths and Entrances*. Dent. 1946)

# CHAPTER 10

# Anatomy

D O NOT worry unduly if the lengthy catalogue of anatomical names in this chapter appears a little formidable at a first glance. The chapter of necessity is the most specialized in the book and for that reason reads more as a technical statement than a piece of straight writing.

If you digest it leisurely, a bit at a time, in preference to reading it straight through, it will soon make sense. For instance, read the section about the skeleton in conjunction with a study of the appropriate diagrams, and establish a sound pictorial idea of this aspect of anatomy firmly in your mind, before passing to a consideration of the muscles. Here too, complete your study of each section in turn. Thus, you should possess a clear visual picture of the muscles of the head, face, and neck, before moving on to a study of the remaining sections.

To facilitate this method of study I have broken the chapter into parts.

The reader should refer continuously to the anatomical diagrams, and supplement his studies by making various rough sketches. This is one of the best methods of consolidating a thorough knowledge of the subject. Many of these sketches can be made from one's own person with the aid of a mirror, while attendance at the life-class of a local art school will of course afford invaluable opportunities of studying anatomy at first hand.

As you progress with your drawing and painting you will become increasingly more conscious of the need for a working knowledge of figure construction. You can plod along quite happily with a variety of subjects that will not involve you in figure-work, but the moment you wish—as you certainly will—to introduce a figure, or figures, into a composition, you will find it most frustrating to be at a loss in this respect. A knowledge of the figure, purely as a piece of machinery, is an essential part of the artist's equipment. Anatomy fulfils this requirement for the artist, and forms the basis of his work in the life-class. You will of course find it a great help if you can supplement this chapter on anatomy, and the one on figure construction which follows, by attending a life-class at your own school, or

*Above:* **NYMPHS AND SATYRS**
**Isaac Oliver (c. 1556–1617)**

English painting really begins with the Elizabethan Miniaturists. Among the greatest of these, Isaac Oliver is seen here as the painter of a rapturous pagan idyll. The artist has given full rein to a free, and vigorous imagination. Apart from the attraction of the subject in itself, the student might well consider the purely anatomical aspects of this picture when studying the Chapter on Anatomy. The figures are extremely well constructed; the back view of the satyr, and the sleeping figure in the bottom left-hand corner, offering a particularly rich account of the relevant anatomy.

**LIBERTY LEADING THE PEOPLE**
**Eugène Delacroix (1793–1863)** [*above*]

**THE OLD SHEPHERD'S CHIEF MOURNER**
**Sir Edwin Landseer, R.A. (1802–73)** [*right*]

Delacroix, leader of the French school of Romantic painting also uses the imagination as a mirror in which the naked idea is transmuted into a powerful, romantic figment. Not so Sir Edwin Landseer whose imagination is limited by the idea that animals are virtually human.

*Above:* **AUTUMN: THE CHÂTEAU DE STEEN**    Peter Paul Rubens (1577–1640)
On the left of this spacious landscape painted in 1636 we can see the artist's château. The small figures in front of the building are those of Rubens, his wife, and a nurse with a child. The cart lumbering slowly out of the picture suggests the continuance of the panorama beyond the canvas.

*Below:* **THE BEACH AT TROUVILLE: THE EMPRESS EUGÈNE AND HER SUITE**
Eugène Boudin (1824–98)
In this sparkling picture, the feeling of openness is accentuated by the vast sky. The serene lines of sea and headland are offset by the swinging arcs of the dresses and the bobbing parasols.

college of art. Practical experience in drawing from the life is really an indispensable part of your development as an artist, and I would urge you to take full advantage of such facilities as your local art school may afford. While it is relatively easy for the serious amateur to gain admittance to an evening life-class, it is unlikely that facilities for the study of anatomy will be available to the spare-time student. Therefore I have included this chapter on anatomy.

We might start with a question—how much anatomy does the artist need to know? Since we are dealing here with an exact, determinable study, the question is not difficult to answer. He must know enough to ensure that the delineation of his contours, and the structure of his forms, will agree with the "geographical" facts common to every figure. Except in the case of malformation, the "geography" of the body is constant. (See pictures between pages 136-7). There can be no inadmissible lumps, or bumps—no going in or coming out at the wrong places. Whether he works in cool, meticulous detail, or in a rapid spontaneous line, the draughtsman must express hard, anatomical fact. It is only necessary to compare the drawing by the English artist Alfred Stevens (between pages 136-7) with the one by Auguste Rodin (facing page 104) to appreciate this point.

The Stevens' drawing is a relatively detailed study, executed slowly, and methodically; on the other hand, the Rodin drawing has been effected with a minimum of detail and at considerable speed. It is an extremely economical drawing. Yet irrespective of these marked differences in approach, and style, it is immediately apparent that both artists are masters of the anatomical situation. One can clearly see in the two drawings an appreciation of the fat, bulky *deltoid* (the big shoulder muscle at the top of the arm), of the *scapula*'s effect on the line of

"Geographical" facts are common to every figure and every style of drawing.

the back (the *scapula* is the shoulder-blade), and a sense of the boniness of the elbow, and knee joints. The Stevens' drawing also displays a perfect appreciation of the form of the *external oblique* muscle as it pads the region of the pelvis, and of

G

the weightiness of the great *gluteal*, or buttock muscles. While the bent right limb of the Rodin demonstrates clearly the flexion of the *tibialis anticus* muscle in action at the front of the leg. One can literally *feel* its tense, bunched contraction.

All this is dependent upon a thorough knowledge of the anatomical construction of the figure. The detailed Alfred Stevens, and the economical Auguste Rodin, are equally sound anatomically. If anything, the Rodin is the finer achievement, since here the artist's knowledge of anatomy has been employed *intuitively*. It has become an instinctive, inherent element, in his style.

The really good draughtsman will know the topography of the body in the same way that a person knows his way about a familiar town, or city. Without the exertion of any conscious effort, he will thread his way smoothly, and with complete confidence through the maze of streets that to a stranger would prove merely bewildering. Until you know your anatomy, the same will apply to the topography of the body. Ideally, you should be able to delineate at speed, a drawing that will "read" accurately as a piece of anatomical fact. To illustrate this I have made two rapid sketches of the arm (page 100), one with the *biceps extended*, and the other showing the same muscle *flexed*. They show not only how much can be said with the swiftest and most economical of means, but the chief characteristics of muscular action, and inaction. When a muscle is extended—in a state of relaxation—it becomes soft, and merges gently into the context of the surrounding muscles. But when it contracts, in action, it shortens and becomes hard. In this state it presents sharply defined outlines. This is a basic principle to keep at the back of your mind.

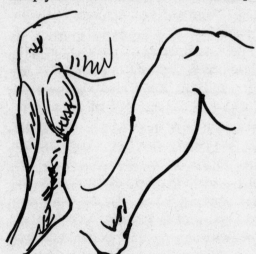

Flexion and extension: an exercise.

It is quite easy to test this principle by a few practical exercises with your own muscles. For instance, raise a leg from the ground—you can do this in comfort while sitting down—and turn the foot upwards with a quick, sharp movement. This will cause the foremost muscle in the anterior group—the *tibialis anticus*—to shorten, and contract into a hard mass. At the same time, the chief muscle of the posterior group —the *gastrocnemius*, or calf-muscle— will lengthen and become relatively soft. Do this a few times while watching the movement, and checking the action with your fingers. You can see, and feel it all happening. As I noted earlier, this particular flexion is well demonstrated in the Rodin drawing.

Now if, on the other hand, you turn the foot downwards, the *tibialis anticus* will extend, and flatten, while the *gastrocnemius* will contract and harden into a tight mass. (See opposite). You can make a similar test by clenching your fist and bending the forearm so that the *biceps* are flexed into a ball. The same action will extend the *triceps*—the large muscle at the back of the upper arm. The contrary will occur if you unclench the fist and let the forearm fall gently into a relaxed state. The *biceps* will soften, and extend, and the *triceps* will harden, and become shorter.

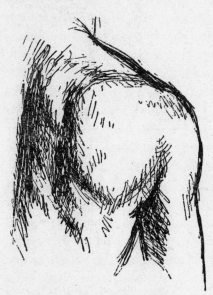

The effect of the scapula on surface form.

Having now established the importance of flexion and extension, let me describe the chief anatomical characteristics, and individual features, of the body. An artist does not need to be submerged in a deluge of anatomical detail, but he must understand the construction of the skeleton, and know the location, and form, of the main surface muscles. The skeleton of course affects the surface appearance of the body at a number of points. For instance, the *malar*—or cheek-bone—is often evident; the *clavicle* (collar-bone), ribs, pelvis, scapula, and patella (knee-cap), are all prominent surface features. But the muscles are in complete command of the scene.

No matter how great the artist, in his figure work he is, of necessity, subordinate to the laws of anatomy. Indeed one great master was so obsessed by this consideration that his art suffered. This was Michelangelo (1475–1564). However, we must remember that anatomy was a re-discovery of the Renaissance, and a feature of an age that had at last broken free from the ruthless control of the medieval Church, a power which for hundreds of years had forbidden any first hand study of the body. The work of medieval artists provides conclusive proof of this restriction. In such circumstances it is hardly surprising that the pioneer work of Michelangelo—and Leonardo—in this challenging new field, should have been treated with a robust enthusiasm. Not since Greek and Roman times had living models been studied by European artists. Both Michelangelo and Leonardo were practical anatomizers, cutting up and dissecting bodies in their quest for knowledge.

Gradually, anatomy grew less self-conscious, taking its place as an effective, integral feature in European art. The debt to Michelangelo, and other keen

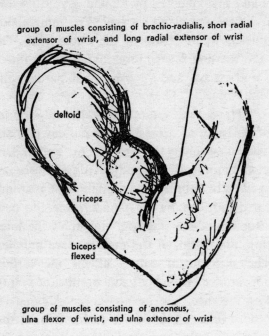

group of muscles consisting of brachio-radialis, short radial
extensor of wrist, and long radial extensor of wrist

deltoid

triceps

biceps
flexed

group of muscles consisting of anconeus,
ulna flexor of wrist, and ulna extensor of wrist

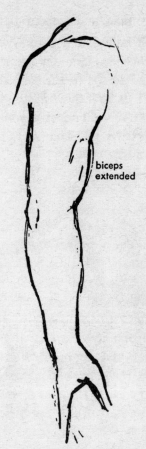

biceps
extended

students of anatomy—like Jacopo Robusti (1518–1594), called Tintoretto—is very considerable. Without their rather self-conscious study of anatomy it would not have been possible for later draughtsmen, as diverse in style as Alfred Stevens and Auguste Rodin (see between pages 136-7 and facing 104), to draw the figure with such an effortless appreciation of the anatomical scene.

### THE SKELETON

The skeleton is the foundation of the body and consists of a number of bones joined together by ligaments. There are four main groups: the bones of the skull, of the trunk, and of the upper, and lower limbs. For artistic purposes it is sufficient to know that the skull consists of two, large, bony areas, one of which, the *mandible*, or jaw-bone, is movable, and the other, the *cranium*, fixed. The *cranium* consists of eight, closely surtured cranial bones, the chief visible feature of which is the *malar.* This affects surface appearances particularly in lean faces. It tends to be obscured by fat, and is seldom visible in the faces of healthy children. On the other hand, it is often a marked feature in the face of elderly people, where the flesh has

100

shrunken, and the skin tightened over the bone. But there is of course no set rule about the extent to which it is discernible. Every face has to be studied as an individual case. One frequently hears passing references to high cheek-bones, and fine bone structure, and these are both instances in which the *malar bone* plays a part. It does in fact often impart an extremely subtle, and beautiful quality to a face, with its delicate line, and the gentle shadow cast by its form in the softly hollowed flesh.

The trunk consists of the following elements. The *spinal*, or *central vertebral column*, the *thorax*, or rib cage, and the *pelvis, clavicles*, and *scapulae*.

The spinal column is composed of a number of bones, twenty-four of which are separated, the remainder being closely knit in two masses known as the *sacrum*, and *coccyx*, which together form an inverted triangle of bone, terminating in a sort of tail. The individual vertebrae, separated by discs of cartilage which assist the articulation of the spine, are divided into three groups. Seven *cervical*, or neck vertebrae, twelve *dorsal* vertebrae (to which the ribs are attached), and five *lumbar* vertebrae. The *thorax* consists of twenty-four ribs, twelve each side of the *sternum*, or breast-bone. Ten of these are attached at the back to the vertebral column, and in front, to the *sternum*. The two remaining ribs on either side are unattached in front, and commonly known as the floating ribs.

The *pelvis* is composed of the two hip-bones fixed at the back to the *sacrum* and *coccyx*. It forms a bowl-like shape which holds and protects the organs in the lower part of the abdomen. Each hip-bone is divided into three parts, The *ilium*, which is the flat upper portion, the *ishium*, which is the knobbly lower portion, and the *pubes*, which forms a bony ridge directly in front. The lower part of the hip-bone is socketed to receive the head of the *femur*, or thigh-bone. This cavity is known as the *acetabulum*. The upper ridge of the hip-bone is known as the iliac crest. The angle of the *pelvis* across the line of the *iliac* crests is an important checkpoint in the construction of the figure.

In a standing position, if the weight of the body is evenly distributed upon both legs, the line across the crests of the *pelvis* will be horizontal. If, on the other hand the weight is taken by one leg, so that the other hangs loosely, flexed at the knee, the angle of the pelvis will be inclined downwards on the side which is free of weight. This is a very important point, and one to which I shall refer later, in my chapter on figure construction. The *pelvis* then is composed of four bones: the two hip-bones, the *sacrum*, and the *coccyx*. Bear in mind also that the female pelvis is wider than that of the male, and this accounts for the characteristic breadth across a woman's hips.

Two other skeletal features complete the trunk. The *scapulae*, and the *clavicles*. The scapula, or shoulder-blade, is a flat, triangular shaped bone possessing three

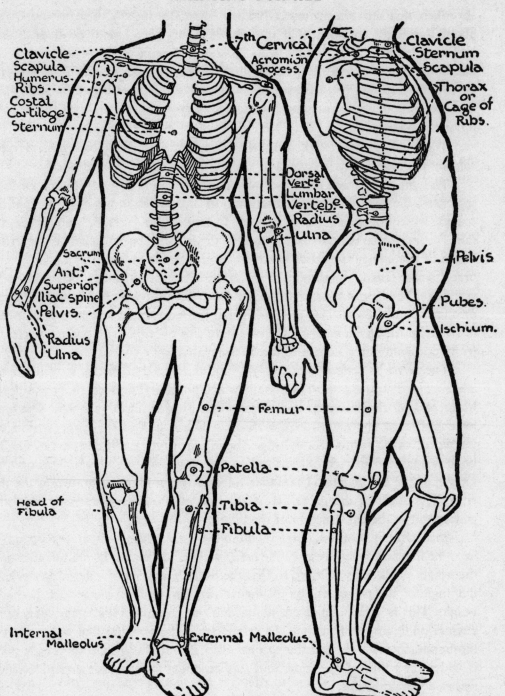

The Skeleton: by F. J. Glass from *Modelling and Sculpture*.

borders: the upper, or *clavicular border*, the *vertebral border* which faces the spinal column, and the *anterior border* which faces the arm. The *scapulae* are clearly visible at surface level. The *clavicle*, or collar-bone, is joined at one end to the *sternum*, and at the other to the outermost point of the spine of the *scapula*, called the *acromion*. The spine of the *scapula* is a bony shelf that slopes upwards from the *vertebral* border.

Now let me describe the bones of the upper and lower limbs. The upper arm consists of one bone, the *humerus*, which articulates freely in the *glenoid* cavity of the *scapula* to form the shoulder-joint. The *glenoid cavity* is situated at the upper extremity of the *anterior border* of the *scapula*. At its lower end the humerus articulates with the *radius*, and the *ulna*—the two bones of the forearm—to form the elbow-joint. The lower extremity of the humerus is wide, and marked by two bony prominences, known as the *condyles*. One is situated on the outer side and one on the inner side. They serve as points of attachment for certain muscles which I shall describe later. When the forearm is *supine*, that is to say, when the palm of the hand faces upward, or to the front, the *radius* and the *ulna* are more or less parallel. But when the hand is turned over in the *pronate* position, with the palm facing downward, or to the rear, the *radius*, which is the outer bone, crosses inwards over the *ulna*. You can carry out this demonstration yourself. Sit at a table with forearm bared, and resting, palm upward. Now just turn the hand over so that the palm lies flat on the table. If you carry out this movement a few times, quite slowly, carefully considering the action of the two bones, you will appreciate the way in which the *radius* crosses over the *ulna*. When the palm is in the *pronate* position you can see, and feel, the prominent, knobbly head of the *ulna* which in this position will be on the outer side of the wrist. This is a clear instance of the skeleton's effect on surface appearances. Once you have learned the location and general appearance of such landmarks, you will be in a position to introduce them correctly, even when working from memory. This is the vital knowledge that makes for informed draughtsmanship.

The wrist is composed of eight small *carpus* bones, and the hand of five *metacarpal* bones—one to each digit—and fourteen *phalanges*. There are three of these small *phalange* bones to each finger, and two for each thumb.

It might at this point be of interest to the reader to appreciate that a great many anatomical names derive from the Greek and Latin languages. Thus the word "carpus" from the Greek "karpos", meaning wrist. In combination with the Greek "meta", meaning "with, after", we get "metacarpal", meaning the bones of the hand between the wrist and the fingers. The name "phalange" too is Greek in origin, from "phalanx" meaning "banded together for a common purpose". Thus, the bones of the fingers and toes unite to perform their respective functions.

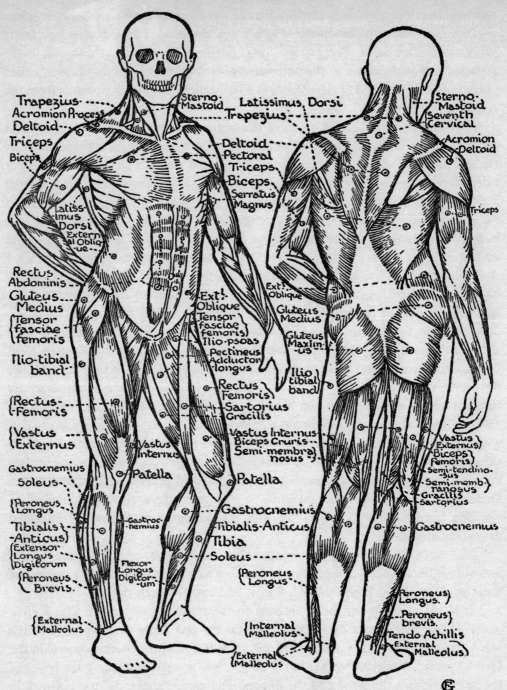

The Muscles of the Body: by F. J. Glass from *Modelling and Sculpture.*

*Right:* **DRAWING**    **Auguste Rodin (1840–1917)**
One of the greatest of all European sculptors, Rodin also left a number of unique figure studies. Drawn at speed in a sensitive, revealing line, they were often tinted with pale washes of delicate colour. His power of anatomical description is profound, yet extremely subtle.

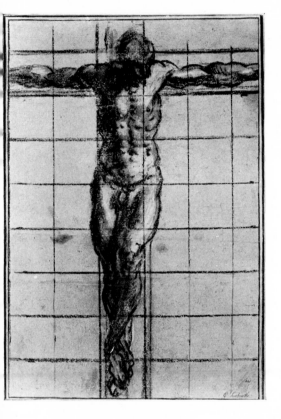

*Left:* **STUDY FOR A CRUCIFIXION**
**Tintoretto (Jacopo Robusti: 1518–94)**
The name of this great Venetian artist derives from the fact that his father was a dyer: in Italian, *Tintore*. His compositions, often intensely dramatic and violent in movement, point to the Baroque style of the seventeenth and eighteenth centuries, with its theatricality and flamboyance in opposition to the classicism of the Renaissance. Anatomically more obvious than Rodin's conception, this drawing is of course a painter's study, and not an end in itself. Yet it also expresses the exaggerated anatomical detail characteristic of Tintoretto, and directly inspired by Michelangelo.

*Right:*
**MALLORCAN FIGURINES AND ORNAMENTAL VASE (1957)**
Through its folk art the community as a whole is able to express itself creatively. These charming pieces, produced by the islanders of Mallorca, express the sense of fun, and simple gaiety, which inspires the inhabitants of this beautiful Spanish island. The current enthusiasm for painting for pleasure, common in Britain today, is a comparative phenomenon.

*Above:* **MAJA DESNUDA**     Francisco Goya (1746–1828)
Goya's friendship with the Duchess of Alba has led to the
belief that she posed for the *Maja* (in Spanish "a fashionable flirt") *Desnuda*. There is no conclusive proof of this.
It is however likely that she inspired this idealized conception of the eternal, seductive female.

*Right:* **WOMAN ON A DIVAN**   Albert Marquet (1875–1947)
A realistic and informal conception which breaks with the
more formal, classical tradition of the reclining nude.

*Below:* **THE BIRTH OF VENUS**   Alexandre Cabanel (1824–89)
In Cabanel's titillating nudes the eroticism is veiled in
allegory. Compare this "double think" with the frankness
of Botticelli's conception (see facing page 24).

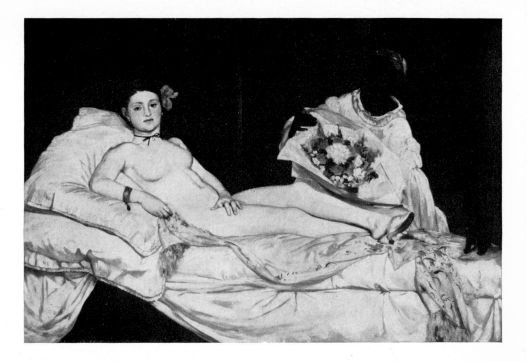

*Above:* **OLYMPIA**      **Edouard Manet (1832–83)**
*Below:* **LUNCHEON ON THE GRASS**      **Edouard Manet (1832–83)**

The modern movement in painting begins with Manet, whose *Luncheon on the Grass* exhibited in 1863, and *Olympia* in 1865, struck the first blows at the moribund conventions of the day. These paintings profoundly shocked both critics and public, and became at once the centre of scandal and fierce controversy in which the writer Emile Zola rallied stoutly to the support of the painter. The artist's use of a young girl, probably a prostitute, as the model for *Olympia*, and his unconventional conception of a naked woman in the company of clothed gentlemen was too much for a society conditioned to accept female nudity in the hypocritical disguises employed by Cabanel and others.

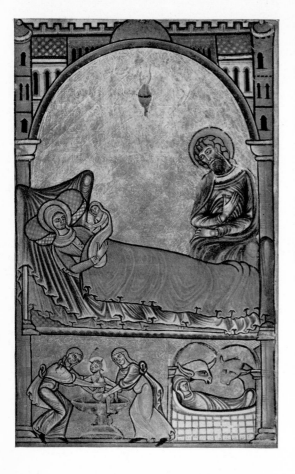

*Above, left:* **THE NATIVITY (Possibly German)**
  Cotton Ms.: 12th century

*Above:* **A GAME OF POLO**
  Persian Illumination. 16th century

*Left:* **ODALISQUE**
  Henri Matisse (1869–1954)

In medieval painting, two-dimensionalism is the direct result of a lack of any real knowledge of perspective. In Persian painting of the 16th century this deficiency is amply compensated for by the beauty of pattern and design. Flatness for its own sake has also been employed by many modern painters. Here, Matisse intentionally abandons three-dimensionalism for the sake of decoration.

An interest in the etymology of anatomical terms will add touches of colourful interest here and there to your general study, and naturally, the greater your knowledge of the details of any particular subject, the more clearly and excitingly it will come to life. A good dictionary will of course provide you with the etymological source of your various words, and terms.

The effect of the metacarpals on surface form.

It is also important, always, to check, so far as possible, the location and appearance of the bones and muscles either on your own, or on the body of a live model. Married couples, especially if they are both interested in painting, and figure construction, are of course in a happy, and privileged position since they can act as models for each other. However, in such a simple matter as a study of the metacarpals and phalanges, it is only necessary to examine your own hand. You can easily feel, and to some extent, see, the long metacarpal bones and the smaller phalanges. The spaces between the metacarpals are frequently visible as a series of long, shallow indentations, on the back of the hand. Muscular tendons will also be clearly visible overlaying these bones and running down to their attachments in the fingers.

The lower limb contains the longest bone in the body—the *femur*. As I mentioned earlier, this bone is articulated with the *acetabulum* of the *pelvis* to form the hip-joint—the largest ball and socket joint in the body. There are two main prominences at the top of the *femur*—the smooth head which fits into the *acetabulum*, and the *great trochanter*, to which several muscles are attached. The *great trochanter* is visible, particularly in thin subjects, and can be felt quite easily a few inches below the *iliac crest*. In general, the prominence of the *great trochanter* plays an important part in conditioning the surface form of the upper locality of the thigh.

If you stand in front of a mirror perhaps just before or after the bath, you can study the effects of the *great trochanter* on surface form, simply by shifting your weight from one leg to the other. It will be clearly visible at the top of the thigh in the leg which is taking the weight, as a marked, knobby protuberance.

The leg consists of two long bones—the *tibia*, and the *fibula*. The *tibia*, situated on the inside of the leg is the larger of the two bones. It articulates with the *femur*, and at its lower extremity forms a marked prominence at the ankle-joint, which is known as the *internal malleolus*. The part of the leg commonly known as the shin is formed by the inner surface of the *tibia*. The upper end of the bone which is composed of two tuberosities, forms a marked prominence on the inner side of the knee. The *fibula*, or small bone of the leg lies on the outside. Its head can be detected a little below the level of the knee, the prominence being known as the *styloid process*. At its lower extremity the fibula forms the outer protrusion of the ankle-joint, known as the *external malleolus*. This falls below the level of the *internal malleolus* of the *tibia*, and contributes to the characteristic angle which is a feature of the alignment of the ankle. You have only to stand in front of a full-length mirror with bare feet and ankles to observe this interesting angle. The fibula is articulated with the *tibia*, and with the *astragalus*, one of the bones of the foot.

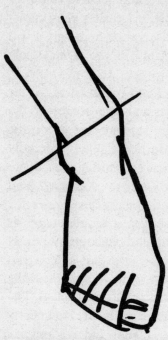

Alignment of the ankle.

The bones of the foot are constructed in the form of an arch, and divided into three groups. The *tarsal*, *metatarsal*, and *phalange* bones. The *tarsus* is made up of seven bones, the largest of which is the *os calcis*, or heel bone. It is to this bone that the Achilles tendon is attached. Officially, it is known as the *tendo achilles*, and I shall mention it again later when I describe the muscles, and their attachments. The *astragalus*, which is next in size to the *os calcis*, rests on the front portion of this bone, and forms the keystone of the arch of the foot. The lower extremities of both *tibia* and *fibula*, articulate with the *astragalus*. There are five *metatarsals*, and they correspond to the *metacarpal* bones of the hand. There are fourteen *phalange* bones, and these too correspond with their equivalents in the hand. Each toe has three phalanges, and the great toe, two. They are of course correspondingly smaller than the *phalanges* of the hand.

Finally, a word about the *patella*, or knee-cap. This is a small, triangular shaped bone with a smooth, flattish, posterior surface, secured at the front of the knee by tendons. The triangle is set with its apex pointing downward, and is always a visible feature of the knee-joint. Its effect on surface form can be seen in Tintoretto's study facing page 104.

# ANATOMY

As you can see now, the skeleton affects the surface appearance of the body in a great many ways, and at a number of points. The muscles affect the body no less. Broadly speaking, the function of the muscles is to act upon the bones like pulleys, action being effected by muscular contraction. For instance, the *zygomaticus major*, a small facial muscle, pulls the corners of the mouth inwards, and upwards, when we laugh. This is superbly demonstrated in the Rubens drawing of Elizabeth Brandt. (Facing page 64). On the other hand, when we feel, so to speak, "down in the mouth", another facial muscle, the *depressor of the angle of the mouth* comes into action, pulling the corner of the mouth downward, so creating a miserable, or dejected expression.

Let us now consider the main muscles of the body, starting with those of the head and neck, followed by the muscles of the trunk, and of the upper and lower limbs. I will describe only those muscles which I feel are important from the point of view of the beginner in anatomy. Later, if you feel the need for a more comprehensive and detailed survey of anatomy you may consult some of the many specialist works on the subject.

## MUSCLES OF THE HEAD, FACE, AND NECK

Generally speaking, the muscles of the head and face do not greatly affect surface appearances. It is bone structure that tends to determine the form of the head, and the face. Fat, of course, also plays its part in conditioning the final shape and form, especially of the face. But fat is not muscle.

Above the eye is the *frontalis*, and surrounding it, the *obicularis*. The former facilitates the movements of the eyebrow, and the latter, a thin, wafer-like muscle, somewhat elliptical in shape, opens and closes the eyelids. The most important muscles in the region of the nose are the *levator of the nostril and the upper lip*, and the *levator of the upper lip*. The mouth is surrounded by a number of extremely supple, and subtle muscles, which facilitate a wide range of movements and expressions. Chief among these, apart from the *levators* of the upper lip, are the *zygomatic* muscles, major and minor, the *depressors* of the lower lip, the *buccinator*, and the *obicularis of the mouth*. This latter muscle, which facilitates eating movements, for instance, is also thin, and wafer-like, corresponding in this sense to the *obicularis of the eye*.

Another of the important muscles of the face is the *masseter*. This is a short, thick, powerful muscle, originating from the *zygomatic arch* of the *malar*, and inserted at its lower extremity, into the jaw-bone. It assists the clenching of the jaws. You can watch this action in your own face, by standing in front of a mirror and clenching your jaws tightly a few times. You can also feel the action with your finger-tips.

107

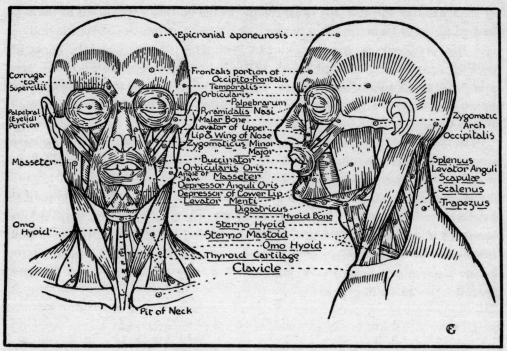

The Muscles of the Head and Neck: by F. J. Glass from *Modelling and Sculpture*.

The most prominent muscle of the neck is the strong, thick, *sterno-mastoid*, which starts from the mastoid process of the skull behind the ear, and sweeps downward with a graceful line to the pit of the neck. In the lower third of its length the muscle divides in two, the outer branch being attached to the *clavicle*, and the inner, to the *sternum*. Both branches of the sterno-mastoid are clearly visible when the head is turned to one side. When the head is facing the front, the muscles present a V-shape enclosing the hollow of the neck, and above it, the Adam's Apple. This is sometimes referred to as one of the two *triangles of the neck*. In this case an inverted triangle. The other is the triangular depression between the sterno-mastoid, and the trapezius, which folds over the shoulder to its attachment at the *clavicle* in front. The *trapezius* is a great, flat diamond-shaped muscle which covers a substantial area of the back. I shall refer to it again later.

Just below the lower jaw is a small, horse-shoe-shaped bone known as the *hyoid bone*. This is not a visible feature at surface level, at least from the artist's point of view, but is important as the point of attachment for a number of muscles passing into the jaw, tongue, and neck. Muscles which facilitate eating, swallowing, and talking. One muscle, however, which originates from the *hyoid bone* is often apparent in the neck. This is the long, ribbon-like, *omo-hyoid*, which runs more or

108

less at right angles in relation to the *sterno-mastoid*, under which it passes. It is attached to the *scapula*.

### THE FRONT OF THE TRUNK

The front and sides of the trunk are covered by a number of prominent muscles which are particularly apparent in the male figure. For this reason, anatomy is always taught in conjunction with a male model.

The chief muscles of the front of the trunk are the *pectorals*—or chest muscles —the *serratus magnus* which ripple below the *pectorals*, and to the side of the trunk, the *rectus abdominis* (muscles of the abdomen), and the *external oblique*, the fleshy muscle which cushions the *pelvis* on either side of the trunk. The large, fan-shaped *pectorals* cover approximately the top half of the thorax. Usually they hide the ribs completely. However, the rounded form of the rib-cage beneath is a factor which determines their curvature around the body. The *pectorals* spring from the *clavicle* and the *sternum*, the fibres converging outwards towards the arm where they are attached to the *humerus*. They can be seen forming a thick band across the armpit. Immediately below the *pectoral*, the lower digitations of the *serratus magnus* interlock with the upper digitations of the *external oblique*. The *serratus magnus* springs from the rib shafts at the side, and is attached behind to the *vertebral border* of the *scapula*. It comes into action when the arm is raised, or outstretched. The *rectus abdominis* is a flat muscle lying on either side of the abdomen, and divided by the centre line which passes through *sternum* and navel. The *recti* start from the ribs, tapering away at the lower extremities to their attachment with the *pubic bone* at the front of the *pelvis*. The whole muscle is divided into segments by three horizontal strips of tendinous membrane. Thus we have eight segments in all, the longest being those from the navel to the pubic bone.

The *external oblique* which forms a hillock of flesh at the side of the trunk lays across the *iliac crest* of the *pelvis*. As I mentioned earlier, the *external oblique* dovetails with the *serratus magnus*, and originates from the ribs. At the rear of the trunk it is partly covered by the *latissimus dorsi*. The muscle is a prominent anatomical landmark, plainly evident from front or rear.

A notable feature of the front of the trunk is the *thoracic arch* of the rib-cage, which is often visible.

Its curve can be easily traced with the fingers, and is particularly noticeable when the stomach is drawn in, and the chest thrust outwards. This superb and subtle arch is specially noticeable in the male figure, and should always be taken into account when constructing the figure from memory. The chief function of the rib cage is of course to afford protection for the vital organs of lungs and heart, and points of origin and attachment for a great variety of muscles.

## THE BACK OF THE TRUNK

The chief muscles at the back of the trunk are the *trapezius,* a part of the *deltoid,* the *latissimus dorsi,* and the *gluteal* muscles. The *external oblique* is also prominent on either side of the lower half of the *latissimus dorsi,* and above the *gluteal* muscles. Partially concealed by the *trapezius,* the *deltoid,* and the *latissimus dorsi* is a group of relatively small muscles. The *levator of the scapula* and the *supraspinatus* are completely hidden by the *trapezius,* but the *rhomboid major,* (the *rhomboid* minor is also hidden by the *trapezius*) *infraspinatus,* the *teres major,* and the *teres minor,* are all surface muscles contained in the area bounded by the *trapezius,* the *deltoid,* and the *latissimus dorsi.*

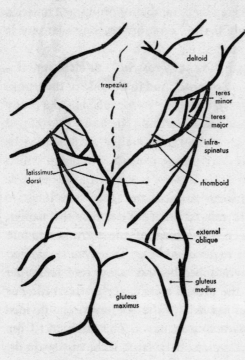

The Muscles of the Back.

The *rhomboids* originate from the *cervical* and *dorsal vertebrae,* and are attached to the *vertebral border* of the *scapula.* The *infraspinatus* and *teres* muscles are part of the *scapular* group with attachments at the *humerus.* The *infraspinatus* is often visible as a bulge on the blade of the *scapula.*

The trapezius originates from the neck, and the base of the skull, and from the *cervical* and *dorsal vertebrae* of the spinal column. Its fibres converge outwards to their attachment along the spine of the shoulder blade, and the collarbone. The *latissimus dorsi* is a thin muscle covering the lower regions of the back, and part of the sides of the trunk. It arises from the lower dorsal and lumbar vertebrae, from the *iliac crest* of the *pelvis,* and from the lower ribs. Its fibres converge outward and upward, winding and twisting to its attachment with the *humerus,* under the armpit.

The *deltoid,* or shoulder muscle, is a prominent, bulky form which springs at the back from the spine of the *scapula.* At the front it is attached to the *clavicle,* its fibres converging downward to their attachments at the middle of the *humerus.*

One of the most prominent and beautifully formed muscles of the body, the *deltoid,* whose actions facilitate the raising of the upper arm, is visible from any aspect. It is of course less prominent in women.

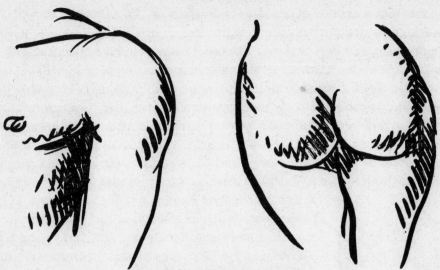

The Deltoid and Gluteal Muscles.

Most pronounced of all the forms at the rear of the trunk are the great *gluteal* muscles, popularly known as the buttocks. They lie on either side of the centre line of the back, each buttock consisting of a *gluteus maximus*, and a *gluteus medius*. The *gluteus maximus* originates from the rear of the *iliac crest*, and from the *sacrum* and *coccyx*. Its fibres converge on the prominence of the *great trochanter* where they flatten and join with the fibrous tissue of the thigh known as the *ilio-tibial band*. The *gluteus medius* is a fan-shaped muscle which is situated in the shallow depression below the *iliac crest*, at the side of the thigh. Like the *maximus*, the *gluteus medius* also starts from the *ilium*, its fibres merging with the tissue of the *ilio-tibial band* at the *great trochanter*.

On the forward side of the *gluteus medius*, and at the side of the buttocks is the *tensor fasciae femoris* which runs downwards with a backward inclination from the *anterior spine of the ilium* to blend with the fascia of the *ilio-tibial band*.

A characteristic feature of the back is the deep furrow which extends down its centre line. This is caused by the mass of the *erector spinae* muscle which bulges on either side, increasing in width, but losing prominence as it ascends. In the small of the back the furrow spreads into a flattish, slightly depressed area, which is again transformed into a deep groove separating the buttocks.

The muscle originates from the *sacrum*, and the *ilium* of the *pelvis*, extending upwards to a series of attachments with the vertebrae, the ribs, and the base of the skull.

## THE THIGH

The thigh is our next consideration. This member tapers downwards from the buttock to the knee, a feature which is especially prominent in the female. At the front of the thigh a number of muscles are conspicuous. The *sartorius*, a long, tape-like muscle, runs obliquely across its entire length, originating from the *anterior spine of the ilium*, and sweeping over the *vastus internus* to its attachment with the *tibia*, just below the knee. Running behind the *sartorius* and parallel with the inner contour of the thigh, is another long, narrow muscle, the *gracilis*. This starts from the *pubic bone*, descending steeply to its insertion into the *tibia*. The *vastus internus* is always clearly discernible as a fleshy mass on the inner side of the lower half of the thigh. It originates from the whole length of the *femur* and joins with the tendinous fibres of the *vastus externus* and the *rectus femoris* to form a common attachment with the *patella*. Together, these muscles comprise the *extensor group*.

The curves of the *vastus internus* and the *vastus externus.*

The *vastus externus* originates from the neck of the *femur*, and the *great trochanter*, and viewed from the front imparts a graceful curve to the line of the thigh. The *rectus femoris* is a long muscle which adds a distinct fullness to the front of the thigh and is visible from the side elevation as a beautiful, sweeping curve. It originates from the *anterior spine of the ilium*, and apart from its common attachment with the *patella*, it is also fastened by a ligament with the head of the *tibia*.

Certain other muscles less conspicuous than those already mentioned are involved at the front of the thigh, and these have been noted as a matter of general interest in the diagram on the left.

At the back of the thigh is a pronounced muscularity composed of three muscles, known as the *flexor group*. All the muscles originate from the *ischium*, the tuberous lower portion of the *pelvis*, their source being concealed beneath the *gluteus maximus*. The group, which imparts a marked fullness about the middle of the *femur*, consists of the *biceps femoris*, the *semi-membranosus*, and the *semi-tendinosus*. They descend the thigh, tapering into tendons, and dividing above the knee joint into two, conspicuous strings. For this reason they are sometimes called the *hamstring muscles*. The *biceps femori*, which also originates from the *femur*, is inserted into the head of the *fibula*, while the tendons of the *semi-membranosus* and *semi-tendinosus* are attached to the head of the *tibia*. Also located at the back of the thigh, between the *gracilis* and the *semi-membranosus*, is one of the deeper *adductor group—the adductor magnus*.

112

*Above:* **STUDY OF FARM BUILDINGS**
   Giovanni Tiepolo (1696–1770)

*Right:* **GIRL SLEEPING**    **Rembrandt van Rijn (1606–69)**

*Below:* **FIGURE STUDY**    **Mervyn Levy (born 1915)**

A combination of pen, brush, and wash, is ideal for the rapid sketch: it is a partnership which encourages spontaneity and the direct, uncompromising approach which is the essence of the art of sketching. Simply, the technique is to lay in a fast, loose drawing with pen, or brush, then to add clear, fresh washes of ink, or water-colour. The general effect can be sharpened with a few deft touches of line when the washes are dry. The more direct the drawing and limpid the washes the greater the life and luminosity of the sketch. Tiepolo's study is a striking example: working with crystal lucidity the artist has captured pure sunshine and shadow; perhaps the first pale sun, and delicate, liquid shadows of early morning?

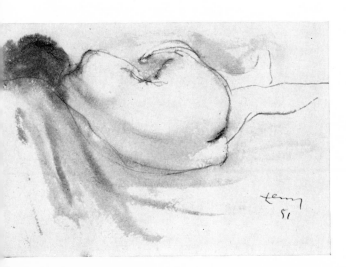

*Left:* **WOMAN AT A FOUNTAIN**
**William Etty, R.A. (1787–1849)**

Although William Etty is one of the most distinguished British painters of the nude, this particular work is chosen not for its own sake, but simply as a convenient basis upon which to establish an important theory. Drawing is a science, and, as such, perhaps the only really concrete thing a teacher of art can offer his students. When I say that drawing is a "science", I mean that it is founded upon an immutable principle. It consists of the systematic application of mathematical fact. The science of drawing is based upon the relationship of the direction of certain lines to any given series of master verticals and horizontals. The first thing is to establish in the subject a system of key verticals and horizontals, and then to plot all the other alignments in relation to these. A study of the various lines which I have superimposed upon Etty's nude will reveal how the system operates. The ideal of course is to train the eye to "read" into any given subject—especially a life study—a suitable system, first of master lines, and then of supplementary directions.

*Right:* **VENUS, CUPID, FOLLY and TIME**
**Agnolo Bronzino (1503–72)**

Contrast is a vital element in the work of art. In paint, contrasts of rough and smooth; in composition, the contrast of straight and curved. Consider the powerful right angle formed by the outstretched arm of Time, and the vertical contour of the young child's body. These are offset by the long, rhythmic lines that flow gracefully through the figures of Venus and Cupid, weaving their bodies in supple and charming motion. I have indicated a few of these rhythms; there are others to be found.

The *vastus internus*, the *vastus externus*, the *gracilis*, and the *sartorius*, also contribute to the appearance of the thigh from the back.

I have said little about the functions of the muscles because I feel this is a matter for a more specialist study of anatomy, and I am concerned here more with the location and appearance of the muscles. Once you have established these facts in your mind and can relate them to the mechanics of *flexion* and *extension*, you will be in a position to draw muscular forms, either in action, or repose, according to the disposition of the figure. You can check your anatomical facts first hand, either in the life class, or at your leisure by reference to your own body. A full length mirror is very useful for this purpose.

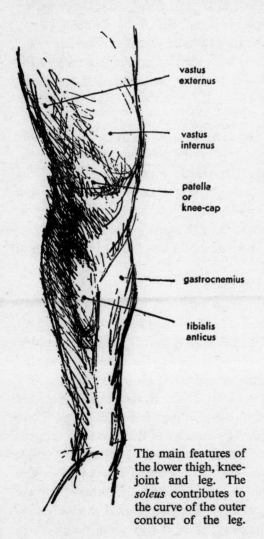

vastus
externus

vastus
internus

patella
or
knee-cap

gastrocnemius

tibialis
anticus

The main features of the lower thigh, knee-joint and leg. The *soleus* contributes to the curve of the outer contour of the leg.

Certain anatomical terms are self-explanatory. I have mentioned the *extensor*, and *flexor* groups of the thigh, and referred to one of the *adductor muscles*. There are, altogether, a number of *adductor muscles*, and the *adductor-flexors*, comprising the *sartorius* and the *gracilis*. It is the function of these two latter muscles to draw one thigh inwards towards the other. The term "adduct", in itself meaning "to draw to a common centre". The *sartorius* and the *gracilis* also join with the *flexor*, or *biceps group* to bend the leg at the knee joint.

The *abductor* muscles on the other hand, such as the *gluteus maximus* and the *gluteus medius*, carry forms away—outwards, as opposed to inwards. The *gluteal* muscles carry the thigh away from the body. The *extensor* group extends the thigh—the *flexor* group contracts it. When one set of muscles is in action its complementaries are in repose.

The knee presents a most interesting, if complex appearance. Its form is largely conditioned by the underlying bone structure; the *patella*, the lower end of the *femur*, and the upper portions of the *tibia*, and the *fibula*, all contribute to this intricate mass. The appearance of the knee is also complicated by the muscles and tendons in its immediate vicinity.

### THE LEG

So far I have described the muscles of the thigh, now let me say something about the muscles of the leg itself. At the front of this member the most conspicuous muscle is the *tibialis anticus* to which I referred earlier. It originates from the *tibia*, descending in a flat tendon to the inner side of the foot. The other muscles of the anterior group consist of the *long extensor of the toes*, the *extensor of the big toe*, and the *peroneus tertius*. They all originate in the leg, their tendons terminating in the foot. The second group of leg muscles is composed of the *peroneus longus*, and the *peroneus brevis*. At the back of the leg the most prominent muscle is the *gastrocnemius*. This is the only muscle of the leg which originates from above the knee. It starts in two heads from the condyles of the *femur*, swelling into the full, graceful curve of the calf, and terminating in a broad, tapering tendon, at the heel. This is the famous *tendo achilles*.

The remaining muscles of the posterior group consist of the *soleus*, and the *long flexor of the toes*, while the *peroneus brevis* and the *peroneus longus* both contribute to the form of the leg at its rear. The *soleus*, which is overlaid by the *gastrocnemius*, is prominent at either side of this muscle whose tendon it joins in a common descent to the heel. The *soleus* is also visible from the front of the leg, at the sides of the *tibia*, and the *fibula*. The *soleus* and the *gastrocnemius* are responsible for raising the *oscalcis*, and play an important part therefore in the action of walking.

### THE UPPER LIMB

Finally, let us consider the muscles of the upper limb. At the front of the upper arm is the *flexor group*, and at the rear, the *extensor group*. The *flexor group* consists of the *biceps*, and the *brachialis*. The *biceps* rises in two heads, one passing directly over the top of the *humerus* from its origin inside the shoulder joint, the other starts from the *coracoid process* of the *scapula*. The muscle terminates in a tendon which is inserted into the head of the *radius*. The *brachialis* springs from the lower half of the *humerus*, and is inserted into the upper part of the *ulna*. These then are the muscles that bend the forearm. The muscles of the second group, the *extensors* of the upper arm, consist of the *triceps*—which is also partially visible from the front, on either side of the *biceps*—and the *anconeus*. The *triceps* originates from three heads. One springs from the *scapula*, and the others from the *humerus*. The muscle is inserted into the upper end of the *ulna*, at the *olecranon*. This prominence is a very important landmark, since it forms the point of the elbow joint. It is of course, easily seen, and felt. The *anconeus* is a short, triangular shaped muscle extending across to the *ulna* from the *external condyle*, at the lower extremity of the *humerus*. These two muscles assist the extension of the lower arm. The *deltoid*, of which the sources of origin, and point of attachment I have already described, is also a pronounced feature of the upper arm, covering in the region of the shoulder the top portions of both the *flexor*, and *extensor* groups. The *flexor* group is also partially concealed by the fibres of the *pectoral* as it crosses the *axilla* (armpit), to its insertion into the *humerus*.

Earlier in this chapter I described the effects of *supination* and *pronation* on the disposition of the *radius* and the *ulna*. Normally, the forearm is in a state of continuous alternation between these two states as it fulfils an infinite variety of common tasks. When we carry a tray, for instance, with palms upward, the forearms are *supine*; when we turn the knob of a door the hand turns over and the arm is *pronated*. Think out a few examples for yourself, it will help you to appreciate the exact nature of these two conditions, and of the movements that bring them about.

*Supination* and *pronation* are effected respectively by two groups of muscles: the *extensors* on the posterior side of the forearm, and the *flexors* on its anterior side. The *supinators* of the forearm are the *brachio-radialis* and the *supinator brevis*. The former rises from the *outer condyle* of the *humerus*, its tendon being inserted into the lower end of the *radius*. It imparts a characteristic fullness to the outer contour of the upper part of the forearm. The *supinator brevis* is situated beneath the *brachio-radialis*. Besides the two *supinators*, a series of *extensor* muscles which operate the wrist, fingers, and thumb, are also involved in this group.

The *flexor* group, which is located on the inward side of the forearm, possesses two *pronator* muscles. One, the *pronator teres*, being superficial, the other, the *pronator quadratus*, deep lying. The *pronator teres* originates from the inner *condyle* of the *humerus*, and is inserted into the *radius*. It forms a band on the inner side of the hollow at the bend of the elbow. On the other side of the concavity lies the swelling of the *brachio-radialis*. All this is quite easy to check on your own arm. The remaining muscles of this group consist of the flexors of the wrist, fingers, and thumb.

This completes, for our immediate purposes, the anatomy of the body. With this knowledge at your finger-tips—for it must become, eventually, an instinctive element—you will no longer find yourself hindered by a weakness which distresses so many pleasure painters—the inability to construct figures. Apart from any consideration of style, which is of course, an infinitely variable quality, the basis of figure work is a matter of determinable fact, solidly founded on anatomy, and the principles of figure construction, with which I shall deal in the next chapter.

CHAPTER 11

# The Science of Figure Construction

I N AN age which professes to be contemptuous of standards and indifferent to the exercise of any rules or conventions in the practise of painting, many people are unaware that the best unconventional artists have always been, at the outset of their careers, masters of academic method. A familiarity with the techniques of painting, a knowledge of the laws of anatomy, perspective, and figure construction, these have always been learned and assimilated through practise, and personal achievement.

We often hear that rules are made to be broken, and if as I suspect there is some truth in this axiom, it must also be argued that you cannot break the law until you know it. This is a very different thing from seeking to excuse bad draughtsmanship on the grounds that an artist is not interested in the conventions, but reaching beyond them to bigger, and more significant issues. It is an argument often put forward by the swindlers who call themselves artists, and by the mountebank critics who peddle jargon in their support. The real reason for such ineptitude is either that the artist cannot be bothered to learn the geography of the body, and the laws of proportion, or what is more likely, that he does not possess the capacity to do so. In such cases, unconventionality is founded on ignorance, whereas knowledge is the only legitimate basis for originality. The exceptions are those curious, and unique manifestations of the aesthetic vision, common to the art of the genuine naïve. However, since we are concerned for the present with the artist whose evolution is plotted through the normal channels, the difference between informed, and uninformed unconventionality, is crucial. It is the difference between the profound, searching iconoclasm of Picasso, and the insolent anarchy of the poseur. Before he was twenty years of age, Picasso had achieved the status of a master draughtsman in the great academic tradition. At this tender age he could draw with the accomplishment of Raphael. Thereafter he was fully entitled to jettison the rules of academic method in his search for those fresh aspects of the truth that lay beyond the scope of the existing order. But first it was essential to know that order—to have used it, and to have exhausted its possibilities.

Picasso could never have foreseen the significance of Cézannes's pleas, "treat nature by the cylinder, the sphere, and the cone", if he had not been already skilled in an appreciation of the purely structural, architectonic qualities upon which nature, in all its forms, is founded. As it was, he discovered Cubism—another aspect of the truth.

The human body is a piece of architecture aesthetically based upon the elements of anatomy, and the science of figure construction. These comprise an alphabet which must be learned before articulate communication can be effected. Skill in draughtsmanship depends upon such knowledge. When this has been acquired you will be in a position either to communicate in known, "grammatical" terms, or to experiment intelligently in the quest for a fresh syntax. But this will not be possible until you have mastered those laws which are the same for *all* artists. Indeed, apart from the aesthetic interpretations superimposed upon the existing order by the artist's vision, certain fundamental laws are immutable. If there is any such thing as objective beauty, it can only exist as a supplementary condition of *fact*. It is the artist who seeks to transmute fact, into *fiction*. The delightful fiction of art. Let us for the moment concern ourselves wholly with fact.

"Drawing" said Ingres, one of the greatest draughtsmen in the history of European art, "drawing is the probity of art". Once we are agreed on a definition of the term "drawing", this statement will be seen as one of the great, fundamental aesthetic truths, as absolute, and constant in effect, as the law of the golden section.[1] By "drawing", I mean, as I am certain Ingres did, the accurate representation on a plane surface of those measurable phenomena which exist for the artist in the *reality* of volume, and the *illusion* of line. The term "drawing" assumes therefore, when used in relation to the science of draughtsmanship, a mathematical connotation. We are concerned with the kind of accuracy that demands precision in the estimation of such matters as proportion, and the degree of the angles created by lines of direction seen in relation to hypothetical verticals and horizontals which vary in accordance with the subject under study. The principle of a series of directional deviations from the master verticals and horizontals which are implicit in the subject, is a rule that will afford you a practical guide of inestimable value. This too, in due course, must become an instinctive element in your work.

Drawing consists of a series of variations on the master theme of the vertical and the horizontal. Let me now demonstrate precisely what I mean. Consider William Etty's "Woman at a Fountain" (facing page 113) which you will see has been overlaid with a series of verticals and horizontals, and with some of the directional deviations from those key lines of reference. The number of references you use is immaterial: they can be few, or numerous, the artist deciding

See Glossary.

how many will be sufficient for himself. It is the principle which matters

Eventually, the eye will be in a position to superimpose this system in the abstract, so that the act of drawing becomes a fluent activity in which rapid mathematical assessments are verified by a network of imaginary key lines. After a while the eye grows adept at superimposing the master verticals and horizontals upon the subject, and skilled in plotting the various lines of deviation, and the angles dependent upon them. Long study in the life-class produces in the best draughtsmen an intuitive awareness of this mathematical framework which is, ideally, independent of any literal, or even abstract system of configuration. Ideally, the eye and the mind should act simultaneously, without any time-lag between the seeing, and the statement. But first, naturally, you must master the two preliminary stages in this gradual progression to the ideal state. Continuous practise in figure drawing is essential.

Since this chapter on figure construction is designed expressly for those who at the present time are students in a life-class, or who may become students in the future, I would suggest one or two practical methods of checking your key lines of reference, as the stage prior to the visualizing of these in the abstract. A pencil, held either vertically, horizontally, or at an angle, about a foot, or eighteen inches from the eye (one eye should be closed for this operation), is one method of carrying out these checks. Anything straight will do—a ruler is splendid, but a pencil of course is the most expedient implement and facilitates a sense of continuity in drawing, since it is simply lowered from the checking position, and the drawing continued immediately. Another method of checking the verticals is by the use of a *plumb line*. This consists of a length of thread, or thin string, with a weight at one end; a piece of metal, a rubber, a latch-key—anything of this sort will do. "Plumbing" the figure affords a vital check on poise and balance. In a standing pose a line dropped from the pit of the neck to the point of the *inner malleolus* will give you a reference against which you can measure the relative positions of such other key points as the nipples, the navel, the *patellae*, and so on.

But while it is vitally important to establish a series of master lines, I cannot over-stress the importance of assessing the deviations from the vertical and the horizontal. The untrained eye is apt to jump to quite inaccurate conclusions, and to imagine that such and such a direction is simply a straightforward horizontal, or vertical. Often, it is true that certain deviations are extremely subtle, but just as asymmetry is the salt of good composition, so alignments away from the vertical and the horizontal are the spice of good drawing. The real value of the various methods of checking I have described consists in their power to help the artist in determining even the most fine deflections from the perpendicular and the horizontal.

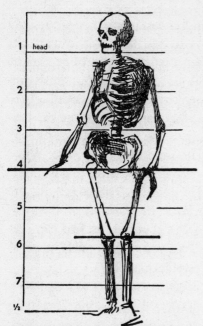

The Proportions of the Figure.

The proportions of the figure provide our next consideration. These, while varying a little with the individual, are constant in the main. Usually, in the adult, the height of the figure is equal to seven and a half heads; or if you like, from the point of view of a check with your outstretched pencil, the head will go into the total height of the figure, seven and a half times.

The figure is divided into equal halves at the level of a line drawn across the hips from the prominence of one *great trochanter* to the other. The lower limbs are divided into halves at the level of the *patellae*. The *clavicle*, *scapula*, and *sternum* are all rather less than a head in length. The *humerus* is one and a half heads in length, and the *radius* and the *ulna* about a head's length. The *femur* is two heads in length, and the *tibia* one and a half heads long.

One of the most characteristic differences between the male and the female figure exists in the greater breadth of the female *pelvis* with the consequent tendency towards a slight "knock-knee". This is so because the female *femora* are more sharply inclined towards each other in the region of the knees. The female face tends to be smaller than that of the male, while in general, the muscles are far less distinguishable and clearly defined in the female figure.

"Studies of Details" by Hans Holbein.

Considering the figure in terms of volume, and form, it is perhaps best thought of as a series of articulating cylinders and tubes, surmounted by an ovoid, the head. These ovoid, cylindrical (the neck for example), and tubular (the fingers for instance) forms, are in turn broken into a series of planes. The head in particular lends itself to this form of structural analysis. There is the front plane across the face, on which the features are set, and the side plane along the line of the cheek-bone, to the ear. The nose possesses a front, and side planes, and the hand and fingers are easily simplified into a series of planes as you can clearly see in the "Studies of Details", by Hans Holbein the Younger (c.1497–1543).

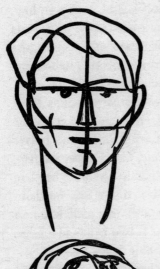

Constructing a Head.

The construction of the head is based on a number of points. If the ovoid is halved both vertically, and horizontally, it will be seen that the vertical line passes through the centre of the nose and mouth, while the horizontal line cuts through the line of the eyeballs. The ears are set between the level of a line drawn across the cheek from the eyebrow, and the level of a line drawn across the same plane from the base of the nose. With these few, simple rules in mind it is possible to construct a head in any position you require. The angle, tilt, or inclination of the ovoid, and the position of the two centre lines is the key to the problem, as you can see from a study of the Holbein drawings, and Raphael's head of "St. James the Great". (Page 121).

The construction of figures depends not only upon concrete fact, but frequently upon illusion as well. Unless the forms we are observing, or constructing from memory, lie parallel with the *picture plane*, (the plane of the surface upon which the artist is working, or through which the spectator views the subject), they will be subject to the *foreshortening* which is due to their apparent recession *into* the picture plane. This principle is clearly demonstrated in Sir William Orpen's "The Draughtsman and his Model" (between pages 136-7) which contains a number of examples of the foreshortening of forms. First however, study the left side of the model, and the right leg of the artist as they present themselves to the spectator; both are parallel with the picture plane, and are subject therefore to no foreshortening. The model's left arm recedes *into* the picture plane from the point of the elbow, as does the artist's left leg which is in recession from the knee-joint. Both these forms are clearly foreshortened. So also is the artist's left arm which recedes into the picture from the wrist-joint.

When correctly applied, the principle of foreshortening will enable you to create the illusion of the recession of forms into the picture plane. All forms of course, even those which lie parallel with the picture plane appear to diminish in size as they move into the distance, but foreshortening is a further condition of visual perspective, its acuteness depending upon the angle from which the form is

"St. James the Great" by Raphael.

viewed. In the case of the examples in the Orpen drawing, the angles of recession are all in the region of about 30° from the picture plane. Thus, the degree of foreshortening increases as the angle widens, until at 45° from the picture plane, a form will no longer be visible at all. Yet no matter how accurate the construction of your figures may be, no matter how exhaustive your knowledge of anatomy, and your understanding of the laws of foreshortening, your figurework will need to be animated by other elements, and sensibilities, if it is to possess the vital spark that alone can transform the lifeless image into a living force.

Rhythm and movement are an essential part of the life of the human figure. Every pose contains a number of these *lines of force*, and the flow of a dynamic line can often be traced through the full length of a pose, exerting a graceful, and potent vitality. I have indicated some of these in Bronzino's "Venus, Cupid, Folly and Time". They contribute in no small measure to the beauty of this masterpiece. One of these movements commences in the curve of the Cupid's head, passing through the arc of the Goddess's eyebrow, and continuing in a sublime flow right down through the leg to the very tips of the toes. What an ecstatic rhythm is this exquisite line of force. You will find this picture extremely interesting also from the purely anatomical point of view. See how many muscles you can account for. The woman's figure is unusually, though not unpleasantly muscular, as indeed is that of the infant, "Folly", while the outstretched arm of the figure of "Time" displays a superb example of pronation. (Facing page 113).

\*　　　　　\*　　　　　\*

I have endeavoured in this, and the previous chapter, to give you a blue-print for your figurework. Once you have mastered the information and the principles involved in these chapters you will find yourself in a very strong position, for *without* this equipment, the problem of figure construction becomes a nightmare, and nothing is quite so distressing as the impotence of the inspired artist who lacks the technical wherewithal to express his vision.

# CHAPTER 12

# Perspective: Linear and Aerial

THE application of the science of perspective was one of the major contributions of the Renaissance to European painting. It transformed the art of painting from the flat, two-dimensionalism of the medieval period, into a spacious, three-dimensional world of solid forms, organized in space, and depth. Among the earlier practitioners of perspective were the Florentine, Paolo Uccello (*c.* 1396/7–1475), and the Umbrian master Piero della Francesca (1416?–1472), who defined perspective in these terms:

> "Many painters censure perspective because they do not understand the purpose of the lines and angles that are constructed by it, and that enable us to represent with the right proportions the outline and shape of any object. Therefore I think I should explain how necessary this science is to painting.
> "I say that this word 'perspective' signifies objects seen from afar and represented upon certain given planes in various scales depending on their distances. Without perspective it is impossible to foreshorten anything correctly."[1]

Let us take this fifteenth-century definition a little further and see just what it means today for the practising artist.

Linear, and aerial perspective, are the means through which the artist represents the relative positions, magnitudes, and appearances of objects and other phenomena, in depth, on a plane surface. The *picture plane* is the more exact way of describing the flat, two-dimensional surface upon which the artist works, and this may be thought of also as an imaginary, and transparent plane—a large sheet of glass if you like—set between the eye of the spectator, and the subject. As objects recede from the observer into this picture plane, they appear to diminish in size, and linear perspective is the science of delineating this illusion by means of a geometrical method.

The basis of linear perspective is the vanishing of parallel lines on the *horizon line*, or *eye level*, as it is alternatively known. The points at which parallel lines converge to meet on the horizon line are known as *vanishing points*. The position

[1] From *Artists on Art*, compiled and Edited by Robert Goldwater and Mario Treves.

of the horizon line will vary of course, according to the position of the observer. In all probability you will be reading this book in a sitting position, in which event your eye level will be lower than if you were standing up. Relative to this consideration, parallel lines *below* the eye level converge upwards to their vanishing points, while those *above*, converge downwards. Only the parallel lines of planes that lie

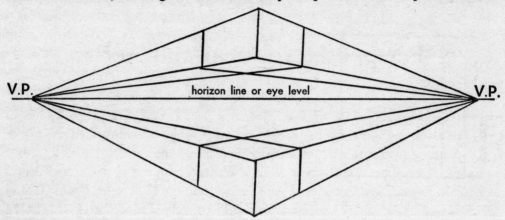

horizon line or eye level

V.P.                                                                V.P.

*oblique* to the picture plane (the elevations of a house at an angle of 30° to the picture plane for instance) converge to meet at vanishing points on the horizon line.

The horizontals of planes which lie parallel with the picture plane do not converge towards the eye level. An example would be the front elevation of a house when the observer's line of vision is directly at its centre. When a plane lies parallel with the picture plane, it is in *parallel perspective*; but when it is turned at an angle to the picture plane, it lies in *oblique perspective*.

By applying the principle of converging parallels, the artist can accurately describe the apparent, proportional decrease in the size of objects as they recede into the distance. We all know for instance that a line of houses, or telegraph poles are the same size in fact, although when viewed from a particular standpoint, the farthest away will appear to be very much smaller than those close to hand. They will also appear to close up, to telescope: to display *foreshortening*, a common optical illusion when forms are viewed from an angle, the degree of foreshortening depending upon the acuteness of the angle. The principle of foreshortening applies to phenomenon in the horizontal as well as the vertical plane. Think of a straight run of railway line with its sleepers, or a series of hills in a landscape. These appear to telescope as they recede.

Get into the habit of studying the principles of linear perspective during the normal course of your everyday affairs. Whether at home, or abroad in the streets, you will find an endless succession of illustrations. Their discovery will import a fresh interest to the experience of *seeing*.

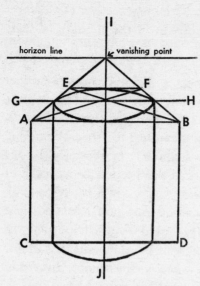

The Foreshortening of Circles.

The perspective, or foreshortening of circles, is also commonly met with, especially in still-life, in which the ellipses of jugs, cups, vases, and the like, often figure. It should be sufficient to be aware of this fact, and to observe in specific instances the various degrees of foreshortening. There is however a simple geometrical method of constructing the ellipses that circles in perspective assume. First, construct a cube as in the diagram. The front elevation A.B.C.D. being in parallel perspective, and the top elevation E.F.A.B. in oblique perspective. Next, draw the diagonals E.B., and F.A. Draw in the lines I.J., and G.H., and delineate arcs in the resulting quarters of the top plane. The line G.H. will be found to halve the ellipse in accurate perspective.

In the academic sense, linear perspective is a complex geometrical science involving a variety of mathematical problems and their solutions. For our immediate purposes however, and indeed, for the usual run of perspective problems that are likely to concern the artist, such principles as I have established so far will prove quite adequate.

\*  \*  \*

Aerial Perspective (sometimes referred to as "colour" or "atmospheric" perspective) is concerned with the changes in the tones and colours of objects and other phenomena in nature, as modified by atmospheric conditions. As they recede into the distance, tones and colours become respectively, paler, and cooler: to change from the relatively strong, warm colours of the foreground (the red-orange-yellow half of the colour circle: see page 89) into the delicate, cool shades of the distance (the green-blue-violet half of the colour circle).

Leonardo da Vinci (1452–1519) was another Renaissance master of perspective, and it is interesting at this point to consider his personal definition of the science:

"The first requisite of painting is that bodies which it represents should appear in relief, and that the scenes which surround them with effects of distance should seem to enter into the plane in which the picture is produced by means of the three parts of perspective, namely, the diminution in the distinctness of the form of bodies, the diminution in their size, and the diminution in their colour. . . ."

In this statement Leonardo summarizes very neatly the fact that the basis of landscape painting is a combination of linear, and aerial perspective. Diminution in the size of objects being supported by a diminution in the strength of their colour.

*  *  *

Whether or not, or to what extent you apply the principles of perspective in your own work will depend upon your aims. It is only fair to note that in spite of its flatness, medieval painting possesses certain purely decorative qualities, as indeed, without any loss of aesthetic value, does a great deal of Oriental painting in which the conditions of formal perspective are frequently in abeyance. In our own time an artist like Henri Matisse often sacrificed perspective for the sake of decoration and design. One thing however is certain: you are in a better position to modify or dispense with the academic niceties when you have mastered their meaning, and have practised their application. One would always hope that the well informed, intelligent, and truly creative student of painting will be catholic enough in outlook and intention to use perspective when it suits his objectives, and to modify, or dispense with its application when it does not.

# CHAPTER 13

# Sketching

WHAT exactly *is* a sketch? Is it an unfinished work? a study for a finished work? or an end in itself? The problem is not an easy one. The diction-ary defines the word sketch as meaning, rough, slight, outlined, or unfinished; yet many of the greatest artists were unable in their so-called finished works to equal the fresh, spontaneous crystallization of vision, and expression, that characterized their preliminary sketches. Constable is perhaps the most striking example of the painter whose sketches almost always outshone his com-pleted works. His flashing, immediate impressions, whether small scale, in oil or water-colour, or large scale, as in the full size oil sketches he executed for many of his most famous works, these one feels, are the essential Constable. In his incredibly lucid, and fluent studies, the master has seized at once upon the dynamic essence of his subject, and with dazzling speed, and verve, captured the very soul of nature. There is a freedom and spontaneity, a sense of kinetic, continuity about Constables sketches, large, or small, that suggests the answer to our problem. Just as nothing is ever *finished* in nature, nothing perhaps ought ever to be *finished* in art? Not at least in the artist's portrayal of organic phenomena; in his depiction in fact, of any living thing. And a landscape of course is as much a living thing, as a person, or an animal.

So the sketch is perhaps closest to the heart and the meaning of "life", since it suggests that continual "coming into being", which is life itself. Nothing is static, everything moves and changes, ceaselessly. In nature, immobility is death: move-ment and change, the true condition of organic being. You have only to compare the static "classical" landscape of the French painter Nicolas Poussin with the mobility of Constable, to appreciate this. (Compare pictures facing page 136 and between pages 24-5).

If we start then by thinking of the sketch as the most vital of all the various forms of drawing and painting, we may then, in respect of our own personal objectives, consider it also, either as the basis for a "finished" work, or as an end in itself. It ought never I think to be thought of as an *unfinished* work.

First of all then, let us consider the sketch as a note for some aspect of a large,

A series of sketchbook notes made on a bus.

and detailed work, and also as a stimulus for picture making: as the source of inspiration, always remembering of course, that even as a note for something more extensive, the sketch remains at the same time, an end in itself. As a note for further reference, or for future inspiration, the sketch has its place, most usually, in a sketchbook. This is an item of equipment which the artist should carry with him at all times, everywhere. The main function of the sketchbook is to record stimulating, unusual, or useful data, such as the artist is likely to meet in the course of his normal perambulations through life, and not just when he is out on an official sketching, or painting expedition. More often than not, the most interesting and important things an artist encounters are those he meets unexpectedly, as he goes about his daily business. That is why it is most important to carry your sketchbook, even to work—and always of course on holiday—for you never know, for instance when you might see that specially exciting face: in a bus, a train, or perhaps, just across the way from you, in your lunch hour restaurant. Wherever you may be, there is almost always likely to be something of interest for your sketchbook. In the park, on the station, at a football match, an endless succession of material presents itself. Once you have trained yourself in the art of reaching for your sketchbook the moment you spot an interesting item, you will feel as lost without it, as a gun-slinger without his pistol.

At first you may feel just a little self-conscious about sketching in public places, but in a little while you will think no more of it, than you would of lighting a cigarette in public. And believe me, it is better to endure a pang or two of self-consciousness, than to sit in impotent agony with some exciting subject right in front of you, just crying out to be captured in your sketchbook. Personally, I have often suffered acute pangs of remorse, simply because I had no sketchbook with me when I saw something I very much wanted to record. The sketchbook then, is the first prerequisite of the complete artist.

128

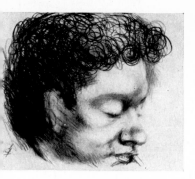

*Left:* In this pencil drawing of Dylan Thomas, made in 1949, I tried to capture the coarsening of the poet's appearance, the sense of weariness and disaster, that even then seemed to be closing about him. The hair is still wild, symbolic of his contempt for the pettiness of conventional things; but the face in John's early portrait (between pages 48-9) is crumbling now into a podgy and shapeless ruin.

*Right:* A fresh, spontaneous drawing, swiftly executed, was the only way to catch this moment of a child's fleeting absorption. I used only a brush, and a brown poster colour, since anything darker would I felt have been too heavy for such a lively, and youthful subject. Here, the most indeterminate suggestion, as in the hands, is adequate.

*Below:* I wanted to express a feeling of the dark intensity that is typical of the bull-fighter. To achieve this I drew first with a sharp, incisive pen line, completing my drawing in washes of watered Indian ink.

*Below:* The draughtsman has an extensive range of materials at his command, and the subject itself will often suggest which is likely to be the most suitable. In these drawings I worked with a delicate, restrained technique, using a plain HB pencil, to capture a mood of serenity, and repose. The models are my wife and daughter.

*Above:* **TAKING IN THE LAUNDRY**      Grandma Moses (born 1860)
*Below:* **YOUNG MAN YOKING AN OX**      Samuel Palmer (1805–81)

The American "primitive" who took up painting at the age of seventy-six ("for company"), bases the beauty of her pattern and design upon a keen observation of detail. The conception is imaginative, the facts are literal. In Palmer's picture, the vision transcends the reality; the dream and the facts are inextricably blended.

You should always have three or four books on hand, varying in size from something about fourteen inches by ten inches, that you can pack with your painting materials—perhaps in an old rucksack—to a small book around seven inches by five inches, that you can conveniently slip into a side pocket (or a hand-bag if you are a woman) for your casual sketching.

The most suitable mediums for casual sketching, are pencil, and pen. Two or three good quality pencils ranging from an HB to a 2B, or 3B, will provide you with an ideal range of hard (but not too hard), and soft (but not too soft). An HB for instance, is perfect for those subjects that require some degree of sharpness and definition, while the softer pencils are ideal for those subjects that can be treated with more breadth. Any subjects for example in which there are strong, broad contrasts of light and dark. Short lengths of pencil are more convenient to carry around in one's pocket, especially for casual work, than the full length pencil which I personally have always found to be inconveniently long. No matter where you carry it on your person—unless of course in a box of some sort, which is cumbersome—the point is subject to damage, while if you carry it sticking out of your breast pocket, it is positively dangerous. I suggest therefore that pencils about three or four inches in length are most suitable. It is also a good plan to carry a razor blade in a match-box, or holder, for sharpening your pencils. In the chapter on "Drawing Portraits" (page 79) I explain why a razor blade is the best of all pencil sharpening implements, and describe the correct method of preparing a pencil for use.

So far as pens are concerned, a ball-point, or fountain-pen (specially reserved for sketching) are most convenient for casual work. So, armed with pencils, pens, and a small sketchbook, you are ready for anything. With these simple tools, you can put down those subjects, or mere detail that can provide you with such valuable inspiration, and data, for your more ambitious projects.

There are so many things that lend themselves to the small scale sketchbook; someone's shoes, an expression—perhaps the twist of a mouth—a hand holding a cigarette, a hat, an ear, a shopping basket bulging with provisions, this is the sort of material that lends itself, ideally, for recording in your small sketchbook. This is just the sort of reference material you may need, especially when constructing pictures from memory. Every artist should build up a little library of sketchbooks to which he can turn for information, as the writer to his various reference works.

Let us now consider the sketch as an end in itself. In this sense, its purpose is to capture the essence of a subject: to crystallize that fundamental vitality, and sparkle, the dynamic surge of energy that is so often lost during the transition from the first sketch, to the finished work. These are the qualities that give life to organic subject matter—to nature, people, animals. Even the temporary immobility of living things is charged with tension: with the resilience of forces waiting like coiled springs to leap into action. We can sense this controlled energy in cats for instance,

as they sit, passive, yet dynamically alert. It can be felt in people when they are concentrating on some task that, for a moment or so, demands a sharp focus of their attentions. It may be simply the threading of a needle—you know how people concentrate on this task, with their tongues sticking out—or in fact, any job that requires a momentary pin-pointing of the faculties of concentration. Try to capture this moment of intense, controlled energy. Look for it in animals, and in human beings; it is the very substance of the rapid sketch.

The dynamic alertness of cats; the concentration of the human being.

The sketch may also take in, and capture, the moment of action—or at least an aspect, or a phase of some action. Draw a cat in motion, perhaps washing itself: or a baby crawling about the floor. And draw them, not just once, but six, ten, twelve times, racing from sheet to sheet of a large sketching-pad, tearing them away and flinging them aside, as your powers of concentration grow more

intense, and each rapid drawing moves closer to the mark. Do not bother about
your drawings while you are in action, do not consider them, or wonder whether
they are good or bad: simply draw. The essence of action sketching is split second
co-operation between the mind, the eye, and the hand. The mind must divine, the
eye must see, and the hand must translate the mental assessment, and the visual
impact, into the aesthetic form. After an hour or so of this rapid, concentrated
sketching, gather your drawings together and lay them aside for a while. Later on,
you can go through them at your leisure, calmly, and coolly, considering the results
of your labour.

In this way you will find it quite easy to make a selection from your dozen or
so sketches, those few that have come closest to capturing the spirit of the subject.
You will probably be surprised to discover that the drawings which appear most
successful in retrospect, are invariably those you had not thought to be the best,
in the heat of action.

The immediacy of the sketch as an end in itself, is its principal attraction. The
imprisonment of some fleeting, but characteristic moment in the life of the subject,
is the quality that imparts such appeal to the sketches of perhaps the greatest
master of this particular form of expression, Rembrandt van Rijn (1606–69). There
is no artist you could study to better advantage in this connexion, than this master
who could crystallize in a few flashing lines, and dashes of wash, the quintessence
of his favourite subjects; the children, and the beggars, the old people, the animals,
and the landscape, that inspired him ceaselessly.

The French sculptor Auguste Rodin (1840–1917) is also a man to study,
particularly from the point of view of the pure action sketch. It was Rodin's
custom to draw from models in movement—from figures slowly circling about
him as he worked, or moving occasionally, while he drew. To sketch living matter
in action is to put your finger on the very pulse of life itself, while the temporary
suspension of motion—as in Rembrandt's "Girl Sleeping" facing page 112—is
immobility charged with the quiescent forces of action. At any moment the sleeper
may stir, or turn.

Because the artist must anticipate these possible changes, he will draw even
"static" subjects, with the same intense, nervous concentration that he must give
to subjects in motion. So the sketch deals with *life*, and with that pattern of ceaseless change that is the condition of life. Eyelids flickers, sleepers turn, animals
twitch; the face of nature changes more often than the face of man, yielding to
every vagary of sun, and cloud, wind, and rain.

The sketcher moves through this undulating forest of action, and change,
seeking to fix in his sketchbook, those moments of truth which pass almost as soon
as they come into being.

A sketch from the television screen.

Today, there is one source of subject material that offers the artist the most unique, and stimulating opportunities for sketching, and that is the television screen. The human face, in action, is particularly absorbing—and revealing too—and there is something deeply satisfying about having a celebrated personality at the mercy of your pen, or pencil. If you use your television in the right way you will soon possess an interesting collection of portrait sketches of famous people—even of people whom *television* has made famous, which of course is a rather different sort of fame from that which a person has to win if he—or she—is to achieve recognition the hard way. So your television portrait gallery will be doubly interesting, containing studies of the genuinely celebrated—Bertrand Russell for instance—and that phenomenon peculiar to the age in which we live, the pseudo-celebrity of television fame.

My impression of Mr. Harold Macmillan was made during a television political broadcast. It was the third in a series of three sketches executed with brush and indian ink, and while in no sense a superficial likeness, it has I think captured a fresh aspect of an old subject: the hardened politician seeking to project a somewhat untypical, and contrived *bonhomie*. The faint smile is the key.

Mark off in your weekly television journal those programmes such as panel games, discussions, and talks, that will bring before you anyone you feel you would like to sketch. In such circumstances you will have them at your mercy sufficiently long to enable you to make a series of rapid sketches. Television is one of the most exciting sources of supply for the artist's sketchbook, and I use the term sketchbook in its figurative as well as its literal sense, since you can of course, sketch on paper pinned to a drawing board. Certainly for sketching at home you need a much larger working area than a pocket sketchbook will provide. Either a large sketchbook, sketching pad, or sheets of paper and a drawing board are the most suitable, and the size of your working area should range from something like sixteen inches by twelve inches, and upwards.

132

Improvising a "donkey".

A good system is to pin a dozen or so sheets of the thinner cartridge paper to a drawing board, using large, good quality pins at the top only so that you can rip away the sheets as you race from one drawing to the next. You will also greatly facilitate your movements, leaving a hand free in which to hold a bottle of ink for instance, if you improvise a "donkey". In schools of art these are a common feature of the studio scene, but you can devise an admirable home substitute simply by placing two chairs as you see in my diagram. On one of these you sit, while propping your drawing board against the back of the other.

For sketching at home you can supplement pen and pencil with *conté* and, if you like, with pen and wash, or brush and wash, both most effective, and dramatic combinations. An ordinary pen with a cheap nib is usually preferable to the ballpoint, or fountain-pen, which I suggested you should use for your small scale, casual sketching, simply because they are more expedient for this type of work. Let me say just a word about the technique of wash drawing. The best method is to draw your contours in pen, or a fine brush, and then, with a larger brush, to lay in your darks, breaking them swiftly into the middle tones, and carrying them off into the lights by diluting the strength of your ink, or wash, with clean water. It is important to have two or three containers of water to hand while working with wash, since you will need to cleanse your brushes frequently, and the essence of the operation is of course to work with speed. You will need plenty of rag with which to wipe the surplus liquid from your brush, from time to time. Brushes will not always require to be saturated with liquid when working in wash. For while you may conveniently apply the main area of deep tone with a heavily loaded brush, you will need a drier one with which to blend this into the lighter tones. The dark will need to be run into a damp, rather than a saturated paper, so having applied a juicy area of dark, you will require a clean, wet brush, rather than one brimming with liquid. But all these things are a matter of practice—of trial and error.

One other source of subject material might be mentioned—and that is the zoo. Not every town possesses one I know, but if you live in London or Manchester, for instance, I warmly recommend a visit now and then, with your sketchbook.

Sketching is the *breath* of art: it is the most refreshing of all the more impulsive forms of creative self-expression and, as such, it should be as free, and happy, as a song in the bath.

133

# CHAPTER 14

# Technique and Style

## *by Colin Moss*

BEFORE embarking upon the discussion of these two rather difficult terms, it would seem essential that we should know, with some precision, what they mean. One thing is certain—they do *not* mean the same thing. Having cleared away this somewhat widespread misconception, the obvious opening gambit is to consult the dictionary, which states:

> *Style*—Manner of writing, speaking, painting or musical composition; distinguishing a particular person, school, period, etc.
> *Technique*—Mode of artistic performance or execution, mechanical skill in art.

With this clear-cut information before us, we may set forth to consider our terms in relation to the particular art of painting. The French, with their customary lucidity, say that "Style is the man", and this is certainly true in the light of the undoubted fact that painting is the most revealing form of autobiography. A painter's style is, in other words the visible expression of his personality. It is as particular to him as his fingerprints, or the colour of his eyes. It is, therefore, latent within him at the outset of his career, and though he may modify and develop it at various stages of that career, it remains, to the end, a constant factor. Of course, it is by no means impossible to discover examples which seem flagrantly to contradict this view; I have in mind, for instance, certain early works by Gauguin which could easily have come from the hand of Pissarro. The explanation is simple: at the time that Gauguin made these pictures, he had only just begun to paint, and working alongside a much more experienced painter, with a mature and powerful vision of his own, he (Gauguin) merely parroted, quite skilfully, his master, producing, if one may be seemingly paradoxical, talented pastiches of Pissarro, which bore no relation to the personality of Gauguin.

Oddly enough, a similar curiosity occurs in Pissarro's own work. Late in life he fell under the spell of Seurat (whose style we shall discuss later) and produced a series of landscapes in the Pointillist manner, which merely mirrored the younger painter. Pissarro later saw the error of his ways, and reverted to his own style. Many more examples of this sort of aberration exist in the history of painting, but I quote these two in order to show that, when an artist apparently changes his style completely, he is merely, as it were, putting on another man's clothes for a time.

Now, if it is satisfactorily established in our minds that an artist's style is nothing less than the vision personal and peculiar to him alone, we must next endeavour to relate our dictionary definition of technique to the particular needs of painting; furthermore, we must look for the link between technique and style. The words "execution" and "mechanical skill" are, I think, the keys to the first part. They indicate clearly that we are now considering an activity which is strictly on the level of manual dexterity. A painter without this mastery of his tools and materials, no matter how powerful his potential style—call it originality if you wish—is in the position of a dumb poet who has never learned to write. In short, he is inarticulate. Hence the rigorous training undergone by young aspirants in the studios of the Old Masters.

Some four or five hundred years ago, a boy would be taken into the workshop of a master painter at a very tender age (probably about ten or eleven) and would serve a very long and arduous apprenticeship, lasting perhaps for ten years, during which he would learn, among other things, the complete craft of painting. The word "craft", which occurs here for the first time, is of cardinal importance to our purpose, since it is a good, old-fashioned term for "technique" and, in my view, much more easily intelligible and apt.

Before ever he began to draw, paint or design—that is, to develop his style— our apprentice would learn to grind colours and prepare panels (there were no shops from which such things could be bought in those days) for the use of the master and the older assistants and apprentices. Later he would make copies of drawings and paintings by his own and other masters, for the purpose of gaining skill in the handling of chalks, brushes and the other tools of his trade. Eventually he would be allowed to execute minor portions of the master's pictures. Only in the latter years of his apprenticeship would he graduate to the execution of original works, since in order to become a fully-fledged member of the guild of master painters (a sort of trade union, usually under the patronage of St. Luke) he would be obliged to carry out a sizeable composition of his own to the satisfaction of the examining masters. I have dwelt at some length upon this "Bottega"[1] system in order that we may see that the masters of the great age of painting held the sound belief that if a solid, thorough technical training was provided, style would look after itself.

[1] Studio or atelier. From the Italian meaning "work-shop"

If I may be permitted to assume that we now have a clear picture of the differences between style and technique as applied specifically to painting, I shall pass to the consideration of the relationship between the two, that is, how the one influences the other. It becomes clear that his style is the inspiration or creative aspect of an artist's make-up, and that his technique or craftsmanship is merely the handmaiden of that inspiration, the means whereby he physically communicates his vision to his fellows. Given this, it is easy to understand that style dominates and dictates to technique.

To illustrate this point, it is only necessary to consider any great artist who worked in different media, for instance, Rembrandt. Rembrandt painted in oils, made drawings, mostly in pen and wash or chalk, and also executed a very large number of etchings. Now the technical procedures for producing oil paintings, drawings and etchings differ very widely, particularly the first and last; yet the overwhelming power of Rembrandt's style so unifies the whole of his output that nothing from his hand, whether it be the gigantic so-called "Night Watch" or the little etching "Six's Bridge" could ever have been mistaken for the work of any other man.

As an artist's vision grows and matures his technique almost invariably becomes simpler and broader, because he learns to express what he has to say more directly and thus achieves the maximum impact upon his audience with the utmost economy of means. We see that, towards the close of their careers, such painters as Titian, Velasquez and again Rembrandt, had learned to dispense with all extraneous detail, and to make their statements with summary brevity and breadth.

So far, all those men whose names have come up lived during or after the Renaissance. In any discussion of style, the implications of the Renaissance must be carefully considered. (Only one other period, namely Periclean Greece, *circa* 450 B.C., provides a similar intellectual and spiritual climate). I refer, of course, to the emergence of the artist as an individual. Since individuality is only another word for style, it is necessary for us to examine the course and development of painting in those epochs when the artist seems to have been regarded in the same sort of light as the carpenter, mason or other anonymous artisan. Perhaps the most astounding example of this kind is provided by Ancient Egypt. There, on the banks of the Nile, for three thousand years and more, a huge quantity of art was produced. What is incredible is its terrifying unchanging quality. A statue or painting made in Egypt in 3,000 B.C. is in all essentials precisely similar to one made 2,000 years later. This seems, at first sight, to be a drastic refutation of our contention that each artist possesses his own inimitable style, but there are, as we shall see, very good reasons for this seemingly paradoxical state of affairs.

There existed in Ancient Egypt an absolute and rigid censorship in what an

*Above:* **WEYMOUTH BAY**
  **John Constable (1776–1837)**

*Right:* **LANDSCAPE STUDY**
  **John Constable (1776–1837)**

It is in his sketches rather than his finished paintings that the genius of Constable is most clearly demonstrated. No other painter has ever moved closer to the heart of nature, or captured more perfectly in paint, some aspect of her ceaselessly changing appearance. It is the intangible, rather than the concrete which Constable imprisons: the pure spirit that swells and surges through cloud and rain, rock and sea, leaf and branch. Nowhere is this little miracle more apparent than here, in these two dynamic studies, wherein the fleeting, spirited moment is endowed with immortality.

Even in black and white it is possible to convey the sensation of colour. To this end I used a strong, soft pencil, rubbing with my finger to suggest a feeling of the floridness which marked the appearance of the poet in his late years.

I treated the hair crisply to convey a sense of the restless energies that drove the writer both in his art—and to his early and tragic death.

*Below:* PIETSIE
**Stephen Bone (born 1904)**

In this fresh, charming study in oils, note the directness of the paint handling, especially in the treatment of the hair; and the simple, but unusual, organization of light and shadow. The pale background gives the portrait a buoyant perkiness.

*Above:* DAME EDITH SITWELL
**Mervyn Levy (born 1915)**

Dame Sitwell's face, so rich in character and form, has often been portrayed; its long shape, with the hooded eyes, and huge, commanding nose, has changed little, basically, with the years. The structure and the forms remain constant producing a curious, impassive serenity, which age has done little to alter. It is that rare phenomenon, the ageless face, cool, deep, and close to the static forms of carved stone.

*Right:* **LIFE STUDY**
 **Alfred Stevens (1818–75)**

*Below:* **THE DRAUGHTSMAN AND
HIS MODEL**
 **Sir William Orpen (1878–1931)**

Irrespective of period or individual style,
the basis of good draughtsmanship is the
artist's understanding of anatomy. At
best, as in these drawings, this should
suggest an instinctive familiarity with
the subject. Whether he works in cool,
meticulous detail, or in rapid spontaneous line, the draughtsman must
express hard, anatomical fact.

*Left:* **THE POND: REGENT'S PARK**
Phoebus Tuttnauer, M.D. (born 1890)

The painter of this remarkable picture is a busy West End consultant who started to paint for pleasure and relaxation only three years ago, at the age of sixty-five. His unique, intensely original vision places him high in the ranks of the modern primitives. The charm of his naïveté lays in a departure from academic conventions, such as perspective, with the resultant intensification of pure pattern.

*Right:* **LANDSCAPE WITH CYPRESS TREES**
Vincent van Gogh (1853–90)

A leading Post-Impressionist, the art of van Gogh is primarily concerned with the expression of emotion. The violence of his colour greatly influenced the Fauvists, while the whole stream of modern Expressionism stems from the intense verve of his explosive style.

*Below:* **THE LIGHTHOUSE, HONFLEUR**
(Detail)    Georges Seurat (1859–91)

Also known as Neo-Impressionists and Divisionists, the Pointillists were concerned with the principle of "optical mixing". Whereas the Impressionists had mixed their colours on the palette, the Pointillists argued that maximum luminosity and brilliance could be best obtained by juxtaposing spots of unmixed colour on the canvas and making the *eye* do the mixing. The technique is seen in the Seurat detail.

*Above:* **THE BATHERS**
Georges Seurat (1859–91)

In collaboration with Paul Signac (1863–1935), Seurat extended Impressionist theory into Pointillism (see page 171). In the hands of this "second generation" of Impressionist painters, the vague, diffuse qualities of the earlier masters were hardened into something more definite. "Art is harmony", wrote Seurat: an axiom superbly borne out by the immaculate composition of his bathers.

artist could or could not do. This was dictated by the priestly hierarchy, of which the Pharaoh was the head. Art was, almost without exception, solely at the disposal of the State, whose interest it was to preserve the status quo. This it did by maintaining a ruthless grip upon the minds of the people through religion, and beyond the prescribed formulae, the artist had absolutely no freedom of self-expression. Here we have a condition in which style has, as it were, become petrified in its own image. Technique (and the Egyptians were expert craftsmen) likewise remained static. That those unknown masters of antiquity who made the prototype which their unfortunate successors were condemned to reproduce in perpetuity, were superb stylists is self-evident; the wonder is that that style could be artificially imposed upon the art of a whole civilization for such an incredible span of time.

That it was artificially imposed is proven during the reign of Akhenaton (c. 1375–58 B.C.) the so-called "heretic king", who made a spirited effort to reform and humanize the robot religion of his ancestors. For a few years a new vitality and enjoyment manifested itself in Egyptian art, but soon the old, overpowering conventions re-asserted themselves and it lapsed into its former state of mummified perfection. Similar conditions prevailed in the contemporary Assyrian civilization, and later, to some extent, in Byzantium. Thus history shows that it is perfectly possible to impose a style indefinitely upon an epoch, provided that, for one reason or another, an authoritarian government, with the power to enforce its dictates is in being. The standard of artistic production may remain high under these conditions, at the expense, however, of nearly all warmth and human feeling, and of course there can be no development, progress or spirit of exploration under such inhibitions.

It is, I think, reasonable to assume that the greatest heights of achievement in painting have been scaled during those periods in history in which the artist has been recognized and honoured as an individual. In Christian times this did not really happen until the Renaissance flowered in Italy. In Western Europe, following the collapse of the Roman Empire, there is no name of any note in painting before Giotto (c. 1266–1337), Cimabue (c. 1240–1302) and Duccio (c. 1255–1319) the forerunners of the High Renaissance, and although a considerable heritage of medieval painting survives, it is relatively small when compared to the immense output of the fifteenth and sixteenth centuries in Italy.

I state these seemingly superfluous historical facts in order to stress the point that it is only possible for style and technique to flourish, develop and change rapidly when the community in which the artist lives is sympathetic to him and appreciates his creations: when, in short, it encourages him as an individual. It will repay us to study the Renaissance from this standpoint, and to note how technical discoveries relate to the styles of certain painters and also schools of painters.

Giotto, the first great Florentine, is a figure of such immense portent in European painting that we can do no better than begin by examining his influence upon our twin subjects. Previous to him, painting in Italy was, with the exception of the great Sienese, Duccio, still under the sway of the rigid, two-dimensional, convention-ridden art of Byzantium, a dying art, which had begun to lose its creative fire and become stereotyped.

It is difficult, after the lapse of some six centuries, to realize the immense revolution in style which Giotto initiated. Put at its simplest, he suddenly realized that men had bodies, with weight, substance, bulk, that they stood with their two feet firmly planted on the earth, and that they moved among houses and trees which equally possessed corporeal solidity. Not only did he give his figures solidity; he gave them, too, humanity. He was much influenced by the teachings of that great humanist, St. Francis of Assisi, whom he actually portrayed in a number of his paintings. Instead of the rigidly solemn masks and gestures which the Byzantine creed imposed, he gave his subjects a liveliness and warmth of gesture and expression which had not been seen in painting since pagan times.

So much then for Giotto's revolutionary stylistic achievements; it remains to examine the methods he applied to the materials available in his time. The bulk of Giotto's work consists of large-scale mural paintings, executed upon the walls of churches and other buildings. They were carried out in a material known as "Fresco", since at that time, oil painting as we know it had not reached Italy.

The technique of fresco is roughly as follows—an area of plaster is laid on the wall at the beginning of the day, and the paint is applied while the plaster is still wet. The paint is thus fused with the plaster as it dries, and in a warm, dry climate such as Italy enjoys, will endure for many centuries. The tonal range, i.e. the scale from light to dark, permissible in fresco is not very great compared with oil paint, and will often induce an average painter to take the easy way out, and paint in decorative flat areas, as had Giotto's predecessors. Giotto was no average painter. By skilfully opposing massive planes or surfaces of light and dark, he managed to convey, within the limited tonality at his disposal, a monumental weight and density to his figures which laid the foundation upon which the whole of the great Florentine tradition was built. In fact, he made a virtue of his small tonal scale. It is of cardinal importance in designing any large wall painting to prevent sudden heavy darks from punching "holes" in the wall surface. The easiest method of preventing this is, as I have said, to paint in flat decorative areas, and to avoid modelling from light to dark altogether. Not the least of Giotto's technical innovations was his power to portray his forms in the round, and at the same time to preserve the total unity of the picture over the whole wall.

138

Another great Florentine of immense importance and interest from the stylistic view-point was Allesandro Botticelli (1444/5–1510). Botticelli stood somewhat outside of the main tradition of Florentine painting as founded by Giotto in that his style was based upon the exploitation of line. The rhythmic undulations, vitality and repose, all the counterpoint which line is capable of expressing, provided that two-dimensional surface-design is the aim, were Botticelli's delight. His problem was, in a sense, easier than Giotto's in that he had no need of the creation of massive form, and therefore did not require such skill in the juxtaposition of his light and dark planes. What he did need was a material which would take crisply a sharp, incisive linear gesture of the brush. Such a material, namely tempera, was to hand. The technique of tempera painting is briefly as follows—a panel, usually of wood, is given a smooth surface of gesso (a kind of plaster). The pigment is mixed with the yolk of an egg and applied usually with a pointed brush. The paint dries immediately upon application, so that there is no possibility of producing any of the blurred atmospheric, impressionistic effects of which oil painting is capable. It is, however, ideally suited to the linear style of which Botticelli was such a consummate master, and although, within his lifetime the technique of oil painting had been fully developed by such Venetian masters as Giorgione (c. 1478–1510) and Titian (c. 1477–1576) many of his most superb creations are carried out in tempera. Botticelli's is a singularly felicitous example of the happy marriage of technique and style.

The history of the development of the technique of painting in oils is somewhat blurred in its early stages, but it seems fairly certain that it was first widely used in Flanders and that Jan van Eyck (c. 1385–1441) and his somewhat shadowy brother, Hubert, were among its pioneers. Early oil-painters favoured a mixed method, in which they did a preliminary underpainting in tempera, then coloured it with transparent oil glazes. This procedure bound them down, more or less, to the linear style already ascribed to Botticelli, and Jan van Eyck's famous "Jan Arnolfini and His Wife" (National Gallery), splendid masterpiece though it is, pays no attention to the atmospheric possibilities of the medium. Antonello da Messina (c. 1430–79) first popularized oil painting in Italy, but it is not until we reach the high noon of the school of Venice that we find masters who fully realized its possibilities and adapted them to a new way of seeing.

The outstanding genius of the Venetian School is Titian and it was he who brought to its apex the style which Giovanni Bellini (c. 1430–1516) and the regrettably short-lived Giorgione had foreshadowed in their work. They saw that light and colour fused in an atmospheric envelope, and that distant objects were not sharply defined, nor even were closer ones under certain conditions of light and that the oil medium could simulate these effects in a way to which fresco and tempera could not possibly aspire. This was both a stylistic and technical innovation to which the Florentines, with their insistence upon sculptural form and drawing, had never attained, although they had the use of the oil medium; they saw painting in terms of drawing with colour added. At the end of his very long life, Titian was painting pictures, e.g. the small "Mother and Child" (National Gallery) which hinted at possibilities which were not fully exploited until the French Impressionists came on the scene nearly four hundred years later.

This last observation prompts me to take a leap forward in time and to examine the characteristics of two men who fall into the somewhat negative and unsatisfactorily named category of "Post-Impressionism". They were Vincent van Gogh and Georges Seurat. Although they were contemporaries who knew each other personally, and are both classed as Post-Impressionists, no two men could have been more dissimilar. Vincent van Gogh (1853–90) was really one of the great exponents of the style called "Expressionism" which describes him far more aptly than "Post-Impressionism". Briefly, Expressionism means that the artist gives paramount importance to his own emotional reactions to the subject, and that such objective values as correct drawing, and colour, are swept away in the cataract of his spiritual intensity, being replaced by distortion and caricature in drawing, and violent, disturbing, and "unnatural" colour. Most of Van Gogh's greatest paintings were made in the South of France, in the last two years of his brief life, and at a time when he was suffering from intermittent bouts of insanity. Typical of this period is his "Cypresses" (Tate Gallery) which I propose briefly to discuss. The features which I list above are all admirably displayed in this picture, with its writhing, tortured trees and clouds, convulsed landscape and strange, searing colour. It is said to have been painted during the season of the Mistral, that hot, blasting wind from the south which drives the most matter-of-fact person to the edge of frenzy. (See picture facing page 137).

It is our special interest to consider the technical means which Vincent used to communicate this frenzy, and the journey which led up to them. In his early days in Holland, he used a dark, somewhat monochromatic palette of earth colours, but the thick impasto and long, slashing strokes of paint were already there. Later, in Paris, he met the Impressionists, learned from them about colour, and for a time painted fairly orthodox Impressionist pictures. However, this method did not suit his violent temperament, and in his last phase he elongated the Impressionist dots of pure colour into disquieting swirls and rhythms for strictly emotive purposes. Although he retained the use of brilliant colour which he had learned from the Impressionists, it was based on no scientific theory as employed by him, but was dictated by his mood. Van Gogh is an almost too perfect example of an aggressively original vision forcing the medium into an absolutely new format.

Georges Seurat (1859–91) is popularly remembered for the invention of an ingenious, quasi-scientific method of painting called Pointillism, or, alternatively, Divisionism. His technique was an extension of the Impressionist practice of juxtaposing small, irregular streaks and dabs of pure colour, in such a way that they resolved themselves into secondary and tertiary colours when the canvas was seen from the viewing distance.

Seurat painted in small round dots of pure colour, which gave his paintings somewhat the appearance of a cheap postcard colour reproduction when the latter is seen through a magnifying glass. He worked out the proportions of different coloured dots needed to give the sensation of any colour he required when viewed at the correct distance, and claimed that he could paint by gas or lamplight with impunity, because he knew beforehand how that colour would appear in daylight. This clever device was not, however, his chief contribution to painting. Seurat was a master designer in the great classic tradition; he sought an ideal, balanced and serene composition, which aim he placed above any display of personal passion or emotion. He magnificently achieves this ideal in his large "Bathers" (Tate Gallery). The relevant point is that Seurat's style ensured that he would become a great designer, no matter whether he had painted in dots or not, and thus his arduous and elaborate technical researches were, to an extent, beside the point. I quote him as an example of a great painter whose technical development was not particularly helped by his infatuation with an ingenious but essentially unimportant device. (See picture facing page 137).

Our survey has now brought us within measurable distance of the present day, and it is time to consider the facts revealed in relation to the personal problems and needs of the amateur. Admitting the original premise that style is inherent, much can be done to foster it, and promote its healthy growth. Modern methods of publicity and production have made available to the public an unlimited number of books and reproductions which, if selected with discernment, can broaden and deepen the knowledge and stimulate the individuality of the embryo painter.

We have already seen how, for instance, Giotto's style served as a foundation for that of many of the great Florentines who came after him, the debt which Titian owed to Giorgione and Bellini, and it is a commonplace of art history that all great masters have, at some time in their careers drawn upon the discoveries of their illustrious predecessors; that is what is meant by "tradition". Everyone who sets out to paint will find among the masters, certain kindred spirits whose style provides him with clues to the development of his own. It is, I hope, unnecessary to warn the reader against the many false prophets of painting whose activities have been studied elsewhere in these pages.

Even more fruitful is the study of original works, and those who have access

141

to the great public galleries of London and other cities should make the fullest use of their opportunities.

The problems of technique have been fully dealt with in other sections of the book, and it would be tedious to repeat them. The moral to be drawn from this chapter, which I leave the reader to digest and put into practice is this—style is innate, technique can be learned.

# CHAPTER 15

# Framing and Mounting

N O PICTURE is really complete until it has been suitably framed and, if it is a drawing, or a water-colour, it will need mounting as well. Many amateur artists make the mistake of placing their water-colours straight into a frame, without any mounting, but this is a most unsatisfactory procedure since the relative delicacy of the medium needs that isolation from the frame itself, which a mount provides. Drawings too, require to be "separated" from their frames. Water-colours and drawings need to be isolated, and contained by a mount, so that their comparative fragility can be savoured, like a good spirit, in a fine glass. A drawing without a mounting is like brandy in a tumbler.

An oil painting demands different treatment. The natural strength and robustness of oil paint, its rugged and forceful character, are sufficiently powerful to compete directly with a suitable frame. Indeed, with an oil painting, the frame should be an *extension* of the painting. The relationship is a very close one, suggesting rather the compatability of beer, or stout, with a tankard, or heavy mug. In the texture of its finish, one can even match the *matière* of the picture itself, so that the frame becomes a sort of organic outcrop of the painting.

The texturing of a moulding in its relationship to an oil painting is a most important aspect of the aesthetics of picture framing. First of all then, let us consider the framing of pictures painted in oils. Far too many artists, professionals as well as amateurs, are inclined to look upon a frame as something impersonal, whereas in fact, a frame should complement with its own distinct personality, the characteristic qualities in the painting of which it is an intrinsic part. The relationship is rather that of a perfectly matched husband and wife. Both will have their separate identity, yet each will complement the other. If you are more romantically inclined, you can think of the simile in terms of the lover and his mistress.

Four cardinal points must be taken into consideration when selecting, or preparing the frame for a painting; they are—*proportion, form, texture, and colour*. The width and moulding of the frame must be proportionately just right for the total area of the painting—for its size as a square, or rectangle: it must be neither too heavy, nor yet, too light. The "weight" of the painting itself is also a determining factor; by this I mean the relative weight of its impasto—has it been thickly, and heavily executed? The form of the moulding must suit the type of subject, the manner of composition, and the style of technical execution. For instance, a rhythmic painting in the romantic vein could take an ornate, baroque moulding, whereas a restrained, comparatively classical canvas, would be best served by a plain, straight moulding.

These considerations are of course very much a matter of personal taste, but it is essential that the artist should appreciate the aesthetic principles which under-lay the art of framing, since, as I say, they are so often neglected. You will, naturally, adapt or modify the broad principles to suit the circumstances peculiar to yourself, and to your type of painting. But the *form* of a picture moulding is psychologically most important. The curve excites emotion—the straight line induces a mood of quiet contemplation. You must decide very carefully what you want your frame to do, as a complement of the painting which it contains.

In brash, vulgar, Victorian times, almost everything went straight into heavy and ornate, gilt, or gilded frames. Gold suggested affluence, even though it was, so to speak, only skin deep. Victorian hypocrisy was satisfied by surface appearances, and the prevalence of the gilt frame in this period is yet another manifestation of this ugly psychological defect. The gilt frame as such is of course no longer fashionable, although the mouldings themselves can provide the basis for excellent frames in the contemporary idiom, if they are first stripped of their gold leaf, then renovated, and redecorated. They may require a little physical repair after stripping, but I will deal with all the phases of renovation and redecoration later in the present chapter. The texture of a frame as I have already indicated, is also extremely important. A rough texture for a picture painted with bold impasto, and stimulating textural contrasts in its brushwork; a smoother surface for a less thickly painted picture, or one in which texture plays a more restrained role.

Finally, the colouring of a frame should echo, or supplement the predominant colour note in the painting, although of course, as a general rule, in a lighter tone. Thus a picture which contains a predominance of ochres and browns, shall we say, would be well served by a frame that had been tinted a pale mustard, with perhaps a white inset. A strip of white between the painting and the colour of the frame, can be extremely effective, and since many mouldings possess some such inset, this can be weaved into the relationship between a picture and its frame.

Now you can come by your picture frames in a number of ways: (a) You can buy them new—"off the peg", so to speak; (b) You can have them "made to measure"; (c) You can buy second-hand frames, and redecorate them; or, (d) You can make your own.

Frames can be a costly business if you buy them new, or have them specially made, and I personally recommend, either that you buy your frames second-hand, or make your own. Apart from the saving in cost, which can be very considerable —a new, or specially made frame for a 24 in. × 20 in. canvas can quite easily cost five pounds or so—preparing your own frames at home can be the source of great pleasure. It completes the conception of the artist as a craftsman, and once you have really appreciated the extent to which a frame can be an intrinsic part of the picture, contributing immeasurably to its appeal, you will almost certainly wish to take some personal part in the creation of its aesthetic appearance. Old frames, often gold leafed, and of excellent design, are almost always obtainable at second-hand, or junk shops, for a few shillings. Basically they are usually in good condition, and find their way on to the second-hand market from families and homes grown tired of the pictures they contain, and who look upon them as so much lumber. The pictures themselves are almost always worthless, but the frames can prove most valuable to the painter. They can also be bought in lots, quite inexpensively, at the smaller auction rooms. It is all a matter of exploring the sort of shops and sale-rooms where such bargains are continually turning up. The best buys, naturally, are obtainable in localities where there is little general interest in pictures, or picture frames, and if you are lucky enough to find the right source of supply— and keep it to yourself—it may well stand you in good stead for some time. Frames, as such, mean very little to the dealer who is not specially concerned with their sale; for him, they will be merely so many clumsy objects cluttering up his valuable space, and he will often be only too glad to sell them for a song, just to get them out of the way.

It is a good plan to build up a comprehensive stock of second-hand frames, ready for treatment as you require them. Since many of these second-hand frames will be odd in size, it is sound procedure to paint pictures for frames which you have in your stock.

This simply means cutting your wood, or stout cardboard, to fit a particular frame, or you may of course be lucky enough to find a canvas stretcher that happens to fit an odd-sized frame, but this is unlikely. So it is better to paint on wood, or cardboard panels, for your odd sized frames. New frames, and a limited number of second-hand ones are of course obtainable in a range of standard sizes, to take canvases of corresponding dimensions, but you are lucky indeed if you find more than an occasional second-hand frame in this range of stock sizes. When buying frames that have been gilded, go for those that have been treated with gold leaf rather than gilt paint. Gold leaf is easy to strip, besides which you can so organize the process if you wish, that you will be able to sell the stripped leaf, in the form of gold dust, to a commercial refiner.

Gold leaf is easily distinguished from gilt paint by the quality of its appearance, which is soft, and gentle to look at, whereas gilt paint is clearly harsh and metallic to the eye. Gold leaf also tends to come away if rubbed with a dampened fingertip.

The method of removing gold leaf from a frame consists of energetic scrubbing with a hard brush in a solution of caustic soda. The process should be carried out in a large metal bath, and it is most important to protect the hands against the burning action of the solution by wearing rubber gloves while stripping the frame. A number of frames should be cleaned in the same solution, and when a couple of dozen or so have been treated in this way, siphon away the surplus liquid, a process which will leave a thick, muddy sediment in the bath. This deposit will contain a quantity of pure gold dust. The sediment is next transferred to a bucket, and the remaining liquid slowly evaporated over a heater, or gas-jet. This process will leave you finally with a dry, earthy substance, speckled with gold. The "earth" is then boxed and either taken, or sent, to a commercial gold refinery for treatment. The refiner will pay you the current price per fine ounce for the quantity of gold dust he is able to extract from your "earth". I merely suggest this procedure as the source of additional interest, and indeed of a little extra revenue, which is usually welcome these days.

Having removed the gold leaf you are now ready to renovate, and redecorate your frame. First of all, make good with plastic wood, any parts of the moulding that may have been chipped, or otherwise damaged. Almost certainly the best method of redecorating old frames is to give them a coat of white, or tinted gesso, and finally, a thin coating of a cellulose finish, which will act as a permanent fixative.

Gesso is a substance which was widely used by the early masters (The Flemish School of the fifteenth century, for instance) as a ground for wood panels, and later for canvas, prior to painting. Basically, it is simply a white pigment, such as chalk, plaster of paris, or gypsum, mixed with a glue size. Today, it provides the basis of an excellent finish for picture mouldings. Gesso is obtainable in ready mixed compounds from all stores that supply the painting and decorating trade. In this form it is easily prepared for immediate use.

Before applying a coat of gesso to the moulding, the surface of the wood should be roughened with a coarse sandpaper to provide a grip for the mixture. On occasions, if you want such an effect, it is a good plan to streak the moulding here and there, with red and gold paint, before gessoing. When this colour is dry, the gesso is applied on top, covering the red and gold completely. When the gesso in turn has dried thoroughly, you can create the most striking effects by carefully scraping, or sandpapering the dry gesso, so bringing through the most subtle and attractive flecks and flashes of red and gold. These can be most effectively woven into the final appearance of the decoration. A sculptor's modelling tool, preferably of metal, is ideal for scraping gesso, although it is quite likely that you will find some other implement that will serve you equally well. The technique however is one that demands considerable skill, and it is only by personal familiarity with tools, and materials, that you will learn by experience how to produce the most satisfying results. This however is all part of the enormous pleasure which is bound up with the preparation of your own frames. Gesso should be applied with a brush—a flat, one-inch paint brush is excellent—as a thick, creamy substance, and the brush-marks themselves should be allowed to play their part in creating the texture of the finished surface.

When the gesso is dry, it should be thoughtfully scraped and sandpapered until all unpleasant lumpiness and roughness has been removed, and a refined surface created. As I say, this should take in the life of the brushmarks. This latter process is the one in which considerable skill and sensitivity are required in order to create those subtle, and delicate effects that are obtainable by the exercise of this particular technique. They will be unique, unrepeatable effects and, as such, will be aesthetically comparable with the uniqueness of style in painting, for however unified by personal style the total of an artist's work may be, every piece that he paints will be an unrepeatable experience, a form of aesthetic existence distinct from all others. It is this element of uniqueness which adds such character and distinction to the gesso technique. Finally, the frame may be given a thin, transparent tinting with a *cellulose* paint, a product which is obtainable from your decorator's supply store. Cellulose dries with a hard surface, and provides an excellent, and permanent finish for your frames. However, you can if you so wish quite well leave the scraped and sandpapered gesso as it is. I should mention also that gesso can be tinted any colour, or tone of colour you require, simply by mixing a powder colour, such as tempera pigment, with the gesso paste before it is applied.

Now for a word about making frames yourself. The first step is to procure lengths of picture moulding—the simpler in design and section the better—from one or other of the many sources from which these are obtainable. Builder's yards, and frame makers will usually be able to offer you a selection of raw, untreated wood mouldings.

For the actual making of the frames themselves you will require the following tools, and of course, if you have a small workshop of your own, such as one often finds in a garage, or shed, then you are in a very good position indeed, since this will greatly facilitate your work. You will need:

1. *A mitre-box*. This will enable you to cut your mouldings to an angle of 45°. This is the angle at which they are joined to form the overall corner right-angle of the frame.

2. *A saw.*

3. *A small vice* for clamping the mouldings together while they are being glued, and nailed.

4. *A stop block* for the mitre-box. A device which enables you to cut mitred pieces of identical length.

5. *Miscellaneous items:* Carpenter's glue, nails, a drill, a hammer, and a crack filler, such as plastic wood.

I will not discuss in detail the precise method of using these various tools since this is really an exercise in pure carpentry, and there are certain to be a number of text books in your own public library which will deal with frame making from the point of view of carpentry. Then again, many of my readers may well be competent sparetime carpenters themselves. The main factors to be borne in mind are the following:

(a) The mitred ends of your four pieces of moulding must be cut at exactly 45°. To ensure this accuracy the saw must be held absolutely vertical when making the cuts.

(b) Correct measurement of the lengths cut, in relation to the size of picture you wish to frame. Certain mathematical allowances are essential, and these you will have to calculate.

(c) The procedure for gluing and nailing is highly technical, and here you should certainly consult a specialist work, unless of course the method of making these attachments is already known to you.

When your frame has been completed, it may be treated with gesso in precisely the same way as I have already described for the treatment of more ornate, second-hand mouldings. Water-colours and drawings after mounting, should be framed in simple, delicate mouldings. Light oak is one of the most effective woods for this purpose, and can be treated with a very thin brushing of gesso, which can be sandpapered so that the natural quality and character of the wood plays its role in the finished appearance of the frame. Light oak is extremely pleasing to look at in itself, and there is really no reason why it should of necessity receive any treatment at all. If you feel that it needs some relief, another method of giving it that little something else, is to rub into the grain, a spot of powdered chalk.

In considering the presentation of water-colours and drawings, perhaps the only types of frame to avoid like the plague are those in the black lacquered finishes that were once so popular for the framing of etchings, and prints. They are psychologically depressing, and their smooth, shining, unrelieved, and featureless surfaces, positively repulsive. On the other hand, the grain and texture of a natural wood is aesthetically most satisfying; in its natural state, wood possesses very distinct features, and I use the term in the sense that lacquered wood has literally *no face or expression*, whereas the grain of raw wood, *is* literally a face.

If you wish to depersonalize wood, your best plan is to paint it a pure white, a method of treatment which often adds considerable luminosity to a water-colour, and acts as a superb foil for a drawing in red *conté*, for instance. A white frame is of course unobtrusive, and helps to concentrate the spectator's attentions upon the water-colour, or drawing itself. By far the best type of mounting for water-colours and drawings is a plain, white, or off-white board, the aperture being cut with a 45° bevel. Mount-cutting is an activity which demands considerable technical skill, and a steady hand, but there is no reason why the technique should not be mastered with practice. A special mount-cutting knife is pretty well indispensable for this job, and with this, a steel rule, and a firm hand, you will, after a while, be able to cut excellent mounts for your pictures, so saving yourself a great deal of added expense.

Mount-cutting is another challenge to your sense of craftsmanship; a method of developing that technical skill which is so much a part of the joy of creation, and of those incidental activities which are an integral aspect of the creative experience as a whole. Today, craft lags behind art; this is perhaps the crucial, and central tragedy of the artist in our time. He has lost, not only his sense of purpose—but also his sense of craft. That is why I lay so much emphasis on the importance of craft, especially in the pursuit of those incidental activities which are bound up with the presentation of pictures. You will I am sure, derive profound satisfaction from a combination of the freedom you may indulge to the full in your painting, with the discipline, and method , that are essential to the production of your frames, and mountings.

Having cut the mount, your picture should be laid on another sheet of card, and attached to this by its top edge only. This is best effected by hinging the picture to its bed with a strip of gummed tape. The mount, with the aperture cut a little under the actual size of the water-colour or drawing is then placed over the picture, thus holding down its unsecured edges. The main advantage of this method of mounting is that it enables you to remove the picture easily should you wish, at any time, to put another one in its place. A water-colour or drawing which has been glued to its bed is of course impossible to remove, and although pictures are sometimes laid down in this way, it is less damaging if they are only temporarily secured. The mount itself may also be hinged to the bed card, a particularly useful scheme if you are preparing a series of pictures for display purposes. In this way they may be stored in a portfolio, and produced, when required, for show.

Finally, a word about the making of *canvas mounts*. These can look most attractive as a setting for the more lush and colourful water-colours, and for that

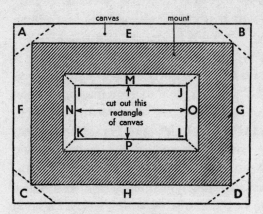

Making a canvas mount.

specially luxurious drawing. The texture of a canvas mount is delightful, and set in a pure white frame, can look positively ravishing. To cover a mount in canvas—an ordinary hessian is ideal —first of all lay it upon a piece of canvas that is somewhat larger in size than its overall area. For example, a mount measuring 20 in. × 16 in., with an aperture of 13 in. × 14 in., might conveniently be set upon a rectangle of canvas measuring 24 in. × 20 in., thus providing an overlap on each side, of 2 in. From the centre of the canvas exposed in the aperture of the mount, cut a smaller opening, say 13 in. × 12 in. Next, cut away the corners A, B, C, and D, gum the overlaps, E. F. G. and H, fold them over, and secure them to the back of the mount. Then make four cuts with a sharp knife, or razor blade, along the lines I, J, K, and L, apply gum to the surfaces M, N, O, and P, fold over, and secure these also to the underside of the mount. When the various adhesions are dry, the mount is ready to lay over the water-colour or drawing, and for placing in its frame.

# CHAPTER 16

# Your Studio: About Varnishing

ONE of the major considerations so often overlooked by enthusiastic protagonists of spare time painting, is the whole question of *where*, in the average house, the inspired amateur is going to get down to his work? With the professional painter, the studio is of course as indispensable for the conduct of artistic business, as the city man's office: but the artist painting purely for pleasure may find himself in something of a quandary here. One thing is certain; he must be able to find some location in a private dwelling, where he can work, both without fear of disturbance, or of causing damage to such items as carpets, and furniture. Painting, especially in oils, is quite a messy business, and unless you take protective measures, both your own personal clothing, and some part at least of an ordinary living room, are going to wear the scars of the painter's battle. For such indeed is the activity of painting: a thrilling tussle between the artist's materials and his inspiration in the course of which an intrinsic part of the whole delicious, exuberant fun, and joy of painting consists in simply not having to bother about making a mess, either of one's person, or of the surroundings in which one is at work. In the face of this, one might even list the first preventive measure as the necessity, either to wear a painter's overall or smock of some sort, or a pair of old trousers, and a pullover. Jeans are ideal, and combined with a sweater, afford a simple, and effective attire, which of course lends itself equally well to painters of either sex.

What about your studio, or a possible substitute for one? Naturally, no enthusiastic pleasure painter is going to be put off for want of some official space in which to paint; after all, improvisation is very much a part of the joy of painting for pleasure, and rather than not paint, for want of suitable accommodation, I would certainly argue that you should boldly prop up your painting surface on the mantelpiece, or the sideboard; provided you first put some newspaper down in the right places. But I doubt if the problem is quite so acute as to call for such drastic action. Naturally, a great deal depends upon the size, and design of your home: on whether for instance you possess either an attic of some sort, or a spare room in the literal sense of the word; that is to say, a spare room that is not simply a guest room, but of the kind that was once referred to as the lumber room. Both the attic and the lumber room held great joys—and terrors—for me as a child, but I fear that in this age of graceless and compressed living, of tiny houses and dwarf flats, this romantic hide-away from the vulgar hurly-burly of daily life, is a vanishing feature of the home scene.

If you do possess any such accommodation, then your studio problem is very happily solved. Lighting is of course a most important aspect of the studio scene, but this too will depend upon what is structurally available. An attic top light often is excellent. If you possess neither an attic nor a lumber room, then you will need to adapt some part of the most convenient room available at home. Usually this is an extremely simple procedure, and one of course that will need to suffice only while you are actually painting. Having chosen your room, and the best position for your easel—the location of the light will determine this—all that is really necessary is some protection for the floor, or carpet. A covering of old sheeting will serve this purpose admirably, although even newspapers will suffice at a pinch.

If you are going to use an ordinary table as the area on which you propose laying out your painting materials, this too will need protection, and here, newspaper is the ideal covering. You should put down at least two layers. I do suggest however that wherever you work, whether in the attic, the lumber room, or the living room, the best plan is to fit yourself up with a permanent *painting table*. Ideal for this purpose is an old tea-trolley—provided it is not too small—so that you will have the benefit of at least two decks to take your various items. If your trolley possesses wheels or castors into the bargain that will greatly facilitate its movements in and out of action.

If you are using an ordinary blackboard easel for your painting, it is a good plan to suspend a weight from the apex of the tripod to ensure stability while you are at work. The easel should be placed near the window, allowing sufficient room for the painter to step back from time to time and scrutinize his progress—or otherwise. This is a very important part of the activity of painting in oils since you cannot really consider your work critically when you are right on top of it.

There is one other item that every painter ought to include in his studio equipment, and that is a mirror. Something about 12 in. × 8 in. is a splendid size. Not only of course is this essential for self-portraiture, but it provides an extraordinary, almost uncanny way of checking up on the accuracy of your work, especially in relation to portraiture. If you hold the mirror so that it reflects both the subject and your representation *simultaneously*, you will be surprised at the way in which faults in general drawing, such as angles of direction, distances, proportions and so on, are revealed.

152

*Right:* **AFTER THE BATH**
**Edgar Degas (1834–1917)**
With Degas, the realistic and informal approach to the problems of figure painting, first broached by Manet (see between pp. 104-5), reached its perfection. Nothing could be less contrived, or more natural, than this spontaneous pose. The painting as a whole is a superb composition in which curves, straightnesses and angles are opposed with great subtlety. Drawn in pastel, it is easy, even in reproduction, to see how the artist has exploited the peculiar qualities of the medium to produce a variety of rich textures. Note the way in which the strokes of the pastel describe the form of the figure.

*Left:* **Detail from THE BAR AT THE FOLIES BERGÈRES**
**Edouard Manet (1832–83)**
The student of painting frequently over-organizes the still-life group, arranging and rearranging its elements until the whole thing grows leaden and dead. The first objective in still-life painting should be to find a group, such as here, which quite naturally and without more than the simplest of adjustments, is ready for painting more or less as it is. It is the chance, rather than the artificially contrived relationship, that should provide the inspiration for the still-life painting.

*Right:* **APPLES AND POMEGRANATES (Detail)**
**Gustave Courbet (1819–77)**
Of peasant extraction, Courbet was imprisoned for his part in the Paris Commune of 1871. His favourite dictum, "the art of painting can consist only in the representation of objects visible and tangible to the painter", is clearly demonstrated in this simple, earthy group.

*Above:* **THE TOWER OF BABEL**    **Pieter Brueghel (c. 1525/30–69)**
Brueghel was one of the great masters of Flanders; his vision of the building of Babel illustrates the craziness of an impossible undertaking.

*Right:* **THE GHOST OF A FLEA**
 **William Blake (1757–1827)**
Blake is perhaps the most consistently and purely imaginative artist in European painting. He drew little upon the objective world, and almost all his drawings, paintings, and engravings spring from an inward vision. Mystic and seer, he claimed that many of his illustrations for Dante and the Bible were divinely inspired. Apprenticed to an engraver at the age of fourteen, he later designed and produced his own books. He spoke of his power to commune with spirits, and *The Ghost of a Flea* provides a link with the visionary world that played such a conspicuous part in shaping his art.

*Above:* **VENUS ASLEEP**
**Paul Delvaux (born 1897)**

*Left:* **GIRAFFE AFLAME**
**Salvador Dali (born 1904)**

Surrealist painting unlocks the doors of the unconscious; the submerged kingdom into which, involuntarily, we repress many of our most fundamental and characteristic desires. This is the penalty which a civilized society imposes upon its members. Only in dreams—or waking fantasy—can we achieve at least a partial liberation and fulfilment of our true nature. Even then, conscience, or a sense of guilt, ensures that the naked identity of a repressed impulse or idea, is suitably disguised. So we dream in *symbols*, and if we are to understand such intriguing paintings as these, we must first interpret the symbolism involved.

*Right:*
**THE OLD TREE,
ARUNDEL PARK**
R. O. Dunlop (born 1894)

*Below:*
**IN THE WOODS**
R. O. Dunlop (born 1894)

A fresh and spontaneous handling of oil (*right*), and water colour (*below*), contributes much to the success of these landscapes. Each captures a feeling of the constantly changing face of nature. Sun and shadow, wind and rain, the continuous alternation of damp and dry, these typical characteristics of the British countryside are easily sensed.

It is interesting to note that both Leonardo da Vinci, and Leon Alberti (1404–72), one of the most cultivated of the Renaissance *dilettanti*, refer in their writings to the employment of the mirror by the artist. First, let us take Alberti's remarks:

"A mirror will greatly help you to judge of relief-effect. And I do not know why good paintings, when reflected in a mirror, are full of charm; and it is wonderful how any defect in a painting shows its ugliness in the looking glass. Therefore things drawn from nature are to be amended with a mirror."

Now compare this with Leonardo's observations and you will get a good idea of the esteem in which the mirror was held by painters during the first great scientific era in western history. It is a typical Renaissance touch, an empirical observation closely linked with the whole exploratory spirit of the age of discovery:

"When you wish to see whether the general effect of your picture corresponds with that of the object presented by nature, take a mirror and set it so that it reflects the actual thing, and then compare the reflection with your picture and consider carefully whether the subject of the two images is in conformity with both, studying especially the mirror."

Both these quotations are taken from a remarkable book, *Artists of Art* (Robert Goldwater and Marco Treves), in which the artist speaks for himself. It is, I think, an invaluable pendant to your studies.

So much then for your studio and its equipment. Improvisation, as I say, is an important part of the whole business of painting for pleasure, and what you lack in the way of official equipment, whether an easel or a studio, you will soon make up for with a little ingenuity. For instance, I am personally acquainted with one well-known London doctor who has designed a removable lid for his bath, on which, for his painting, he stands an easel with shortened legs. All his work is thus very satisfactorily carried out in the bathroom.

*     *     *

## ABOUT VARNISHING

Not only does a coat of varnish add a certain warmth and lustre to a painting, it also protects its surface against the various atmospheric attacks to which pictures in modern industrial towns and cities are continually subjected. The great art galleries of the nation are situated mainly in localities where there is a high degree of atmospheric pollution, and a coat of varnish absorbs the dirt and other harmful waste matter that would otherwise be deposited on the "flesh" of the painting itself. After a long time the varnish becomes discoloured, whereupon it may be removed, usually with alcohol—a highly specialized task by the way—and a fresh coat applied.

Before it became fashionable to clean the discoloured varnish from old paintings—Sir Philip Hendy was a notable pioneer of this practice during the early years of his present Directorship at the National Gallery—it was commonly thought, especially by the layman, that the darkened surface of such paintings was in fact the "mellowing" of age. It was of course nothing of the sort. Dirty varnish has often been mistaken for the ripe gold of time. I mention these facts about the use of varnish as a form of prophylaxis against the ravages of atmospheric disease, by way of general interest; the average spare time painter, less concerned with posterity than with his immediate pleasure, will employ it rather as a means of enhancement, than of protection. Although of course it will serve both ends automatically.

Some months after painting—there is no fixed time about this—an unvarnished picture in oils will start to lose some of its initial sheen and vitality; it may even go matt, and dead in patches. What it needs is a coat of clear varnish to restore its lost brightness. In fact, it will need a tonic. However, no picture should be varnished before it is thoroughly dry, and although it will dry *superficially* in a week or so, it is better left for at least six months before varnishing.

The best varnish is *Mastic*, and in no circumstances should *Copal Varnish* be used, as this yellows very badly. Varnishing should be carried out with a flat brush, at least an inch in width. It is most important that the brush should be free from any hair shedding. During the process of varnishing the picture should be laid flat, and scrutinized carefully while the liquid is being applied to make certain that no part is missed, and that the coating is covering the surface evenly. The varnish should be poured into a shallow dish for the work involved, and the whole of the brush saturated with the liquid. After use the brush should be carefully cleansed in turpentine, alcohol, or surgical spirit. Before varnishing, a painting should be gently warmed, and the work is best carried out in a heated room. After varnishing the painting should be allowed to stand facing the wall of a room that is not in use, until it is dry. This will protect it from the dust that would otherwise settle in the tacky varnish. Only when it is quite dry is it ready for display.

# CHAPTER 17

# Modern Art

MODERN ART is closely related to creative pleasure painting since it forms, chronologically, a period of intensive experiment. In its many exploratory aspects it provides a variety of stimulating precedents for the spare time artist who may, while seeking his own personal direction, himself explore the ground already covered by modern painters. He may even uncover some entirely fresh feature of the road already travelled.

Today, the aesthetic, emotional, intellectual and technical possibilities of genuine pleasure painting are in fact the logical complement of the achievements of professional modern art. I say "genuine pleasure painting" to distinguish between decadent academic illusion—so called "naturalistic painting"—and the truly creative eye moving in complete freedom, beyond the limitations of any stifling convention, or lifeless tradition.

We each possess the power, however slight, to contribute some unique ingredient to the vast ocean of what has already been achieved, in painting. If there were not this possibility it would be pointless to take up painting, especially for pleasure. The human spirit is something more than a series of hollow echoings, of parrot-like repetitions. True, we are inevitably the sum of all that has been, both in biological and psychological terms; we cannot escape our hereditary destiny. But we are also all that only we ourselves can be: all that never was before we were: all that in turn will become part of the inheritance of the next generation. In conjunction with this *unique*, personal "we", modern artists have experimented and explored, and at length, by a process of trial and error, resolved many of these experiments into solid achievements.

Now that the modern movement is largely a matter of art history, we can consider in detachment, the extent of the achievements—and the failures too—that have been wrought by this enormously virile, often violent period of intensive searching. After all, only through trial and error is progress a possibility. This fact has of course always constituted a condition of evolution, irrespective of the field of research, since there cannot be progress without the *changes* effected

155

ceaselessly, by exploration and discovery. Progress is a continuous becoming, and it would be wrong to think of a finding, conclusive as it may superficially appear, as an end. Success is merely a stepping stone, a springboard to something else. Yet curiously, the law of change is a fact that many people are loathe to accept. Consider painting. During the four centuries that lay between the Renaissance and the mid-nineteenth century (from Michelangelo to Manet) the objectives of European painters were reasonably consistent and their productions during this period display little in the way of any radical departures from the basic principles of space-and-form painting established by the masters of the Italian Renaissance.

How far the fulfilment of those objectives was debased by a degeneration in conception and technique, is a matter we shall consider in our stride. Certainly the use of space and form by Leonardo and Michelangelo was incidental to the nature of their respective messages, and they were not of course naturalistic painters in the sense that the most banal of Victorian painters were. Their realism was not an attempt to reproduce or simulate existing appearances; they employed three-dimensionalism in reaction against the flat, rigid and sterile formalism of medieval painting, and as a means of heightening the significance of their own personal conceptions. Leonardo strove to create an ideal human type—to establish an ultimate amalgam of physical and spiritual beauty, impeccably blended. Michelangelo sought a symbolic conception of the Christian story peopled by the supra-muscular bodies of men and women. How else could a densely populated, essentially anthropomorphic mythology be depicted? There had to be bodies— masses of creatures, writhing and knotted like serpents in a pit. There could be no creation and no fall from grace, no judgement and no damnation without the living, heaving swell and stench of human flesh.

Space and form, anatomy and perspective, were bent by Leonardo and Michelangelo to specific ends, largely symbolical. But for Landseer, by way of sharp comparison, realism had to be linked with craven versimilitude and that sentimentality which constituted the apogee of his art; if such you can call the degraded rot that so captivated the hypocritical Victorian middle-classes with their brutal indifference to human suffering (in the 1840s children of five and six were still being worked and beaten to death in the pits and mills), and their depraved lust for sentiment in the arts.

Mankind, unhappily, has one crucial blind spot, which is I think, the chief reason for the inability of the race, generally speaking, to effect any notable degree of advancement. Man is the willing slave of habit. Custom and convention are the shackles with which he has so often fettered his mind and his heart. He is always liable to become the bondslave of a mode of thought, or even of seeing. When a living force has become a bloodless trickle, he continues to admire the brittle husk, mistaking an empty bottle for a full one. Thus, even today, to return to Sir Edwin Landseer R.A., many people still mistake the shadow of Victorian naturalism for the substance of Renaissance symbolic realism.

By the mid-nineteenth century, the habit of equating all naturalistic appearance in art, however degenerate the technique, style, or subject content, as the only admissible standard of aesthetic excellence, was a lunatic *idée fixe* in the public mind (as it still is, very largely), and few could see how urgently a change was needed. Habit had at length bred delusion, and nothing rang so hollow as the stupefying artificiality of Victorian anecdotal painting, which the public of the time blindly mistook for art. Where the painters of the Renaissance, of seventeenth-century Holland, and of eighteenth-century France and England employed a living message to illumine the lantern of their symbolic realism, nineteenth-century naturalism was simply a veneer, an appearance no deeper or more profound than the pigment itself; a façade better simulated by the new fangled camera than by the paint brush. *The fire in painting was out.* In fact, one might say that since the invention of the camera, no artist of real worth has bothered to compete with these machines, preferring to explore those reaches of vision, feeling, and thought, which lay beyond the range, or scope of cameras.

In many ways the camera was a crucial factor in the evolution of the modern movement in art, and it might be as well to quote from a note by a great authority on painting, Mr. R. H. Wilenski. The extract is from his introduction to a retrospective exhibition of the work of Mr. Merlyn Evans which was held at the Whitechapel Art Gallery in 1956. Mr. Evans is a distinguished abstractionist.

"Abstract painting became a necessity for artists as soon as the camera arrived. It has thus been a necessity for more than a hundred years. Today it is more of a necessity than ever, because the camera now means (a) modern cameras with marvellous lenses and various attachments for increasing their efficiency, (b) the cinema-camera recording in black and white or colour, and (c) television which speaks the camera's language. As everything that can be done by these machines is more efficiently done by them than by the human hand, no intelligent original painter now attempts to do anything that these machines can do; and this means that no such artist now speaks the illusionist language.

"The fellows who use the cameras have also robbed the painter of a large proportion of his traditional subject matter. For newspaper photographs, the cinema and television now provide the world with all and more than it asks for in the way of descriptive social records and romantic, dramatic, sentimental and semi-erotic illusionist images."

Mr. Wilenski was not perhaps quite right in suggesting that there was any dire need for abstraction to coincide precisely with the invention of the camera

(J. N. Niepce produced what was probably the first photograph, using silver chloride, in 1822—ten years before Manet was born). It is jumping the gun somewhat to imply this, since it inevitably takes some while for practice to implement theory, or to react positively to the possibilities of new situations, and circumstances. But Mr. Wilenski is certainly right to note, and in the very strongest terms, just what the coming of the camera has meant for the painter during the past century, and most particularly during the past fifty years.

With this fact clearly established in our minds, let us now return to that point in the nineteenth century when illusionist painting was expiring in the arms of Sir Edwin, and his fellow Victorian painters. In France too, the dead hand of degraded academic illusionism was apparent in the work of such painters as Bouguereau, Cabanel, and Meissonier.

The need for change—some change, at any rate—was a matter of vital concern to Manet, and the Impressionists. Although Tennyson, with penetrating good sense, wrote:

> "The old order changeth, yielding place to new,
> and God fulfils himself in many ways,
> lest one good custom should corrupt the world."

no one really wanted to change the existing order. Humanity is notoriously indolent, and to effect change inevitably requires effort, such effort as only the relatively few enlightened ones are prepared to make: at least initially.

Enlightenment in itself is not the prerogative of the few: it is a lodestar which all may follow who are prepared to practise the arts of criticism, and analysis. Every convention should be periodically subjected to the most searching scrutiny, and when it is found wanting, it should be jettisoned. Yet, as I say, few people are willing to effect change, or even to question the nature, or the validity of the existing status quo. It is important to establish this fact before embarking upon our examination of the modern movement in art, since no appreciation of this phenomenon is possible until the reader has purged his mind of existing prejudices and preconceptions, until he has liberated his intellect from the chains of those constricting thought patterns that precondition, and so limit, our appreciation of the multifarious objectives and possibilities of painting.

At present, how many of us enter adulthood, equipped to think, to feel, or even to see, creatively? We live by proxy, taking on trust conceptions and ideologies, systems of thought and of action, in whatever the field, that are founded, not upon our own unique experiences, but upon those that come to us at least second-hand.

Our entire system of education is at fault. As I see it, the function of education is twofold. To present a range of pure facts, modified in relation to specific age groups, and to present, with detachment, suitably modified symposiums of existing opinions and belief. These should be presented with completely impartial guidance by an expert, or "interpreter", but in such a way as may best equip, and train the young, impressionable mind, to arrive at its *own* syntheses. . . .

Let us consider the nature of progress. It is always the few who break new ground, who explore new directions, and who finally effect those radical changes that give fresh impetus and momentum to the thin tendril of human progress, as it feels and noses its way forward. Society as an entity moves into contact with each new creative precedent usually obliquely, to benefit gratuitously from the achievements of genius. This applies particularly in science and medicine, and also nowadays, in relation to the application of the new aesthetic vision in the many fields of applied design. Picasso and his colleagues have greatly influenced and conditioned our daily lives for the better. The entire stream of simplification in modern design flows from those initial experiments with the shapes and forms of nature, and with the attempt to reduce their complexities to fundamentals, which absorbed the attentions of Picasso and his fellow cubists during the early years of the present century. It was these experiments and explorations into the fundamental nature of shape, and form, that was to have such a far reaching effect upon the whole course of commercial and industrial design.

So far as individual members of society ever come consciously, and independently to terms with the innovations of genius, they do so only by paying a kind of delayed action lip service to modes of thought, or of seeing, which have long since lost the volition and fire of their initial revolutionary thrust.

This time-lag is part of the tragedy of the human situation, since where on the one hand there is evidently no reason why we should do other than absorb scientific advances obliquely, there would seem on the other, to be every need for us to keep abreast of aesthetic and philosophical progress, and for that matter, with the practical, day to day applications of modern psychological and psychoanalytical schools of thought. Our capacity for purposeful awareness, unless of course we are content merely to *exist* as a form of impassive, negative vegetation, is largely conditioned by the extent of our ability to perceive the *living* significance of current aesthetic, psychological, and philosophical trends.

To be *really alive* we must come to grips for instance, with the art of Picasso, with the psycho-analytical theory of Freud, and with the existentialist philosophy of Jean-Paul Sartre; even though we ultimately reject them. We cannot exert this right until we have understood just what it is they are trying to do, or to say. We cannot even reject Landseer until we can understand the futility of what he was trying to do. We cannot claim to have lived in any positive sense of the word until

159

we have thought profoundly about those forces that fashion the general climate of the *milieu* in which we live. I have therefore, drawn a distinction between two different kinds of "knowing"; *oblique knowing*, which demands no positive exertion on our own part, and *direct knowing*, which is the result of our own efforts to rationalize in relation to ourselves, the various facets of objective knowledge.

There are still a great many people who do not think at all about any of these things, and certainly not about modern art, preferring to join in the chorus of inane academic clowns who loudly, and vulgarly denounce "the moderns" as mere poseurs and charlatans. True there are some—but there are many more among the traditionalists whose conventions are now only dry bones in a wilderness.

For many people painting would still seem to possess only one function: to represent some obvious, trite subject, *naturalistically*. A horse cantering, an old gentleman reading a heart-breaking letter, roses in a cut-glass bowl, this sort of thing is still for many, the full measure of their conception of aesthetic reality; the maximum extent of the painter's universe. How wrong they are. Few people pause to consider the nature of reality, if only in relation to the problems of painting. Yet there are so many realities. "Being" has a million faces, "coming into being" as many more. Although we are as yet unable to apprehend more than a fraction of these infinite states of grace and illumination, reality can still present to the eye of the painter a splendid range of possibilities.

Every subject can be interpreted and conceptualized in a thousand different ways—that is why the living objectives of painting must never be confused with the mechanical dead powers of the camera. Just consider for a moment a few different states of "reality", any of which could provide a basis for painting. What of the reality of the dream, the waking fantasy, the double-vision of the inebriate, the intellectual or emotional conceptualization that can produce either abstract, or expressionist variations on the theme of any given subject? What of the reality of the stylized image produced by the painter to supplement an ideology, such as the rigid formalism of the figure in Byzantine painting? How wrong it would be on this showing to postulate the existence of a *single* reality. We are neither humble, nor imaginative enough.

In the 1860s the Impressionists, sick to death of an old reality, constructed a new one. They intended a more realistic transcription of appearances in nature than had been seen in landscape painting before. Impressionism was just this: but it was also a fresh reality in its own right. For although an Impressionist landscape looks like a *real* landscape, and more so than in non-Impressionist painting, it also looks like a *real* Impressionist painting. In short, like Renaissance symbolic realism, it fulfils both a scrupulous purpose, and itself. Only when art is motivated by a

*Right:* **THE MARRIAGE**
Georges Rouault (1871–1958)

*Below:* **K.K.K.**
Arthur Haffkin (born 1902)

In Expressionist painting the artist uses distortions of form and colour to heighten the emotional and psychological significance of his work: to intensify its message. The caricaturist and the cartoonist also resort to distortion, while children employ similar devices in their own painting. In his biting satire on what appears to be a rather decrepit marriage of convenience, Rouault, the outstanding French Expressionist, uses a remorseless distortion to describe the mockery which is sometimes made of the marriage ceremony. The people here involved are hypocrites, and the artist's brutal exaggerations drive home the point with maximum impact. Arthur Haffkin, by profession an optician, and a painter only in his leisure time, uses distortion in a more controlled form to describe the obscene brutalities of the American K.K.K. The violence of the attack upon the Negro in the centre is emphasized by the long, swinging lines of the composition, and the clawing hands of the attackers.

*Above:* **AIX: PAYSAGE ROCHEUX**
  Paul Cézanne (1839–1906)

Although Cézanne was for a while closely associated with the Impressionists, he found their objectives too transitory, vague, and insubstantial. He broke from the group to develop his own approach to the problems of painting, which consisted primarily of trying to reduce nature to a range of elemental shapes, forms, and planes. His search for the inherent geometry of nature provided the flashpoint of the Cubist movement which was to follow immediately upon his death.

*Below:* **PEACHES ON A DISH**
  Georges Braque (born 1882)

A collaborator with Picasso in pioneering the fields of Analytical and Synthetic Cubism, Braque arrived finally at his own unique syntheses of arbitrary shapes, forms, and colours, orientated with a keen sense of their purely decorative possibilities.

*Left:* **PAINTING: 1937**
  Ben Nicholson (born 1894)

In the delicate, refined art of Nicholson, classical abstraction achieves a striking purity. The simplest geometric shapes are organized, often two-dimensionally, with great economy. As paintings they are particularly successful when keyed into a background of modern architectural, and interior design.

*Right:* **WHARFSIDE CONSTRUCTION**
  Merlyn Evans (born 1910)

Drawing to some extent upon Cubism, the sharp, pointed forms of this harsh, sinister conception derive also from Wyndham Lewis. Unlike the coldly impersonal art of Nicholson, Evans frequently invests his creations with an acute sense of menace. He has been profoundly influenced by the Kafka situation, in which man has to submit to the terrors of an incomprehensible and evil fate.

purpose which is above suspicion can it possess any real significance. If it merely panders to some degraded requirement, such as most commercial portrait painting does, its purpose is trash.

The Impressionists and Manet re-invested European painting with an honest purpose, gave it back the self-respect it had lost in the lucrative pursuit of decadent versimilitude and crude sentimentality. They raised painting once again from the gutters of flashy rubbish, to the heights of serious aesthetic intent. In fact we may say that two primary functions distinguish any significant art form. There must, as I say, be an honourable purpose—expressed through a vital, unmannered technique and style—and the art form must contain some element of timelessness that can raise it above mere transience. So it is that any superlative work of art is not only *of* its own time, and place, but also *out* of its time, in the sense that it will inevitably contain some quality or qualities, that are perennial, or if you like, universal. For instance, the classical simplicity, harmony, and proportion, that one can find in the work of the English abstract painter, Ben Nicholson. Here are qualities which have their roots in classical Greece.

Modern artists have relentlessly explored every depth, and facet of the character of the epoch in which they live. They have reacted, inevitably, to the moods of disquiet, and bitter uncertainty, to the climate of violence, chaos, and *angst* that comprise, whether we like it or not, the backcloth of Western society today. *Angst* from the German, meaning fear, anxiety, anguish, is a term commonly used in existentialist philosophy and writings to describe the anxiety state peculiar to the modern age, and closely related to the condition of the disinherited mind, and the consequent sickness of the soul, which stems from the destruction of "values".

It is the interim sense of *lostness*, of *nothingness*, which nibbles at the soul of man while he seeks a *new* set of values. *Angst,* or "dread" as it is also known—the dread of *nothingness*—is nevertheless an essential preparation for an awareness of the destiny of man which, according to existentialist thought, lays in his acceptance of ultimate responsibility for his actions and their consequences. Responsibility in fact for *all* that befalls mankind. The "nothingness" of the disinherited mind is therefore really a form of initiation into the state of pure responsibility.

In his book *Existentialist Thought*, Ronald Grimsley writes:

> The true function of dread (*angoisse*) is clearly revealed as soon as I realize that I am a being that is compelled to decide the meaning of its being . . . Dread reveals my condition as a being that is "thrown" into responsibility.

The artists of our time have reacted also to the methodical spirit of science and technology, with its emphasis on discipline and order. On the one hand they have found themselves adrift in the roaring seas of psychological romantic art (Expressionism and Surrealism are the two most apt examples), on the other, drifting serenely among the cool, still lagoons of the classical approach. Either way, whenever these various forms of expression have possessed any real meaning, a quality of perenniality has automatically existed. The universal, timeless element, is always apparent in art of any consequence. The springs dry up, only when *the artist becomes more important than the work*. When he loses humility. In the light of this concept, it might be helpful to consider an aspect of Plato's philosophy of the significance of abstraction in art, before we settle down to our examination of the modern movement in detail.

The idea that modern art is something entirely contemporaneous is one of the erroneous preconceptions we need to dispel. Abstraction, which is often thought, quite wrongly, to be a typically modern phenomenon, is of course, one of the most constant and timeless of all aesthetic elements and makes its appearance in a variety of art forms, as that quality which, beyond the significance of any subject content, endows a work of art with those shining inter-relationships of shape, form, and colour, which in themselves constitute the source of pleasure, and beauty.

They are easiest to discern in classical, rather than romantic art, which is of course more conditioned by emotional complications, and lacks the clarity, and simplicity of the classical manner. Abstract qualities are therefore far more easily discernible in the work of the early Florentine and Siennese Schools than in Rubens, or Delacroix, for example. In recent times however, these qualities have frequently been extracted from the totality of the subject and presented as an essence. So, for instance, in certain of the early still-lifes of Picasso, Georges Braque, and Juan Gris, we move close in to the abstract quintessence of the subject. Interpretation is cleansed of those superfluities of detail which confuse the fundamental issues. Frequently, once the painter has discerned the basic potentialities of pure shape, form, and colour, the subject is completely reconstituted, and represented as a fresh reality. Or it may disappear altogether, leaving a residue of pure abstraction, in the crucible of the canvas.

But modern refinements apart, the quality of abstraction was spoken of as long ago as the fourth century B.C. Here is an extract from the *Philebus* of Plato which I quote from Sir Herbert Read's *Art Now*.

"The best classical expression of the theory of abstract art is naturally to be found in Plato. I would like to quote a significant passage from the *Philebus*: Socrates and Protarchus are the speakers:

'S. True pleasures are those which arise from the colours we call beautiful and from shapes; and most of the pleasures of smell and sound. True pleasures arise from all those things the want of which is not felt as painful but the satisfaction from which is consciously pleasant and unconditioned by pain.

'P. But again, Socrates, what do we mean by these?

'S. Certainly what I mean is not quite clear, but I must try to make it so. I do not now intend by beauty of shapes what most people would expect, such as that of living creatures or pictures, but, for the purpose of my argument, I mean straight lines and curves and the surfaces or solid forms produced out of these by lathes and rulers and squares, if you understand me. For I mean that these things are not beautiful relatively, like other things, but always and naturally and absolute; and they have their proper pleasures, no way depending upon the itch of desire'."

(Trans. by E. F. Carritt: Philosophies of Beauty, Oxford, 1931, pp. 29–30).

When Plato speaks of those things that are beautiful, "always and naturally and absolutely", he means beautiful in themselves, as abstract qualities, and quite apart from any incidental descriptive or literary meanings which they may also possess. In other words, Plato is arguing the existence at the heart of all visual phenomenon of ultimate abstract graces. These one can also argue are presumably the apogee of beauty—at least visual beauty—since they transcend both the temporality, and the topicality of the subject. They are outside of time and place, and one can hardly conceive of a definitive beauty which is less than omniscient. Of such a calibre is the beauty of the central figures in such of Leonardo's works as "The Madonna of the Rocks", (between pages 24-5) and "The Virgin and Child with St. Anne." Here then is an aesthetic essence which is equally common to the art of Greece to that of the Renaissance and that of our own time.

Two and a half thousand years after Plato expounded his doctrine of abstraction Paul Cézanne wrote—"treat nature by the cylinder, the sphere, the cone. . . ."[1] Cézanne too, believed in, and sought, diligently, this perennial essence. For him, this quality was conceived as the incipient geometry which he argued underlies the complexity of superficial appearances. Cézanne, although originally an Impressionist, reacted later against the diffuse, atmospheric character of Impressionism, which he found to be too amorphous, too transient to satisfy his search for universals. In fact he was pursuing the Platonic idea. He sought an essence that was virtually abstraction, and which did in fact, as we shall see, largely through his own unfulfilled quest, lead eventually to the purest forms of abstract immanence. For although Cézanne was to glimpse the goal, he was never to reach it. In 1903 he wrote, "I am working obstinately, for I am beginning to see the promised land. . . ." He died in 1906, within a few paintings, I would estimate, of achieving his objective.

[1] From a letter to Emile Bernard, written at Aix-en-Provence, 15 April, 1904.

As it turned out, it fell to Picasso and his fellow Cubists to complete the journey.

Already then, we can see something of the ancient, and honourable roots of modern art. Indeed, there are precedents at various points in the long history of art for many of the "isms" we are inclined to classify too arbitrarily, as modern. Whatever new directions the modern movement may have beaten through the petrified forest of dead traditions, of obsolete and exhausted conventions, there remains the fact that evolution and advancement consists in synthetizing certain irreducible and perennial elements, with the specific, and variable demands of a particular era, or way of life. Thus, the living present, if it is to possess any vital consequence, must admit these perennial elements into the main stream of its life force, while at the same time ensuring that obsolete, and useless matter is trimmed, and pruned away. Compare this conception with the situation in mid, and late Victorian England. Because they were not prepared to carry out such trimmings, and prunings, Victorian society was literally choked to death by the weeds and debris of the past. By those futile attempts in painting and architecture, for instance, to reconstruct the spirit of Medievalism, and the Gothic. Nothing is more ludicrous, or more hypocritical (unless it is *twentieth-century Gothic*) than certain aspects of pre-Raphaelitism, or of the Gothic revival led by Victorian architects like Sir George Gilbert Scott (1811–78).

Out of their morbid longing for the past sprang those psychological diseases, and maladjustments, that attend all backward lookers; hysterical nostalgia, gross sentimentality, self-pity, a sense of sin and guilt, phantasies of redemption and damnation, all the hideous paraphernalia that arise from the conflict between good and evil, right and wrong. If only I were this, If only I'd done that. All these conditions are inevitable by-products both in persons, and societies, who measure the present with the yardstick of the past.

The Victorians, those sentimental, self-righteous, ghost-hunting humbugs, had no room in their congested bedlam even for a breath of that cool, timeless sanity, for that leavening of simplicity, harmony, and proportion, that characterizes the classical aesthetic. It is this clean, astringent quality which, while completely missed by the Victorians, and indeed by Europe generally during the mid-nineteenth century, is applied today in every branch of modern design from architecture to gas cookers. The Georgians of course were aware of it in their architecture, and town planning, and Bath is a superb example of the adaptation of the classical aesthetic in practical terms. This quality of grace, and simplicity, is an aesthetic phenomenon which constantly reappears: an element whose function seems primarily to cleanse and purify. *To make clear again.*

Classical revivals inevitably follow orgies of romanticism. When it is no longer possible to see the wood for the trees, there is of necessity, a reaction against the confusion of romantic idioms, such as the emergence of the classical movement in French painting led by Jacques Louis David, which followed the Revolution of 1789. By the same token, the reaction against middle, and late-nineteenth century romanticism which reached its final crystallization in the Purism of 1918, and the Neo-Plasticism of 1920, was also inevitable.

Classical revivals, unlike their romantic complements, are relatively impersonal. There is little hankering after the particularities of the past, and a greater desire to recapture, or perpetuate, simply an *essence*. Thus the application of the classical element in modern design is not coupled with any corresponding wish to emulate the day to day working of Greek society. The idea is of course preposterous. Yet Victorian painters, and architects, did in fact consciously contrive to recreate an atmosphere in which they imagined it might be possible to relive the life of the past in its everyday sense. This is an important psychological aspect of the Victorian aesthetic ideal, and the reaction against decadent nineteenth-century romanticism, whatever else it may be, is also a reaction against hypocrisy and humbug.

I have indulged in this preliminary digression upon the nature of abstraction in art, primarily to make it clear, at the outset of this important chapter, that the term modern is purely relative, and one that indicates a combination of the best of two worlds—the proven, "out of time" qualities of the past, in fusion with the peculiar requirements, and aesthetic vision of the present; the precedent, or prototype establishing present. The Greek art forms of the fourth and fifth centuries B.C. were modern by contrast with the archaic forms of preceding centuries. For instance the transition in sculpture from stylization to a supreme naturalism, never since in my opinion equalled by any succeeding generation of European sculptors, is comparable with the changes that transformed the Medieval flat into the Renaissance round. In a progressive aesthetic, something of the perennial past is always retained, but something *fresh* is invariably added. It is of course this element of the *new*, the hitherto unseen, in the art of our own time, that excites in the conventional, the lazy, and the *envious* mind, such fury and abuse.

It must, I am sure, be the source of considerable irritation, and bitterness, for a member of the Royal Academy with no standing among international, or even *national* experts and authorities, to witness and endure the world esteem in which the name of Picasso is justly held. Picasso was perhaps the first outrageously modern artist of the twentieth century, and although there are few today who could find anything to quarrel with in Manet—himself one of the most maligned artists of the nineteenth century—Picasso is still a thorn in the side of many.

There is another type of abstraction which is not classical, but romantic. This derives from the twin stream of expressionism and romanticism, where the emphasis is upon emotional and psychological manifestations. The workings of the romantic imagination, and the causes and significances of the uninhibited flow of free-expression, are qualities far less easy to rationalize, or to describe in objective terms, than those of the classical idiom, since they are so much dependent upon the personality of a particular artist. Romantic, or Expressionist art, because of its intense, subjective personalism, is always more difficult to assess than classical art which is, by comparison, objective and impersonal.

We can study the origins of the romantic, expressionist prototype as it emerges in the imaginative, emotional distortions, and the agitated drawing, and colour, of the German painter, Matthias Grünewald (1475?–1528). The precedent is continued as a tradition in the Expressionism of El Greco (c. 1542–1614), and the Romanticism of Delacroix (1798–1863) and Géricault (1791–1824). I quote these painters as typical expressionists, and romanticists, although there are of course many others. In each of the cases I have mentioned, the subject content is clearly discernible, in spite of such distortions as were employed by Grünewald and Greco to heighten the emotional and mystical intensity of their depictions, and in spite of the acutely personal vision and conception of Delacroix, and Géricault. Later, painters like Wassily Kandinsky (1866–1944) established a form of romantic, expressionist abstraction, completely non-figurative in character, yet clearly in direct line of descent from the incipient abstract emotionalism of Grünewald and Greco, and the imaginative romanticism of Delacroix and Gericault.

Just as there can exist in painting, elements of pure shape, form and colour,[1] so there can also exist elements of pure abstract emotion—dramatic tensions, dynamic rhythms, explosive thrusts, in fact all the manifestations of mobility and action that stir emotional responses in the spectator. These too can be apprehended in detachment from subject content, however much they contribute simultaneously to its representation. Thus for instance, the classical abstract elements in Lorenzo Monaco's "Coronation of the Virgin" (facing page 24) are comparable with the ultimate classical abstractions of Ben Nicholson, while the emotional abstract qualitites in El Greco are comparable with the non-figurative emotionalism of Kandinsky's modern abstractions.

### MANET AND THE NEW REALISM

The first authentic painter of the modern era was Édouard Manet. It was he who injected into the sluggish veins of the dying three-dimensional tradition a radical new conception of the meaning of realism. He extended a jaded, worn-

[1] In 1890 the French painter Maurice Denis uttered one of the first battle-cries of modern art: "Remember that a picture, before being a horse, a nude, or some kind of anecdote, is essentially a flat surface, covered with colours assembled in a certain order."

out idiom, into a fresh, virile direction. Yet he was to effect no revolutionary changes in technique, or style, in the mechanical traditions of painting; in this sense he was a traditionalist himself, and almost certainly the last great exponent of the formal three-dimensional method which extended from the Renaissance through such masters as Titian, Velasquez, Rubens, Hals, Rembrandt and Goya. But the contribution he was to make, the new direction he was to impart to this great, but failing tradition, was to throw him at once into the full glare of bitter controversy, into the blazing spotlight of ridicule and vilification.

Few great innovators in the history of painting have had to endure the virulence of such abuse as was heaped upon his "Luncheon on the Grass" when it was first exhibited at the Salon des Réfuses (an exhibition of works rejected by the official French Salon: the equivalent of our Royal Academy) in 1863, and upon his "Olympia" when it was first shown at the Salon in 1865. On the face of things, this must seem more than a little surprising, since both these masterpieces are based on traditional models. "Luncheon on the Grass" was suggested to Manet by Giorgione's "Concert", in the Louvre, and there are many prototypes of the "Olympia" composition, outstanding among which we can count Titian's "Venus" and Goya's "Maja Desnuda". (See pictures between pages 104-5).

What then was Manet's "crime"? Certainly he must have up-ended *some* beloved apple-cart, to draw from critic Louis Etienne this brutal comment on the "Luncheon".

> "A commonplace woman of the demimonde, as naked as can be, shamelessly lolls between two dandies dressed to the teeth. . . . This is a young man's practical joke, a shameful open sore not worth exhibiting."

Certainly he must have outraged and flaunted *some* precious convention to have drawn this arrow from Jules Claretie in the May issue of *L'Artiste*, (1865).

> "I like audacity, but not too much. . . . What is this odalisque with a yellow stomach, a base model picked up I know not where, who represents Olympia? Olympia? What Olympia? A courtesan no doubt."

From all sides, anger and insult were hurled at the painter. The Emperor, Napoleon III, and the Empress, were among the first to be shocked, and to condemn the "Luncheon". Critic Theophile Thore wrote:

> "The nude hasn't even a good figure, and one can't think of anything uglier than the man stretched out next to her, who hasn't even thought of taking off, out of doors, his horrid, padded cap. It is the contrast of a creature so inappropriate in a pastoral scene with this undraped bather that is so shocking."

While among the snipers at "Olympia" was Gautier père:

> "Olympia can be understood from no point of view, even if you take it for what it is, a puny model stretched out on a sheet. The colour of the flesh is dirty, the modelling non-existent. What's to be said for the Negress who brings a bunch of flowers wrapped in a piece of paper, or for the black cat which leaves its dirty footprints on the bed? The least beautiful woman has bones, muscles, skin, and some sort of colour.... Here there is nothing we are sorry to say, but the desire to attract attention at any price."

Quite simply, Manet had perpetrated a double crime. He not only drew directly upon the life of his immediate surroundings, using real people as his models, but proceeded to present them in everyday situations, without any gloss or sentiment, simply, and frankly, as they were. His characters were not merely dummies in some ludicrous charade, but real, flesh and blood creatures, living ordinary, mundane lives. In so doing, he broke faith with the prevailing mode of romantic narrative painting. That he should interest himself in such unworthy subjects as a naked woman sprawling in the company of two clothed men, or in the portrayal of some wretched slip of a girl who by all accounts was nothing more than a common prostitute, was unforgivable so far as the French Academy of Painting was concerned. "Luncheon on the Grass" and "Olympia" were considered a scandalous betrayal of the current, widely approved fashion for allegorical and historical painting which at that time was commonly practised in France. (The Victorians were not alone in their hypocrisy.) Provided a subject was painted from imagination and couched in suitably histrionic terms, it was acceptable. Nudes in fact were very much in favour—but not *real* nudes. They had to be concocted—a slippery, pornographic synthesis of allegory and sentimentality, represented in a leaden, eclectic manner, which sought to combine the skills of the Renaissance with the slushiness of painters like Guido Reni (1575–1642).

It was against this conception of realism that Manet revolted. His model, both for "Olympia", and for the "Luncheon", was a young girl of his own time, a Mademoiselle Victorine Meurend, who can be recognized in many more of his best known works, since she was his favourite model. Now listen to one of Manet's staunchest supporters, Emile Zola, on Olympia:

> "Nothing is more exquisitely refined than the pale tones of the white linen on which Olympia reclines. The child's body itself is charmingly pallid. She is a girl of six-teen perhaps, some model whom Manet has quietly painted as she was. And every-one exclaimed that this nude body was indecent. When other artists correct nature by painting Venus, they lie. Manet asked himself why *he* should lie—why not tell the truth? He introduced us to Olympia, a girl of our own times, whom we have

168

met in the streets, pulling a thin shawl over her narrow shoulders. But as usual, the public took good care not to understand what the painter wanted to say."

The secret both of Manet's greatness and of the hatred which his work aroused, is contained in that one sentence of Zola's—"Manet asked himself why *he* should lie—why not tell the truth?" Truth was the foundation stone of the modern movement in painting. Very soon, the Impressionists also were to seek truth. With Manet's new realism the ball started to roll again, the stream of painting was freed from its stagnation among the rocks and boulders of nineteenth century hypocrisy, and a revolution that was to sweep away every vestige of the past had begun.

## IMPRESSIONISM

Although Manet was never an Impressionist painter, he was, nonetheless, a revolutionary. It was only natural therefore that he should be drawn into the circle of young rebels who frequented the Café Guerbois in Paris. He became their rallying point, and out of this group which included the youthful Monet, Pissarro, Sisley, Renoir and Cézanne, sprang the Impressionist movement. The younger men had much in common with the struggles of the older painter, since their work too was subjected at first to abuse, ridicule, and indifference. Indeed, they had a great deal in common, since they also were concerned with realism—and with truth. This they sought, not in relation to the human situation, but in relation to nature— to landscape. Their aims were quite objective, their intention, to represent some fleeting aspect of the ever changing face of nature, saturated with light, and ceaselessly modified by the changes in atmospheric conditions. Out of doors, as you well know, the light is continuously changing—a cloud, a ray of sunshine, a mist, a shimmer of heat, to all these vagaries the face of nature is constantly subject. As an essential part of their method, the Impressionists worked on the spot, and in so doing, popularized the habit of painting out of doors.

This in itself was something of a revolution, since it had always been common practise to paint landscape in the studio, from memory, and sketches. Direct, spontaneous, *plein-air* painting, was an integral part of the Impressionist system. By comparison with the landscape painting of earlier times which was static, artificial, lifeless, and comparatively speaking, colourless[1], Impressionism was fluid and in action. It brimmed with atmosphere and colour, shimmering with the pulsating heat of summer, trembling beneath the cold, grey-blue veils of winter. Nothing was static. Here was a living *impression* of nature rather than a lifeless, detailed report on its component parts. This was precisely the essence that Constable had

[1] The two chief exceptions to this criticism being the English painters John Constable (1776-1837) and J. M. W. Turner (1775-1851 both of whom exerted an influence upon the Impressionists.

distilled in his clamorous, swiftly executed sketches, bustling with breeze, and tumbling clouds. Here, in Impressionist painting, the translucent glory of Turner's limpid colour was harnessed to a thoughtful, scientific theory. For Impressionism was based mainly upon the colour and spectroscopic theories of scientists like Chevreul, and Charles Henry. Consequently, only the colours of the spectrum— red, orange, yellow, green, blue, indigo and violet—were admitted into the Impressionist palette. Black, and brown, were outlawed. By restricting their range of colours to those which in fact constitute the very substance of light itself, the Impressionist painters were able to interpret nature in much more natural, and realistic terms than ever before. They had discovered how to distil the very essence of light. From the point of view of style, they painted their pictures, to quote Paul Signac, a second generation Impressionist and with Georges Seurat, the inventor of Pointillism, with "brush strokes of comma-like or swept-over form".

In the first group exhibition of 1874, Monet showed a picture called, "Sunrise: An Impression", and the term Impressionism was first used soon after by a critic of the group, in a derogatory and malicious sense. It was only adopted later by the artists themselves as in fact, aptly descriptive of their intentions. They wanted to register, not a detailed, piece by piece account of nature, but a general impression of what the eye sees at a first glance. It was a question of seeing *simultaneously*, rather than *consecutively*. Landscape was painted as *a whole*, rather than in individual bits and pieces, each separately painted, and laboriously fitted together like some tedious jig-saw puzzle.

But the Impressionists' main advance was in the field of colour, in the use of pure spectrum hues, in the rendering of the effects of light and atmosphere, and in the important discovery that *shadows* are not simply isolated black stains, but integral colour areas: a composite of the local colour of the object casting the shadow, the colour of the surface on which it falls, and the prevailing conditions of the light and atmosphere in which it is seen. This theory of course applies not only to the colour of shadows, but to *all* colour, since every colour is both affected by, and in turn itself affects, all other colours in proximity. The entire colour situation being finally modified by the existing conditions of light and atmosphere. Thus, if the sun is obscured even for a moment by cloud, every colour is immediately transformed.

The Impressionists *liberated colour* on the basis of scientific fact. They discovered, and revealed its diversity, its purity, and its brilliance. It was an advance that was to have the most far reaching influences upon subsequent movements. The Impressionists held a series of group exhibitions in Paris: chiefly between the years 1874 and 1876. In the first of these, the seven leading Impressionist painters were each represented by about a dozen works. They were Monet, Renoir, Pissarro,

Sisley, Berthe Morisot (the only woman member of the group), Guillaumin (not so well known nowadays), and Cézanne, who was later to abandon Impressionism as too melting, diffuse, and lacking in structure for his own purposes.

## POINTILLISM

### Also known as Neo-Impressionism and Divisionism

Pointillism[1] was an extension of Impressionist theory developed by Georges Seurat (1859–91) and Paul Signac (1863–1935). In its original form Impressionism was, they felt, subject to certain impurities, chief among which was the loss of luminosity and brilliance which followed the mixing of colours *on the palette*. There were also it seemed, structural defects, and a lack of order and discipline which Pointillist theory sought to rectify.

Considerable thought was given to the construction and composition of a picture, which was based on three primary elements: tone, line, and colour. Seurat describes the significance of these elements as follows:

"Gaiety of tone is given by the dominance of light; of colour, by the dominance of warm colours; of line, by the dominance of lines above the horizontal.

"Calm of tone is given by an equivalence of light and dark; of colour, by an equivalence of warm and cold; and of line, by horizontals. Sadness of tone is given by the dominance of dark; of colour, by the dominance of cold colours; and of line, by downward directions."

By such modifications the Pointillists achieved a stability that was lacking in Impressionism. But the most fundamental aspect of their theory was the application of the paint directly on to the canvas in pure, unmixed spots. Thus, let us say, an orange hue was obtained, not by mixing its components, red and yellow, on the palette, but by applying these elements in just the right strength, side by side on the canvas, and forcing the eye to bring them together automatically. This is known as *the principle of optical mixing*. The effect in the instance we are considering is to produce on the retina the sensation of a vibrant, luminous orange: a purer phenomenon, displaying a greater degree of luminosity, and colour intensity, than could be achieved by the admixture of red and yellow on the palette. I have quoted merely one example of course, but the theory of optical mixing is applicable to the production of any colour that has to be mixed.

Signac, the group theoretician, sets down the rules of Pointillism with great clarity:

"1. The same palette as Impressionism.
2. Optical mixture (of colours)

[1] From the French, *pointiller*, to dot: stipple.

171

3. Divided brush strokes.

4. Methodical and scientific technique.

*Result*. By the elimination of all muddy mixtures, by the exclusive use of the optical mixture of pure colours, by a methodical divisionism and a strict observation of the scientific theory of colours, the Neo-Impressionist insures a maximum of luminosity, of colour intensity, and of harmony."

Nevertheless, in spite of these clear rules of procedure, Neo-Impressionism was never really a satisfying or successful method of painting. The formula was too deadening. Signac further complicated the issue when he insisted that each spot of colour should be a square, mosaic-like shape, as distinct from the irregular shaped dots used earlier by Seurat who died in 1891 at the age of only thirty-two. The Pointillist group was never a very large one, probably because the method was so restricting. Whereas it could appeal to the resolute disciplinarian, there was little scope for any spontaneous free-expression. Apart from Seurat and Signac, Henri-Edmond Cross (1856–1910) and Maximilien Luce (1856–1941) are probably the only other Pointillist painters of major standing, and well worth seeking out at the Musée d'Art Moderne when next you are fortunate enough to find yourself in Paris.

As an exercise in the disciplined marshalling of aesthetic thought, and technique, Pointillism is a method of painting worth pursuing from time to time, and especially as a salutary change from the more combustible and violent forms of self-expression.

### POST-IMPRESSIONISM

This is not so much a movement in the sense that Impressionism and Neo-Impressionism, activated by a specific theory, produced groups of painters all working in the light of the same system, as a reaction against the cold objectivism and the stereotyping that inevitably followed, particularly the Pointillist method. Painting, irrespective of the artist, tended to look more or less the same; it lacked a personal *fire*. It was cold—not of course in colour, but in *feeling*. By the middle 1880s, two painters—both destined for immortality—had turned their backs upon Impressionist scientific naturalism to stress other, less cold-blooded values. Paul Gauguin (1848–1903), and Vincent Van Gogh (1853–90), both highly individual painters, were exploring the possibilities of the emotional and symbolical approach to the problems of painting, and pointing the way towards the intuitive and emotive art of the Fauves and Expressionists. Paul Cézanne too must be included among the Post-Impressionists, for he also was in reaction against Impressionism, but for different reasons than those of Gauguin and Van Gogh. Whereas they sought a deeper *subjectivity*, Cézanne was seeking a more fundamental *objectivity*.

172

With Gauguin and Van Gogh an intensification of emotional and psychological factors was the primary consideration: with Cézanne, the reaction against the impermanent, transient qualities of Impressionism took the form of a quest for solid, clean-cut, geometric fundamentals. The two former painters, while making full use of the colour potential liberated by the Impressionists, directed the interest of European painters away from the intellectual objectivism of Cézanne's researches, and into those magical recesses of the mind, and the imagination, from which was to spring the whole future course of subjective, psychological art.

The emotional and symbolic distortions practised by these two masters were a turning point of great consequence in the history of the modern movement. In order to heighten the emotional and psychological significance of his pictures, Van Gogh frequently resorted to distortion and exaggeration (as of course did El Greco). Here, in an extract from a letter to his brother Theo written from Arles in 1888, he touches upon these matters:

" . . . instead of trying to reproduce exactly what I have before my eyes, I use colour more arbitrarily so as to express myself forcibly. Well, let that be as far as theory goes, but I am going to give you an example of what I mean.

"I should like to paint the portrait of an artist friend, a man who dreams great dreams, who works as the nightingale sings, because it is his nature. I want to put into the picture my appreciation, the love that I have for him. So I paint him as he is, as faithfully as I can, to begin with. But the picture is not finished yet. To finish it I am now going to be the arbitrary colourist. I exaggerate the fairness of the hair, I come even to orange tones, chromes, and pale lemon yellow."

Criticizing Impressionism, Gauguin broaches the whole question of the employment of symbolism in painting: appearances, he suggests in this extract from the *Intimate Journals*, should be conceptual, rather than literal, a variable and arbitrary structure through which the painter "clothes the idea in a form perceptible to the senses"[1].

"The Impressionists study colour exclusively, but without freedom, always shackled by the need of probability. For them the ideal landscape, created from many different entities, does not exist. They look and perceive harmoniously, but without aim. Their edifice rests upon no solid base and ignores the nature of the sensation perceived by means of colour. They heed only the eye and neglect the mysterious centres of thought, so falling into merely scientific reasoning. When they speak of their art, what is it? A purely superficial thing, full of affectations and only material. In it thought does not exist."

[1] This definition of the physical nature of symbolism was expressed by the critic Albert Aurier writing in the *Mercure de France* in 1891.

Post-Impressionism is really that interim between Impressionism and Cubism which was lit by the flashing, independent genius, particularly of Gauguin and Van Gogh; but in so far as the term is a synonym for individuality, the period may also be said to include such a highly distinctive and non-conforming painter as Henri de Toulouse-Lautrec (1864–1901) whose portrayal of the personalities and situations common to the Parisian pleasure haunts of the *fin de siècle*, were excoriated to the very bone by his ruthless powers of psychological insight. Lautrec must rank as one of the greatest psychological portraitists in the history of European painting, while his unique, brilliantly lucid style helps to establish him as a genius of the first order.

## SYNTHÉTISME (SYMBOLISM)

Although Gauguin's personal style was always distinct and inimitable, he was in fact the acknowledged leader of a small group originally known as the Synthétists. The movement was founded in 1888 by Gauguin, and the painter Emile Bernard, both of whom had recognized the need for an aesthetic language that could be bent to the service of the painter's ideas. It was a concept which contrasted sharply with the naturalism of the Impressionists—"the abominable error of naturalism" wrote Gauguin—since it sought no imitation of mere surface appearances, but the creation of ideated, as opposed to imitative forms. Thus the term *synthétisme* is derived from the attempt to construct a synthesis of the *real*, and the *ideated*; to temper the actual with the conceptual, or imaginary, and so bring into existence a language of personal symbolism. This would vary according to the personality of the artist, the only common denominator being a recognition of the need for symbolic, as opposed to naturalistic forms.

Even before his departure for Tahiti in 1891, Gauguin had appreciated the tremendous potency of primitive art forms, and of their power to communicate ideas that could never be suitably, or vitally expressed, in naturalistic terms. This of course is true, to cite a perfect example, of medieval Christian art, where the severe, formal imagery, cut to a rigid but simple pattern, is utterly expressive of the rigidly controlled, inflexible mental attitude of the medievalist towards the Christian faith. Certainly this was true of the Christian intellectual of the time, while the plain man's conceptions were scrupulously, and rigorously controlled, by a continual sight of this potent, symbolic, synthetized imagery.

The same is true of all societies where *the image is bent to the service of the idea*. Pre-historic art, Peruvian and Aztec art, Egyptian art, are all examples of the synthetic prototype. Classical Greek art on the other hand does not come into this category since it aimed at, and achieved, a pure naturalism which is the direct antithesis of the symbolic method. Gauguin himself, fully aware of these instances, was greatly influenced as well by the modifications he observed in Japanese prints.

The simplification of their shapes and forms, in no way diminished the ultimate emotional force and vitality of their synthetized imagery.

The philosophy of Synthétisme—or Symbolism, as it is also known today—is summarized in this passage which Gauguin, significantly, took direct from the writings of Delacroix, and incorporated in one of his own manuscripts.

> "In man's soul are innate feelings which will never be satisfied by real objects, and it is to these feelings that the painter and the poet can, by his imagination, give form and life. . . . An impression results from a certain arrangement of colours, light and shade. . . . One might call this the music of painting. This emotion appeals directly to the most intimate part of the soul and it arouses feelings which words can only express in the vaguest way. . . ."

### NABIS AND INTIMISM

The group of painters working in 1895 who called themselves the Nabis, were an offshoot of the Synthetist stream, deriving their inspiration from Gauguin, but practising a modified form of Synthétisme. This modification took the form of a radical change in the nature of subject content, the Nabis preferring to concentrate upon simple, everyday scenes, rather than upon the more esoteric subject matter that had interested Gauguin. Technically, they employed the clean, pure colour of Impressionism. The term *Nabi* was adopted from the Hebrew word meaning a prophet, and the chief theorist of the group was the painter Maurice Denis from whose writings I have already quoted.

Quite simply, the aim of the Nabis—or the prophets—was to charge the simple scenes of daily life with a pervading sense of the mystical inwardness of familiar, homely things. It is something we have all felt from time to time. Suddenly, perhaps under the spell of lamplight, as the daylight fades softly beyond the window, or when the firelight weaves its flickering gold traceries on wall and ceiling, the scene is magically transformed, and we enter for a moment into the bliss of that enchanted province, where time no longer exists, and the soul is at peace in the shining beatitude of a sublime "oneness" with all things. This becoming "one" is perhaps the true condition of paradise; certainly it is the most exquisite and refined state of spiritual grace we can apprehend while in the throes of this mortal coil. This is the quality that was sought by the Nabis, and particularly by Pierre Bonnard (1867–1947) and Edouard Vuillard (1868–1940) who later became known as *the Intimists*. Their subject matter was restricted mainly to domestic interiors, suffused and glowing with gentle, jewel-like colour. The mystical, emotive quality with which they invested these charming, delicate depictions of the homely scene, was achieved through the most subtle blend of the real and the ideated; the true condition of the symbolic image.

However, in spite of the common ideal that bound the Nabis and the Intimists, the group had lost all cohesion well before 1900, its members going their separate ways: Denis to religious painting, Maillol to sculpture, Bonnard and Vuillard to pick up the threads of Impressionism. The chief artists of this group were Paul Sérusier (who had worked with Gauguin), Bonnard, Vuillard, Denis, Roussel, Valloton, and Maillol.

## FAUVISM

The origins of pure aesthetic experiment can I think be traced to Fauvism. The painters associated with the movement were not so much seeking to prove any special theory, or to fulfil an esoteric ideal, as to explore for the sheer sake of exploration, the fascinating possiblities of using colour with the utmost abandon, and in the most dynamic and elemental sense. They sought too, that exhilarating refreshment of mind and soul that was implicit in the unbridled licences which they permitted themselves. The savagery and violence of their colour earned them the nickname, *Fauves*—"the wild beasts".

After the centuries during which the virility of the European aesthetic vision had slowly declined, the complete and final overthrow of convention by the Fauves was immensely invigorating. It was virtually a new lease of life, a becoming young again. There is, of course, much of Gauguin's influence here: "Civilization that makes you suffer. Barbarism which is to me rejuvenation", he had written to Strindberg. Gauguin had turned his back on the complexities of bourgeois civilization, with its hypocrisies and frustrations, preferring to seek regeneration among the primitive—but truly civilized—peoples of Martinique, Tahiti, and the Marquesas Islands.

Fauvism was a final rejection of the over-cultivated, weakened aesthetic eye—an attempt to discover the faraway islands of bliss, where the painter could tear off his shirt and race over pink and turquoise sands, under the bluest of blue skies, down to a pure emerald sea where he could catch if he wished, great scarlet fish, and brilliant yellow crabs. An island in fact where all colour was possible, no matter how extravagant. It was an island in the mind, liberated at last from the shackles of drabness and withering convention. The leading Fauvist painters were Henri Matisse (1869–1954) and André Derain (1880–1954), while others like Maurice de Vlaminck (born 1876) and Georges Braque (born 1882) were for a time associated with the movement.

Derain's "Pool of London" (facing page 33) painted in 1906 is a striking example of the Fauvist approach. The paint handling is loose, and free; the colour violent. The opposition of the complementaries red and green, is the source of the chromatic intensification which characterizes the tiger-like brilliance and daring

*Above:* **GUERNICA: 1937**     **Pablo Picasso (born 1881)**

Painted in protest against the bombing of the Basque town of Guernica by German planes during the Spanish Civil War, this dramatic and terrible picture makes full use of distortion and symbolism to intensify the impact of the artist's message. Painted throughout in black, white, and grey, the bull symbolizes the implacable powers of brutality and darkness, the dying horse pierced by a spear the suffering of the people, and the blazing electric lamp the impersonal eye of an indifferent fate.

*Left:* **"THIS IS WORSE"**
**Francisco Goya (1746–1828)**

During the years 1808–14 Napoleon's invasion of Spain and Portugal drew from Goya an appalling, etched commentary on the horrors of war. Many of the titles used in the series, "The Disasters of War", are obscure and cryptic. But since the element of satire is often conspicuous in Goya's work, "This is Worse" might he held to indicate that the evils of war are worse than the hypocrisy of the priesthood and the stupidity of the people which he stigmatized in the "Caprichos", which was an earlier series.

*Right:* **THE BULL**
**Pablo Picasso (born 1881)**

The agony and degradation of the bull-fight is emphasized here with grotesque distortion. The death of a proud and powerful beast is a harrowing sight, and the much vaunted "moment of truth" so often a bungled and bloody shambles in which death comes slowly, and hideously, to a noble creature.

*Right:* **DAME EDITH SITWELL** **Wyndham Lewis (1884–1957)**
Begun in 1923 but not completed until 1935, this clear, deep, silent portrait, seems to confirm my views on the character of the subject (see between pp. 136-7).

*Below:* **MOTHER BATHING CHILD** **Jack Smith (born 1928)**
An example of the British kitchen sink school, composed with stark economy.

*Above:* **PAINTING: 1947** **Sam Francis (born 1923)**
In Tachiste and action painting the artist relies on the possibilities of accidental effect, such as those created here by the uncontrolled trickling of water-colour.

of Fauvist colour. In 1908 however, Derain abandoned the pure, shrill colours of Fauvism for a palette which thereafter grew increasingly more sombre.

Fauvism, which was invented in 1905, was soon eclipsed by the more scholarly and didactic Cubist movement. It was here, rather than in Fauvism, that Braque was to play such a vital part. Matisse was the only member of the original group to sustain throughout a long working life, a continuous, though infinitely varied manifestation of his avowed ideal to express through the dynamic, and decorative possibilities of colour sensations, and colour relationships, an art of pure relaxation and pleasure that would appeal primarily to the eye, and only incidentally to the intellect, and the soul. He was in no sense of the word a psychological colourist as was Van Gogh before, or the Expressionists later.

"What I dream of is an art of balance, of purity and serenity devoid of troubling or depressing subject-matter, an art which might be for every mental worker, be he businessman or writer, like an appeasing influence, like a mental soother, something like a good armchair in which to rest from physical fatigue."

That is how Matisse described the objectives of his art in 1908. But the main function of Fauvism as a phenomenon had been a loosening up of the aesthetic limbs, an exercise in the thrill of sheer freedom, and the regenerating, anarchical use of the brilliant colour first broached, scientifically by the Impressionists, symbolically by Gauguin, and emotionally, or psychologically, by Van Gogh.

Colour sensation for the pure, shouting joy of it, was the main objective of *the wild beasts*. Fauvist painting is ecstatic and free, boundless in its gaiety. There is much still to be learned from it, and no type of artist has benefited more from the experiments of the original Fauvists, than the modern commercial designer who makes full use of the shock effects of brilliant colour to capture the attention of the public eye. Catching the eye is the primary objective of the contemporary poster. It was also the chief intention, for different reasons, of the Fauvist painters. The modern poster is a direct descendant of this school.

### EXPRESSIONISM

So far, our study of the modern movement has been securely set in France. All the great innovations and advances in painting from the "new realism" of Manet to the colour experiments of the Fauves, originated in that country. It is true that certain of the masters who contributed to the mainstream of evolution were not in themselves Frenchmen (Van Gogh and Picasso, for example), yet the actual flashpoint of creation was France, and usually Paris where, in the late nineteenth and early twentieth centuries, artists could meet in the most stimulating and fertile surroundings, the convivial cafés, there to discuss and hammer out in the cut and thrust of each other's lively company, the radical, often inflammatory ideas that were to bring about such momentous and far reaching changes in the whole structure of European painting—and sculpture.

In the first two decades of the present century, all roads led to Paris, and here were gathered many of the most original and progressive minds of the day. From Eastern Europe especially, expatriates and exiles turned to the capital, as to Mecca, packed their bags, such as they were, for they were all mostly poor men, and made for the greatest, and most vital art centre—at least in those days—on earth. The Bulgarian, Jules Pascin, arrived in 1905, Modigliani, an Italian born Jew, followed in 1906. Marc Chagall, a Russian, drifted into Paris in 1910, and Chaim Soutine came from Lithuania in 1911. Chagall was to become one of the greatest of the mystical and surrealist painters, Modigliani, and Soutine, leading Expressionists.

This movement was an exception—it originated not in France, but in Germany. This is perhaps hardly surprising, since the springs of the Expressionist method are the depths of psychological personality; not the submerged world of the unconscious that was later to provide the raw material of Surrealism, but the energies and urges that manifest themselves in our day to day emotions and feelings, in our psychological responses to the many objective stimuli we meet in our daily lives. It was the interplay of these forces that excited the imagination of the Expressionists. It was an "inward" art form, basing itself on the need to distort, violently if needs be, the shapes, and forms, and colours of nature, not for aesthetic reasons as the Fauvists had done, but as a means of squeezing the inmost essence from the subject: a crucifixation of the natural form of objects, so to speak, so that the artist might extract the deepest possible significance from his subject. Naturalistic qualities were utterly sacrificed in order to get at the *truth*—the soul of the subject. Indeed, Expressionism has been called, "soul painting". The idiom was frequently brutal, grotesque, and macabre, and in this sense it is not difficult to see that Expressionism is much closer to the natural morbidity and introspectiveness of the Germanic mind, than the lighter, more effervescent character of the French psychological make-up.

The task of the Expressionist artist is not to render the already visible externals of life, but to render visible the inwardness, both of his feelings, and of the things that excite him; especially in relation to the way in which they interpenetrate and transform each other. Very often of course this method only renders more visible the inwardness of *the artist*, since the subject is strained through the wine press of the painter's personal emotions and responses. This is inevitably one of the classic hazards of any acutely romantic, or subjective art form. Instead of facilitating communication, an intensely personal vision frequently presents obstacles which are difficult, or even impossible, to negotiate. Nevertheless, as a method of intensifying the psychological significance of a subject, Expressionism is perhaps the most vital of all the forms of aesthetic interpretation, since it recognizes neither bounds, nor limits, and can appeal therefore to the widest range of emotions.

It is I think a method best suited to portraiture, where the painter can render visible the inwardness of personality as the caricaturist, or political cartoonist does, first by a recognition of salient characteristics, and secondly through their wilful exaggeration. Perhaps the best popular analogy would be the comparison between official, professional Expressionism, and the art of children, who tend quite intuitively in their early years to exaggerate and distort as easily and naturally as they breathe. They lack, of course, the maturity of adult workers in this field, yet they often achieve a startling sense of the inner life of their subjects: brutal, violent, relentless, yet penetratingly apt.

The Expressionist movement as an integrated phenomenon can be divided into two phases. Later, its influence was to spread westward into France. In 1904 the first Expressionist group was formed in Dresden by Ernst Ludwig Kirchner (1880–1938), Erich Heckel (born 1883), and Karl Schmidt-Rottluff (born 1884). They called themselves, "Die Brücke" (The Bridge), and were later joined by Emil Nolde (born 1867) an artist of the older generation who was destined to become one of the most important members of the group. The second group was formed in Munich during the years 1910 and 1911, under the name, *Der Blaue Reiter* (The Blue Rider), its leaders being the Russian painter Wassily Kandinsky (1866–1944), and Franz Marc (1880–1916). Paul Klee (1879–1940) joined the Blue Rider shortly after its foundation. He was a painter who carried Expressionism into the realms of pure fantasy. The group almost certainly took their name from the paintings of Marc, whose blue horses, often represented against backgrounds of red grass, provided the subject matter for some of his finest pictures. What did the blue horse symbolize, or express? Certainly a revolt against convention, and a desire to be free. The blue horse was a symbol of the unfettered imagination. Unhappily, Franz Marc, was killed at Verdun in 1916. For him, the ultimate symbol of freedom was the bullet.

The earlier designation, The Bridge, was descriptive presumably of the link between the spectator and the artist's emotion which the picture establishes.

## CUBISM

Apart from Impressionism, no movement has exerted a deeper and more lasting influence upon successive generations of artists, than has Cubism. What the Impressionists had done for colour, the Cubists were to achieve in relation to form. They liberated form, not emotionally as the Expressionists were doing—in time,

179

the two movements are more or less parallel—but aesthetically. Form was to be cleansed, as earlier, colour had been. The main impetus came from two sources; from Cézanne, who in reaction against the insubstantial character of Impressionism had sought the solid, basic geometry of nature (and very nearly succeeded in finding it), and from an enthusiastic study of African wood sculpture with its sharply faceted surfaces, and cleanly defined planes, which was held in high esteem by the early Cubists; in particular Picasso. The movement, which can be divided into two distinct phases—Analytical Cubism, and Synthetic Cubism—was evolved by Picasso (born 1881), Braque, and another Spaniard, Juan Gris (1887–1927), during the years 1907–15.

Cézanne had died in 1906, on the threshold of the "new vision": yet only a year later, Picasso had crystallized the whole of Cézanne's unresolved struggle in "Les Demoiselles D'Avignon", which he painted in 1907, and which clearly demonstrates not only the fulfilment of Cézanne's quest for geometric form, but also the influence of the Negro idiom. It is the first really significant geometric painting of the twentieth century, and as much a landmark in the history of modern painting as Manet's "Luncheon on the Grass", or his "Olympia".

Analytical Cubism was concerned with the simplification and geometricization of natural forms in order to arrive at their essential character. In the more advanced forms of this approach, the painter, one might say, *entered* the picture plane to examine simultaneously, from every point of vantage, the objects he wished to simplify. The result is a curious kind of kaleidoscopic effect, much more complex than the simplifications effected by the Cubist painter studying his subject from *outside* the picture plane, and dealing merely with one aspect of its appearance.

Synthetic Cubism was primarily an imaginary reorganization of the dislocated fragments of nature, recomposed in conjunction with shapes and forms created quite arbitrarily by the painter. So once again, as the Synthétists had done for their own reasons, the Cubists were forging an amalgam of the real, and the ideated; but Synthetic Cubism was concerned solely with the creation of geometric pattern and decoration: it had no symbolic axes to grind.

It is quite easy to appreciate why the Cubist movement was to exert such a profound influence upon the whole course of modern applied design. The simplification of form is the true basis of our best architectural, industrial, and technical design. The chromatic lead that Fauvism gave to the poster artist, was paralleled by the Cubists in the lead they gave to the designers, in form. Countless items, from aeroplanes to telephones, owe their appearance to the new vision of the Cubist painters. It is all a matter of history now, of course, but the facts are still not sufficiently well know.

The by-products of Cubism are not to be found only in the province of applied design, but in every type of abstract painting and sculpture where the emphasis is upon simplification, and clarity. The whole stream of classical abstraction derives from Cubism. Once form has been freed from the need to represent a subject, it can be dismantled, and its elements regrouped in abstract relationships. For instance; two bottles, a table, three oranges, and a window, are not only particular things, they are also cylinders, rectangles, and spheres. These geometric elements can be used either to represent objects, or pure pattern. Once the forms have been freed from the tyranny of the subject, they can, if the artist so wishes, live an entirely different existence.

"Cubism" said Picasso, never anxious to explain or qualify his work, "is an art dealing primarily with forms", and this of course, is the reason why Cubist painting in its original phases is relatively colourless; the painter was concerned, not with colour, but with structure.

Gradually, the complexion of Cubism brightened, and in one of its forms at least, it grew gay and fanciful. The restless and ingenious Picasso soon tired of the austerities of the formative period and by 1910, he and Braque had evolved a subsidiary Cubist technique called "Papiers Collés"—from the French, meaning "pasted papers". Bits of newspaper, coloured cardboard, postage stamps, string, playing cards, and other suitable materials were arranged in pasted designs. The basis of all these patterns remained fundamentally geometric in character, and Cubism, in all its forms, a comparatively classical art. If Picasso, Braque, and Gris were the leading Cubists, many other artists of course contributed works of great importance to the movement. Foremost among these was Fernand Léger (1881–1955) who developed his own, monumental, highly mechanistic version of Cubism, which would seem to derive very largely from the clean shapes and forms of industrial machinery. The wheels, and pistons, and cylinders of the machine age, are strikingly echoed in his art, whatever the subject he chooses to paint.

### FUTURISM

In 1909 Italy was to make her first contribution to the modern movement. In that year, the poet Marinetti published the literary Manifesto of an aggressive, militant movement, which called itself, Futurism. Its main objectives were an utter, and contemptuous rejection of the art of the past, and a vigorous glorification of the spirit of the new age; an age of speed and violence, clothed in the flesh of iron and steel, and administered by men of action. "A racing motor-car" said Marinetti in his Manifesto, "its frame adorned with great pipes like snakes with explosive breath . . . a roaring motor-car which looks as though running on shrapnel is more beautiful than the 'Victory of Samothrace'." The spirit of mechanical power was to be the new life force; dynamic action, the driving force of their art. Violence was to be upheld, therefore war was to be glorified. The battleship and the tank were the most beautiful things on earth. "Italy" wrote Marinetti, "has been too long the great market of the second-hand dealers. We would free her from the numberless museums which cover her with as many cemeteries. . . . We shall extol aggressive movements, the double quick step, the somersault, the box on the ear, the fisticuff". Violence, the intoxication of speed, and all those forms of dynamic action peculiar to the twentieth century were to be press-ganged into the service of art, and focused in the painting, and the poem. "There is no beauty" said Marinetti, "except in strife." From all this it is already quite easy to discern a link between such a drum-banging, sabre-rattling aesthetic philosophy, and the rise of the Italian Fascist movement, with which Futurism was later identified. Marinetti and Mussolini had much in common, and the poet was a fervent supporter of the Duce during the years when he was struggling towards political power.

Marinetti's Manifesto was followed shortly by the painter Umberto Boccioni's Manifestos, countersigned by the artists Carlo Carra, Gino Severini, and others less well known. The first of these written in February, 1910, contained the following:

"To the young artists of Italy!

"We want to fight relentlessly against the fanatical, irresponsible, and snobbish religion of the past, which is nourished by the baneful existence of museums. We rebel against the grovelling admiration for old canvases, old statues, old objects, and against the enthusiasm for everything moth-eaten, dirty, time-worn, and we regard as unjust and criminal the usual disdain for everything young, new, and pulsating with life. . . .

"As our ancestors drew the matter of their art from the religious atmosphere weighing upon their souls, so we must draw inspiration from the tangible miracles of contemporary life, from the iron network of speed enveloping the earth, from the transatlantic liners, the Dreadnoughts, the marvellous flights furrowing the skies, the spasmodic struggle for the conquest of the unknown. . . ."

Two months later, Boccioni published the "Technical Manifesto of Futurist Painting":

"Our craving for truth can no longer be satisfied by traditional *form* and *colour*! Action, in our works, will no longer be an arrested moment of universal dynamism. It will be, simply, dynamic sensation itself. Everything moves, everything runs, everything turns swiftly. The figure in front of us never is still, but ceaselessly appears and disappears. Owing to the persistence of images on the retina, objects in motion are multiplied and distorted, following one another like waves through space. Thus a galloping horse has not four legs: it has twenty, and their movements are triangular. . . . Our pictorial sensations cannot be whispered. We sing them and shout them in our canvases, which ring with deafening and triumphal fanfares."

This then was the intellectual climate of Italian Futurism. In appearance, on canvas, it derived largely as one might expect, from the clean-cut, faceted, sharp angularity of Cubism. But Cubism was a still, silent, static art, it had to be animated, made to kick up a fuss—to move vigorously into action like an army on the move. The kaleidoscope of analytical Cubism was set in motion, rotated before the eyes of the spectator. "Painters have always shown things and persons in front of us. We shall place the spectator at the centre of the picture", wrote Boccioni. The intention was to present every phase of the activity of the subject. The simultaneous analysis of form was extended into the simultaneous analysis of dynamic action: Dynamic Futurism as opposed to static Cubism. That at least was the intention. But theories do not always work out in practice, and Futurism, like Pointillism earlier, soon presented insurmountable difficulties. The attempt to represent simultaneity of action, every phase of a dynamic movement—the twenty legs of the horse in motion—resulted inevitably in confusion: a state of exciting, but largely unresolved chaos. Ironically, the artist who got the most out of Futurism in the long run was not an Italian at all, but the British painter C. R. W. Nevinson.

Marinetti, who often visited London, became friendly with Nevinson, and in 1914 the two artists published the English version of the Italian Manifesto—"Vital English Art. Futurist Manifesto". In this, as in the Italian prototype, the traditions were roundly denounced. It was against the Pre-Raphaelites, against the Aestheticism of the 'nineties, against Oscar Wilde, against, in its own words—"the old, grotesque idea of genius, drunken, filthy, ragged, outcast . . . the Post-Rossettis with long hair under the sombrero, and other passeist filth. . . ."

In his painting, Nevinson, one of the most original British artists of his time, brought Futurism to a tense standstill. He did not, as the early Italian Futurists had tried to do, attempt to represent simultaneously all the successive phases of a movement. Certainly he used as his inspiration the character and mood of the new age, but he employed in a relatively static fashion, the crisp, machine-like forms of Cubism, using their sharp angularity with the utmost clarity, to express his feelings. There was no confusion in his art, everything was superbly resolved. He was always an artist who felt, and saw cleanly.

Writing from the Western Front in the early years of the war, he describes his arrival with the stark simplicity that was characteristic of everything he did. "It was dark when we arrived. There was a strong smell of gangrene, urine and French cigarettes." Nothing could be more to the point—nothing more expressive of the occasion. Later, as an official war artist, many of the pictures he executed in this capacity reflect the misery, and cheerless inhumanity of war. For Nevinson, whatever glory the idea of war may have held for the Italian Futurists, it held none for him. In spite of his avowed and fervent association with Marinetti, and of his obvious indebtedness to the forms of Cubism, Nevinson remained very much an individualist, a painter profoundly influenced by the isomorphism of the twentieth century—the soaring skyscrapers, the streamline of the great transatlantic ships, the swift shape of the aeroplane—yet bringing to bear upon this harsh and strident panorama, a curious personal vision, that saw within the present, a dream of the future.

Nevinson resolved the conflict within Futurism and gave it a stable form: but the spirit of animation was not quenched—it was transformed from a raging, uncontrollable torrent, into a steady, carefully directed stream.

## ORPHISM, OR SYNCHROMISM

In 1911, the French artist Robert Delaunay (1881–1941) painted a picture titled "Simultaneous Windows". Its comparatively geometric appearance stemmed directly from Cubism, but in other respects it differed completely. It was notable for the purity of its rich, glowing, jewel-like colour. Yet unlike Fauvism in which the original subject played a conspicuous part, Delaunay's Orphism was virtually abstract. Such vestiges of reality as remained in the finished work were retained, not for their objective significance, but for their intrinsic abstract quality. In his "Simultaneous Windows" we can discern as an indispensable part of the dynamic life of the composition, the exquisite curves, and the forceful, soaring verticals of the Eiffel Tower, the subject which provided the original source of the artist's inspiration. These lines of movement, of rhythm and force, were divested of their objectivity and woven into the composition as elements of pure abstraction. In this connexion you will recall the Platonic concept of abstraction which was earlier introduced. "True pleasures are those which arise from the colours we call beautiful and from shapes. . . ." Socrates then goes on to say that "for the purpose of my argument, I mean straight lines and curves. . . ."

Colour and shape, line and rhythm, the fundamental qualities of Plato's concept of the nature of aesthetic abstraction are thus clearly discernible in Delaunay's Orphism. As indeed they are in many other kinds of aesthetic abstraction. Quite evidently then, the title "Simultaneous Windows" symbolizes the duality of the final conception which is, at least partially, a window on to reality, and at the same time, a window into the realm of abstraction. But Delaunay's primary concern was with colour; with the organization of pure colour compositions—the orchestration of colour melodies. Orphism can be described as a chromatic equivalent of music. The principle of Orphism—or Synchromism as it is also known—was formulated by Delaunay in 1912. "Colour alone is both form and movement" he postulated. The movement was christened Orphism by the writer and critic, Guillaume Apollinaire, who had discerned the close affinity between Delaunay's orchestration of colour, and the comparative orchestration of sound.

Dissatisfied with the relatively colourless appearance of Cubism, and with its dependence upon the subject, Delaunay and his associates, the Czech Frank Kupka, and the American painters Morgan Russell and Macdonald Wright, sought to extend the potential of Cubism into a less rigid and harsh form; one in which pure abstract colour would supersede derivative Cubist form.

Yet Orphism, in spite of its exciting intentions, proved to be, like Pointillism, too limited and specialized a concept to exert any enduring, or exclusive influence. So far as it has influenced succeeding generations of painters at all, its force must be counted mainly as an instinctual factor in the continuous drive towards an intensification of the chromatic aesthetic.

### SUPREMATISM (1913)—PURISM (1918)—NEO-PLASTICISM (1920)

The three "isms" I want to deal with now have all a great deal in common. They are fundamentally, austere and highly intellectualized forms, making few concessions to the free play of feeling, or emotion, either in terms of conception, or of technical expression. They are for instance, the direct opposite of Expressionism with its abandon, and freedom from all dogma. Formal, severe, and classical in character, their driving force was a rigid pattern of order and discipline. The painting techniques employed by the various exponents of these three systems were neat, trim, and precise. Everything was painted with great care. However, in themselves, they are minor features of the modern movement, and, like Orphism, have long since been absorbed into the broad fabric of the modern aesthetic where their influence can best be seen today, playing an integral part especially in the field of the best architectural design. One has only to consider some of the fine blocks of modern flats—particularly those built in London and its environs under the London County Council—to observe in action, characteristics and qualities that were first broached in painting. The subtle juxtaposition of irregular sized rectangular shapes, the employment of clear, flat colours, the relationship of mass to space, the rejection of all superfluity and the insistence of functional criteria as the basis of architectonics, all these qualities can be traced back to their roots in Suprematism, Purism, and Neo-Plasticism.

Suprematism was founded in Moscow in 1913 by the Russian painter, Kasimir Malevich. In this year he exhibited a picture which consisted simply of a black square, perfectly set, on a white ground. The basis of his aesthetic philosophy was the alleged supremacy of pure geometric forms. It was essentially non-figurative, and non-derivative. No subject was involved, even as a flashpoint. In sharp contrast to the complex geometry of Cubism, Malevich set out to realize and assert the aesthetic possibilities of arranging a few, simple shapes, on the canvas. Certainly this was a severely limited art form, yet one which did at least make it clear that even the problem of superimposing a small square upon the field of another, and larger square, can present an aesthetic problem of considerable magnitude.

You can quite easily put this to the test yourself by cutting a square of black paper, or thin card, say 3 in. × 3 in., and a square of white paper or card, about 8 in. × 8 in. Having done so, try moving the black square about until you feel that its relationship with the white square is aesthetically, just right. It will soon be apparent that you have an extremely difficult problem on your hands, particularly since the one position where the black square would seem to fit quite happily, is really the most unsatisfying of all. If you place your black square at the centre of the white square, you are confronted at once with the least interesting form of composition—the symmetrical. It is generally agreed that asymmetry is far more stimulating, so that your real troubles will commence once you have accepted the fact that the centre is not the right place for the black square.

This is, all other considerations apart, a most intriguing aesthetic problem, and one that will tax your sensibilities to the utmost. Here in fact is the sort of problem which might well, in another field, confront the architect. He too has to resolve similar issues; where for instance will he establish his window, and door spaces, in relation to the overall shape of the building? In this context the problem is of course intensified by the need to combine the functional with the aesthetic.

Malevich was originally a Fauvist, who graduated through Cubism to the austerities and the asceticism of his own, peculiar vision. In his own words— "Suprematism is the rediscovery of that pure art which in the course of time, and by an accretion of "things", had been lost to sight. . . ."

In referring to the accretion of "things", Malevich was condemning the extent to which the fundamental qualities of abstract simplicity, grace, and purity, had been obliterated during the course of time by an increasing insistence on the priority of subject content. At the worst extreme of this particular deficiency one can cite the "historical", "classical" subjects of Lord Leighton, where all aesthetic considerations are relentlessly sacrificed for the sake of "story".

However cold and remote the clinical refinements of Suprematism may seem, however far removed from the idea of painting as we normally understand it, it is important to see this phenomenon as an integral part of the whole process of the cleansing of the painter's vision which had become so clogged with the weeds of subject content, that only the most drastic action could clear away the suffocating debris of the past. Suprematism was a form of aesthetic aperient, if you like, whose action was to wash away a great deal of entirely superfluous, and waste matter. Once the aesthetic vision had been thoroughly cleansed, it was possible for painters and designers to start afresh, unhampered by conventions which no longer possessed any meaning—at least for the progressive artist, working in the spirit of the time.

Purism also had something of value to contribute. The leaders of the move-ment were Le Corbusier (born 1887) a Swiss architect, and the French painter Amédée Ozenfant (born 1886) who had himself been a student of architecture for some years. In 1918 they published the Purist Manifesto "Après le Cubisme" which outlined their intention to impart a fresh, and more purely functional impetus of Cubism, which by this time they felt had declined into a mere decorative formula.

It is significant that both these men should have been trained in architecture— indeed Corbusier is today one of the great figures in modern architecture—since the acknowledgement of the importance of function is one of the chief character-istics of Purism. Ozenfant and Corbusier were never anti-subject, as was Malevich. Many of their early paintings were based on simple still-life groups, painted in clear, bright colours. Bottles, jugs, and glasses figured prominently, because they matched in essence, the functional shapes and forms of the machine age. Circles, ovals, and cylinders—the hard, clean, precise forms of modern machinery were those sought by the Purists. Cubism was to be cleansed of its irresponsibility and refashioned so that its geometric forms ran parallel with those of the mechanical age. In this respect, Léger is virtually a Purist himself, although he was not a member of the original group.

Summing up, one might describe Purism as a pictorial language deriving its motive power from the functionalism of machinery and its aesthetic appearance from mechanical shapes and forms. In this sense it has since exerted a profound influence upon the Industrial Designer, who must necessarily combine beauty with function.

By 1920, when a group of Dutch artists published their manifesto of Neo-Plasticism, it was clear that the motive force of European painting had been sharply cleft into two distinct streams, driving hard in separate, and irreconcilable direc-tions. On the one hand the abstract painter was moving into the most intimate rapport with the applied arts, on the other, the Expressionist was furiously at work in the loose, detached field of acutely personal, non-functional, psychological art. In fact the rift between the extremes of functional abstraction on the one hand, and the comparatively anti-social manifestations of expressionism on the other, has remained to the present time. The remote, relative uselessness of psychological art forms the basis of the critical dilemma of the professional easel painter today. There is of course no question of a return to any form of outmoded academic illusionism. On the other hand, classical abstraction has found a happy, and natural fulfilment, in the applied arts.

The swing towards functionalism reached its climax in Neo-Plasticism, a title which may be interpreted as meaning "the new adaptability". The chief exponents of this method were the Dutchmen, Piet Mondrian (1872–1944) and Theo van Doesburg (1883–1931). Earlier, in Holland, they had with other artists formed the group known as *de Stijl*—"the style". Their aim was to bring painting and sculpture within—for them—the more significant context of architecture, and Industrial Design. Utter simplicity was their creed, and this is expressed with stark finality in the paintings of Mondrian. His pictures were frequently no more than the breaking up of the canvas area into a group of variously sized rectangles, separated by thick black lines, and painted in schemes permitting the use of no more than the three main primary colours, red, yellow, and blue. White was of course also admissible.

Neo-Plasticism is the last phase in the development of the classical abstract ideal which in terms of modern art, originated in Cubism, and was pushed to its logical, and ultimate conclusion, by Malevich and Mondrian.

### VORTICISM

"By Vorticism we mean (a) *activity* as opposed to the tasteful passivity of Picasso; (b) *significance* as opposed to the dull or anecdotal character to which the Naturalist is condemned; (c) *essential movement* and *activity* (such as the energy of a mind) as opposed to the imitative cinematography, the fuss and hysterics of the Futurists...."

With these stirring, sabre-rattling, militant sentiments, Wyndham Lewis (1884–1957) introduced the first, and only exhibition of Vorticist painting at the Doré Galleries, London, in 1915. The first shots in the great art war had been fired by the Italians, and here was a counter-attack from the British lines. It is interesting to note that the neutral power, Picasso, should have come under fire, and ironic that he should remain the only unscathed survivor of the Futurist-Vorticist war. He was of course, completely indifferent to this intellectual struggle.

Vorticism was the English equivalent of Italian Futurism, and whatever Lewis may have said in condemnation of the earlier movement, there are many striking and irrefutable similarities between the two "isms".

They were both militant movements—aggressive and dogmatic. Dynamic action was the mainspring of their vitality, but, as we shall see, Lewis was a far more mature personality than Marinetti. This astonishing man who died on 7 March, 1957, was not only a draughtsman and painter of outstanding brilliance, but a writer and thinker who wielded great power as one of the most formidable and devastating critics of the day. His attack on extremism in the arts—"The Demon of Progress in the Arts" (1954)—is a profound and withering analysis of the sickness of the artist trapped in the fashionable lunatic asylum of extremism.

In 1914 Lewis published the first number of his periodical *Blast* (only two issues were in fact ever published) which, together with his foundation of *The Rebel Art Centre* in Great Ormond Street, he intended should form the literary organ and party headquarters of the English Vorticist Movement. Vorticism—the title was invented by the poet Ezra Pound, himself closely associated with Lewis at this time—was in perfect character with the intellectual *zeitgeist* of the time. It advocated a brutal rejection of the art of the past, the employment of harsh, sharp edged, spiky, machine-like forms and shapes, the use of pungent, disquieting colours, and a relentless insistence upon activity.

These were the characteristics of "the great English Vortex"; the whirlpool swallowing up the rubble of the past, while representing at the same time, the furious pace of intellectual and technical progress which was so notably accelerated in the first two decades of the present millennium.

The intellectual's attempt to keep pace with the swiftly flowing stream of mechanical and scientific evolution, received a shattering set-back in the bloody holocaust of the First World War. Whatever glory the Futurists may have found in the *idea* of war, and violence, was rapidly dispelled by the storm of blood and flying metal that disfigured the bodies and the minds of the men who fought on the Western Front. Futurism could hardly have survived this hellish, practical demonstration of ultimate violence, which made such a hollow mockery of its childish tub-thumping.

By 1916, when Lewis joined the army to serve as an artilleryman, both movements were submerged in the horror and filth that was to breed a new generation of artists, and to produce a very different aesthetic attitude to war. The bitter disillusionment of poets like Wilfred Owen and Siegfried Sassoon, the sense of futility and desolation, the atmosphere of brute destruction that characterizes the war painting of Paul Nash and C. R. W. Nevinson (1889-1946), these were the heralds of the new age: the great era of mechanical progress rattling insanely to its doom.

Yet whereas Futurism was utterly destroyed, an essential part of the Vorticist spirit survived the conflagration of the First World War. The Vorticist, in the purest sense—and only Lewis possessed ultimately the necessary intellectual make-up—is essentially the outsider: an observer, never in the last resort *emotionally* involved or identified with the action he represents. Thus, for Lewis, war was genuinely a stimulating phenomenon, whereas for Owen, it was the supreme hell. For Lewis it was a spectacle, for Owen, an appalling *experience*.

In his "Modern English Painters",[1] Sir John Rothenstein describes Lewis as being "enraptured by the physical splendour of mechanized warfare" and quotes from Lewis's "Blasting and Bombardiering" (p. 120) where the painter is writing about heavy guns in action:

> "Out of their mouths had sprung a dramatic flame, they had roared, they had moved back. You could see them, lighted from their mouths, as they hurled into the air their great projectiles, and sank back as they did it."

It is this quality of remorseless detachment which places Lewis in the privileged position of commentator, rather than participant. Because he is not involved, he is free. His commentaries are pure, and stark. Emotion is not involved, at least in any personal sense. As a means of vital commentary on activity in all its forms, Vorticism occupies a permanent place in the history of the modern movement in art. The diamond hard, razor sharp style, the crystalline imagery of the founder of Vorticism, symbolize the penetrating, intensely analytical quality of modern thought. And although many other artists were associated with the movement, Vorticism remains, in the final analysis, very much the exclusive prerogative of its originator. C. R. W. Nevinson, William Roberts (born 1895), and the draughtsman and sculptor Henri Gaudier-Brzeska (1891-1915) who was killed while serving with the French Army at Neuville, were all included in the Vorticist Exhibition, but no one possessed the intellectual qualifications of Lewis himself. "Essential Movement and Activity (such as the energy of a mind) . . .", that is the quintessence of Vorticism. *The energy of a mind* penetrating like an X-ray to the very heart of the matter, not with the passionate and uncertain fingers of emotion, as in Expressionism, but with the deft touch of the surgeon. In his drawings, Lewis uses the point of pen, or pencil, like a scalpel, excoriating the flesh of appearances to expose the shining bones of inwardness. As an artilleryman, he was deeply impressed by the hard, shining forms of the big guns, and the streamlined shells. The raw material of war inspired many of his most characteristic drawings and paintings. For him, battle was dynamic, it was the great vortex, devouring and spitting, a seething cauldron of action: "the point of maximum energy".

In portraiture Lewis employs the same searching technique, the searing line, the sharp angularities, the metallic curves. Like watches, fully wound, his characters scrutinize the spectator with a pitiless gaze, or simply withhold their judgment, perhaps out of pity, like Dame Edith Sitwell in his magnificent portrait, smouldering quietly with the lean fires of her formidable intellect. (Facing page 177).

Quite irrespective of subject, the art of Wyndham Lewis in all its forms is invariably charged with energy—armed to the teeth. A whirlpool of bristling and

*Modern English Painters: Lewis to Moore.* Sir John Rothenstein.

restless forces superbly marshalled and focused in his highly disciplined, carefully controlled, but brilliantly lucid technique. There is no dissipation of energy as in Futurism, and there now seems no doubt that his original indictment of that movement for its fuss and hysterics, was fully justified.

Vorticism remains, in the work of Lewis alone, the one vital British contribution to the mainstream of modern art.

### DADAISM

If the First World War engendered a spirit of bitterness and disillusionment, it produced also one short lived artistic phenomenon which expressed a curious, satirical, even comic resignation to the collapse of Western society in the maelstrom.

The Dadaists saw the war as the flashpoint for a wholesale rejection not only of aesthetic standards, but of all social, moral, and religious values: a renunciation of the entire fabric of European culture and social behaviour, which, they argued, not perhaps without justification, had failed so miserably to protect mankind from unprecedented slaughter and destruction. Their extraordinary art was the indictment of a way of life, riddled with hypocrisy. The brute forces of materialism had broken through the façade of respectability. The whole rotten system of nineteenth century self-righteousness, pomposity, and chauvinism had finally started to crumble. The Church had failed, the nations had failed, reason had failed. Men were being sacrificed in the name of God, and country, by the power-crazy ravings of the politicians, and the idealistic clap-trap of the clergy. The old men of parliament and church spewed their ludicrous idealism from the safety of town hall and pulpit, while the young men, the flower of European manhood were massacred in their tens of thousands. If this obscene bloodbath was the ultimate fruit of Western civilization, then far better it should be utterly destroyed. Better to obliterate the past with all its revolting hypocrisies. This was the objective of a group of sickened, nihilistic young men who gathered one day in February 1916, at a café in Zurich. Chief weapon in the armoury of destruction was to be *ridicule*. Since *nothing* mattered any longer, why not also a complementary *art form* that did not matter? A completely anarchical art, one that would match the insanity of human affairs. Mock, and destroy—that was the intention.

The irrational forces of the new movement were to be turned, not only against art and literature, but against society as a whole. With such thoughts in mind, the leaders of the group, the Rumanian poet Tristan Tzara, and the Alsatian painter Jean Arp, together discovered Dada, "at six o'clock in the evening" records Arp "when Tzara pronounced for the first time this word which aroused a legitimate enthusiasm in us all. This took place at the Terrace Café in Zurich and I had a roll of bread up my left nostril. . . ."

This ridiculous irrelevance was an intrinsic part of Dada. Everything must be reduced to nonsense. The word Dada, meaning "hobby-horse" was simply taken at random from the Larousse Dictionary, by Tzara. It could equally well have been any other word or term. Here then was the nihilist attack upon the civilization that had failed.

Other groups of artists also sought to change, or to obliterate the aesthetic standards of the past, but the Dadaists wanted to annihilate the past completely, and in every respect. A typical Dadaist picture for instance was simply a reproduction of the Mona Lisa disfigured by a moustache and beard. Marcel Duchamp, who had earlier associated himself with the Futurists, submitted a "ready made" to a Dadaist Exhibition in New York—a lavatory basin. During the years 1916-22, the Dadaists held many meetings and exhibitions throughout Europe. They published magazines and manifestos, and held absurd readings and recitals of Dadaist poetry, and music. One of the most extraordinary of the Dadaist Exhibitions was held at Cologne in 1920. Entrance was through a public lavatory, and visitors were invited to take up hatchets and attack the works of "non-art" which hung, and stood around the gallery. It is hardly surprising that the exhibition was swiftly closed by the police.

The essential spirit of Dada is perhaps best expressed in a statement by the French writer Louis Aragon:

"No more painters, no more writers, no more musicians, no more sculptors, no more religions . . . no more aristocrats, no more armies, no more police, no more fatherlands, an end to these imbecilities. No more anything, *anything*, ANYTHING. Nothing, *nothing*, NOTHING."

This makes little sense unless you see Dadaism as the logical, and indeed the inevitable by-product of a civilization that sustained itself on pretence and hypocrisy, and whose standards in the final analysis, were coined in the base metal of gross materialism. The same problem faces humanity today, on an even more terrible scale, and whatever lunacies we may discern in the art of our own, immediate period, are no more than a reflection of the greater, and far more sinister lunacies organized by the world's "statesmen".

There was after all, no more reason in the ultimate horror of the First World War, than in the Dadaism which it produced indirectly. Dada was a reflection of chaos, and madness. So although you may well ask—"What in heaven's name has all this to do with painting?"—a very important point is proven. Art, for better or worse, is necessarily a reflection of its environment. The art of Egypt was a mirror for tyranny, that of Greece a reflection of grace and proportion. The baroque painting of the Counter-Reformation, writhing with hell-fire and portents of

**BASSIN AUX NYMPHEAS (1899)**     **Claude Monet (1840–1926)**

For Monet, perhaps the greatest of the Impressionists (see page 91), colour was everything. He once said "Colour is my day-long obsession, joy and torment. . . ." Professor Douglas Cooper describes the painter's evolution as "a pure Impressionist phase from 1872 to 1877; an exploratory post-Impressionist phase from 1878–91 . . . and a late, imaginative phase of Impressionism from 1892 onwards, during which Monet became increasingly a visionary, until after 1912 he found all the inspiration he required in the private world of his own water-garden." Here, in one of the first of a long and intensive series of such subjects, the painter is on the threshold of those more diffuse and imaginative interpretations that were to follow. The patterns woven by the floating blossoms, the drifting vegetation, and the reflections from trees and sky above, were to absorb him utterly in later years, clouded by Madame Monet's death, and failing sight.

**THE OLD CAB HORSE**    R. P. Bevan (1865–1925)

The horse figures prominently in the history of art. Leonardo, Stubbs, Delacroix, Morland, Guys, Degas, and many other artists are indebted to this beautiful, and noble creature. But few painters have done more to capture the spirit of the hard working, "everyday" horse, than R. P. Bevan, who carved for himself a unique niche in the history of British painting with his fascinating portrayals of the cab yards of old London. Here, in the mist of the early morning, the old cab horse is being prepared for his day's work. But the painting is also interesting for the light it throws on a British painter's debt to Impressionism. The atmospheric and luminous qualities of this painting are closely dependent upon the employment of the *spectrum palette* (see Impressionism—page 169) with its scientifically controlled range of colours.

damnation, proved an invaluable visual aid in the pattern of Jesuit propaganda. The art of the French Court in the eighteenth century was understandably frivolous and irresponsible, gay and voluptuous.

Can we then blame the Dadaists for holding a distorting glass to the madness of their time? And who shall we blame for the degeneracy of current techniques such as Tachisme which consist, virtually, of flinging paint at a canvas and hoping it will run into pleasant, fortuitous patterns? Is Tachisme *really* more lunatic than the wilful pollution of God's sweet atmosphere with "dirty" hydrogen bomb tests? Who are the bigger madmen, the artists who reflect, or the so-called statesmen who present the image of hell to the mirror?

Quite unwittingly, Dadaism was a forerunner of Surrealism. The employment of fortuitous and random material, of images and objects, associated without conscious thought, reason, or order, in fantastic and irresponsible juxtapositions, was a clear step in the direction of Surrealism with its insistence on the significance of automatic expression; the free flow of the unconscious as it reveals itself in dreams, fantasies, and the psychopathology of daily life. The irrational plays a far greater part in the pattern of our lives than we perhaps realize. Beneath the surface of law and order, of rational behaviour, lies a hidden world of intense psychological activity. Consciousness is a pitifully thin veneer; and the greater part of being is always submerged. We are, what is hidden. However, Dada used the irrational to illustrate and supplement the collapse of aesthetic and social values. The Surrealists on the other hand were to use the key of irrationalism and fantasy to unlock the door into the dark side of personality.

In conclusion, I must mention one Dadaist technique which is perfectly in line with Surrealist practice. This is known as Collage, a method which consists of pasting together, just as they come to hand, and without conscious thought, scraps of newsprint, fragments of photographs, and similar materials, linked with scribblings in pencil and other media. The inventors of the Collage technique were Jean Arp (born 1888), and the German Surrealist, Max Ernst (born 1891). It can best be described perhaps as a fortuitious equivalent of the calculated construction of Cubist Papiers Collés.

## SURREALISM

The word Surrealism, another of the terms invented by the writer Apollinaire, means simply, "super-reality". The *other reality* of the dreams, fantasies, and imaginings which form the major part of psychological personality. Everyone is obliged to lead a double existence, and *consciousness* is by far the least significant level of our being. It is only through the expression of the *unconscious* that we can arrive at a clear picture of the ultimate nature of personality. The dream is an indispensable key to the unlocking of the other reality, and with this phenomenon in particular, Surrealist painters have always been preoccupied. There are of course, other manifestations of the *unconscious*, such as the random thoughts, and imaginings, and the small, seemingly unimportant compulsive actions, and inhibitions of daily life[1], common to us all. With these too, Surrealism is concerned. But unlike Dada, which employed fantasy and inconsequent behaviour for destructive reasons, Surrealism was a positive, and constructive art form, seeking to drive into the open the whole mysterious and intriguing world of the unconscious. It was, of necessity, to be presented *as it stood*, without any conscious modification. The dream was to be painted, however fantastic, illogical, or inexplicable to the painter, *exactly* as it was dreamed. The chance day-dream, or imagining, no matter how curious, was to be recorded with the same fidelity. Reason was to play no part in the production of Surrealist painting, neither was it considered necessary that the painter, any more than the spectator, should be able to interpret the symbolism and imagery contained in his pictures. The intention was simply to liberate the unconscious, in its purest state, and to the devil with interpretations. These could be left to the psychologists and psycho-analysts who specialized in such matters.

The Surrealist movement was profoundly influenced by the psychological theories of Dr. Sigmund Freud (1856–1939) with their insistence on the significance of dreams and fantasies, and the employment of the free association technique[2] as the working basis of psycho-analysis. Surrealist painting was to be the pictorial pendant of Freudian theory.

The movement was officially launched in 1924 when a group of writers and painters under the leadership of André Breton (born 1896) published the first Surrealist Manifesto. The soul of man was to be liberated from the chains of reason and inhibition, and the super-reality of the unconscious given full scope to express itself in words and pictorial images, unhampered by the exercise of reason, or control of any sort. The dream, they argued, was the true reality—fantasies and random thoughts the ultimate state of being. All else was false, and consciousness, merely a part of the expedient and hypocritical façade of extrovert being, which bears little relation to the true nature of personality with its roots in the unconscious.

Surrealism as an art form had one crucial limitation; it could only communicate with the medical psychologist. So for all the interest of its many strange appearances, Surrealist painting can have little ultimate significance for the casual spectator. A fantastic picture by Salvador Dali (born 1904), Giorgio di Chirico

---

[1] *The Psycho-pathology of Everyday Life.* Sigmund Freud.

[2] During psycho-analysis, the subject is given a stimulus, such as a word, which sets in motion a train of spontaneous ideas and thoughts. These are poured out just as they come to mind.

(born 1888), or Marc Chagall (born 1887)—three typical Surrealist painters—may be all very well up to the point where sheer pictorial enjoyment ends, and the need for psychological interpretation begins. Beyond that barrier, only the psychological expert can pass. It is therefore a peculiarly limited art, and today, quite outmoded as a form of professional painting. Nowadays, it is a method of painting frequently used in mental hospitals where patients are encouraged to release the unconscious as an invaluable guide to a deeper understanding of psychological and mental illness. (See pictures between pages 152-3).

For the amateur also, there is a great deal of interest in dream and fantastic painting, and there is no reason why the method should not be used now and then as an exercise in the exploration of the artist's fundamental personality. A compelling, or vivid dream, for all its apparent illogicality can lend itself to the most striking composition. As for interpretation, this can to some extent be facilitated by a study of the many excellent popular books on psychology and psychiatry that are commonly available today. Getting to know yourself through your own fantastic painting is a fascinating aspect of the joys of painting for pleasure. Painting can teach us many things—not least, a better and deeper understanding of ourselves.

During the decade that followed the innovation of the Surrealist movement many exhibitions were held in various parts of the world. The last, and one of the most important of these, was held in London, in 1936.

Surrealism has many forerunners in the history of painting and literature. William Blake, Henry Fuseli, and Goya, in the visual arts, and Lewis Carroll and Edward Lear in the field of writing, are a few of the names that come to mind immediately. Goya's series of fantastic etchings, "Los Caprichos", and Carroll's "Alice" books, are superb examples of surrealist art.

\*       \*       \*

To all ends and purposes the last vital phase of the modern movement in painting was contributed by the Surrealists. Just as the Cubists had exhausted the exploration of objective form, so Surrealism completed, at least for aesthetic purposes, the investigation of psychological personality.

Since 1936, European and American painters have worked mainly *in the manner* of the idioms already established during the fifty years between the first Impressionist Exhibition of 1874, and the publication of the Surrealist Manifesto of 1924.

Nothing new, or dynamic, has been contributed by the present generation, and although certain degenerate movements have laid claim to serious attention, they can be dismissed as mere reflections of the current trend, in so many directions, towards extravagant and hollow sensationalism. Dadaism on the one hand was not, in spite of its strangeness, a piece of trivial self-advertising, but a sincere expression of social decay. On the other hand, movements like Action Painting and Tachisme in which the creation of accidental effects is a primary consideration, are unquestionably debased. Both methods consist of flinging, pouring, wiping, dragging, or otherwise applying paint to the canvas without thought, or any form of conscious control. Each is a system unsupported either by the intellectual anarchism of Dada, or the conscious recognition of the significance of the unconscious, as in the practise of Surrealism. Intellectual purists it is true, distinguish between "action" and "tachiste" painting, arguing that whereas the tachiste must leave all to chance, the action painter may assume control provided the basis of his abstraction is fundamentally fortuitous. As a side thought on the whole business of human automatic abstractionism, it is sobering to reflect on the *natural* tachisme of modern chimpanzee painters. Congo of the London Zoo, and Betsy of the Baltimore Zoo are distinguished ape artists whose work has already been exhibited in London; and very good it is too, as pure, uncontrolled abstraction. Human tachistes are shamed both by the quality, and of course by the unquestionable honesty of chimpanzee artists. A leading exponent of the Action painting technique was the American painter, Jackson Pollock (1912–56) who died in a motoring accident. His method was to dribble paint on to his canvas from a series of cans. The whole system of contemporary extremism is even more suspect when you realize that in the United States, huge sums of money are paid for this sort of "painting".

It is very much as though the painter, in a state of complete exhaustion, has thrown a final absurd tantrum for which, incredibly, he is handsomely rewarded. Can you blame him for taking advantage of the fools, both critics and patrons, who are happy to swallow this ludicrous and costly artistic pill. The charlatan is a notable, and curiously, a respected figure in the world of contemporary art.

In his crushing attack upon extremism—*The Demon of Progress in the Arts*, to which I referred earlier—Wyndham Lewis crystallizes the extremist tragedy in clear terms.

> " . . . there is the enormous quantity of young men of all classes who find their way every year into provincial art schools or into the Royal College of Arts and other large metropolitan academies. There are, of course, nearly as many women as men studying to be some kind of artist. Talent is not often met with; but a great number of more or less youthful people are trained as artists: and it is from this horde that the stunt crusades are recruited—the more violently untalented would no doubt soon drop out, if it were not for the opportunities offered the dud in extremism."

Extremism as a form of vulgar self-advertisement is sharply dealt with:

"Infantile extremist sensationalism (as a by-product of self-seeking) is the curse of the pundit. What every artist should try to prevent is the car, in which is our civilized life, plunging over the side of the precipice—the exhibitionist extremist driving the whole bag of tricks into a nihilistic nothingness or zero."

It is essential that the artist should regain his self-respect—his sense of social and moral responsibility. He must learn to take his place, once again as a useful member of society. This is a state which cannot be achieved by the exertions of the artist alone. If it is to survive, Western civilization must extricate itself from the slime of cheap sensationalism which is the root cause of its moral decay.

Only one group of painters during the past twenty years has made a sincere and positive contribution to the mainstream of painting—the Social Realists. This was a movement which emerged in America during the 'twenties and reached its climax during the great Depression of the 'thirties. Human affairs were represented with a stark and brutal realism. Social Realism stood against every form of art for art's sake, and against every type of egotistical extravagance in the visual arts. It had a message to communicate, and this it did in frank, outspoken terms. Life was grim, bitter, ugly, unjust—all this was depicted accordingly: an unbiased commentary in an era of great social distress, and much human suffering.

Latterly, in a different setting, the movement has emerged in Britain where our own brand of Social Realism is perhaps better known as the painting of "the kitchen sink". Artists like Jack Smith (born 1928), Edward Middleditch (born 1923), and John Bratby (born 1928) have dealt with realistic depictions of the domestic scene. The great, towering houses of London, carved into flats and teeming with tenants, napkins, babies, prams, and milk bottles. The rooms festooned with washing, the landings bare and creaking, the rooms thinly furnished with secondhand junk. The whole, stark, inelegant, expedient, sweating life of humanity, crowded into the crumbling remnants of an age when leisure, and servants, and wealth, produced the very different realism of Victorian painting. It would be wrong to draw any comparisons between contemporary social realism and these depictions of late-nineteenth-century respectability and affluence. This was purely a mask for the spate of evils seething beneath the hypocrisy of "appearances". Social realism is concerned with the *truth*, and it can best be compared with the work of the French realist painter, Honoré Daumier (1808–79) whose depictions of the social scene in his own time are marked by a strain of unflinching realism and satire.

\*      \*      \*

This chapter has necessarily been lengthy. Painting is a highly complex affair, and technical considerations apart, I was anxious to demonstrate the importance of ideas in relation to the production of painting. I also wanted to establish its diversity. In order to do these things I took the modern movement in art as my text, since it is such a many faceted phenomenon, and one in which the idea is always very much to the forefront.

At the outset of the chapter I spoke of the uses to which the pleasure painter can put the modern movement while in the process of evolving a personal vision and style. Experiment is the essence of progress, and the history of modern painting offers an absorbing series of appropriate exercises.

Try your hand at an Impressionist landscape, use Fauve colour—paint a dream picture, or your own kitchen sink. Only by an exhaustive process of trial and error can you hope to arrive at the crossroads where your own, unique direction will be revealed. One must scout in all directions for the right road. Yet most people, unhappily, spend their lives travelling the first road that presents itself. And that, whether in life, or in art, is usually the wrong road.

# THE GENEALOGY OF MODERN ART

The following are the chief movements in modern art from Manet and the Impressionists to Action and Tachiste Painting. They are described and criticized in the previous chapter.

*Medieval Two-Dimensionalism* and *Renaissance Three-Dimensionalism* (The background of the Modern Movement) — *Edouard Manet* (1832–83) The New Realism.

*Impressionism* (1874) — *Pointillism, Divisionism* and *Neo-Impressionism* (the 1880s).

*Post-Impressionism* (the 1880s).

*Synthétisme (symbolism)* (1888).

*Nabis* and *Intimism* (1895).

*Fauvism* (1905).

*Expressionism* — Die Brücke "The Bridge" (1904), Der Blaue Reiter "The Blue Rider" (1910–11).

*Cubism* (1909) — *Papiers Collés* (A Cubist Technique). Abstract, Non-Figurative, or Non-Objective Art in all its forms up to the present time, and including the influences of Abstraction in the various fields of commercial and industrial design.

*Futurism* (1909).

*Orphism,* or *Synchromism* (1912).

*Suprematism* (1913).

*Vorticism* (1914).

*Dadaism* (1916) — *Collages* (A Dadaist Technique).

*Purism* (1918).

*Neo-Plasticism* (1920).

*Surrealism* (1924).

*Social Realism* (American Movement of the 1930s).

*Action Painting* and *Tachisme* (Degenerate Movements since 1940).

# CHAPTER 18

# Vision, Humanity and Distortion:
# The Three Faces of Genius

I N THE introduction to this book I wrote about the creative idea in painting, and illustrated my argument with various examples. In the present chapter I want to delve even deeper into the waters of aesthetic inspiration, and examine the most elemental roots of the creative idea, as we can trace and uncover them in the work of three masters: Leonardo da Vinci, Rembrandt van Rijn, and Pablo Picasso. Painting, as I have tried to show throughout this book, is primarily a matter of ideas. Once you have learned how to use your materials, and have discovered that style of expression which is peculiar to yourself, your key problem will always be expressed in a question very familiar to most artists—"What can I paint?" Technique and style will develop almost automatically; certainly manual dexterity in the use of your technical implements will increase, slyly, and unconsciously, like the control and mastery which comes to the darts or billiards player, the more he practises the pure craft of the activity of playing darts, or billiards. The quest for ideas, and for the subjects that spring from ideas, or conversely, that in themselves suggest ideas, is a matter which is intimately bound up with the conscious development of the mind itself. Mind in its purest state is awareness, and ideas, the sparks, or reflections thrown off by the mirror, or the mirrors of awareness.

Ideas are not mechanical things like the dexterity with which an empty-headed painter may still manipulate his pencil, or brush. They do not just *happen*; they are not virtuosity. An idea is not even an inspiration—but the *extension* of an inspiration: an extension in the special terms in which an artist chooses to express himself. Let me give you an example of what I mean. An artist may be initially inspired, *emotionally* inspired, by a sunset: but that is not an *idea*. If however he utilizes the sunset as the basis for a picture through which he expresses the idea that colour is the most fundamental and dynamic element in nature, then the inspiration has been extended by the breadth of the idea. The painter may of course *start* the other way round, by first evolving the idea, then finding, or creating a sunset which will illustrate the idea. But this is a point I have already made in my introductory chapter where I write about the application of the creative idea, in portraiture, for instance.

What I am primarily concerned with here, is a study of those *absolute* forces which, as I see it, have always played the predominant role in giving a visible shape to the raw, and at first, malleable ideas of the artist. It is only thus that the flexibility, the relative impermanence of the loose idea, can be stabilized, and so take its place as an integral element in the scheme of universal aesthetic order. An order which, if such an idea is no longer acceptable to science, is still apparent as a continuity of constants in the history of art.

Let us for the time being, forget your personal problems as a painter, and consider these "universals" in the hope that later on, an understanding of this ultimate aesthetic order will assist you, not only to pursue your own painting with a deeper perception of ultimate truth, but also to discern, in your general study and appreciation of art, the appearance of these *immutables*, when, and wherever they may present themselves. The artists I have chosen for special reference in the present chapter are of course among the greatest of European masters, but countless other artists, many at lesser levels, approximate nonetheless, either equally, or in varying degree, to the same, ultimate qualities. Not only in European and Occidental art are these universals evident. They will be found at the core of the great art forms of India and China, of Mexico and Peru, and at the heart of the visual arts of many other Oriental, Mediterranean, Oceanic, and even primitive cultures.

What then *are* these immutable, universal qualities that activate the disparate ideas of the arts of mankind? Behind the *personal* idea that a sunset may symbolize a fundamental aspect of the ultimate reality of nature, is the *vision* of that reality, or truth, from which the idea emanates. The idea is merely one of the million faces of truth; a reflection if you like from the *one* face of the ultimate state of reality. The visionary beholds this absolute in its most pure, and diffuse form, and in order to prepare it for expression in more synthetic terms, he must necessarily associate it with a modified idea which in turn is rendered down through whatever medium the artist may choose as his final vehicle of expression. The painter will naturally elect to use pigment, and the poet, words.

Truth, in its purely visionary form can have no counterpart in the world of physical phenomena, so that it must necessarily undergo some diminishment of strength, and modification of meaning, in the process of translation by the artist into the aesthetic form. When the artist—as the saint—in beatitude, perceives the face of truth, he becomes one with the "all"; he achieves, so to speak, for a fraction of *timelessness*, the bliss of that nirvana in which the raindrop of personality mingles with the ocean, and is lost. The bliss of the extinction of individuality in the supreme spirit, is the pivot of Buddhist philosophy. It is this vision of the *impersonal* "becoming one" that activates the ideas of those artists, like Leonardo, who seek to project *in human time*, some evidence of the peerless serenity and peace, of the release from personal striving, which they have beheld.

It is a quality to be found also in much of the art of China. It is detectable in the portrayal of Buddhist subjects, and in those divinely restful and contemplative studies of nature that are peculiar to the art, and of course the spirit of China.

Although the face of the ultimate visionary experience may be the same for Leonardo, as for a Chinese landscape painter of the Sung Dynasty (960–1279), *the idea* through which it is adapted for aesthetic presentation will differ, naturally, both in relation to the personality of the artist, and especially to the society and culture from which he springs. We may say then, that the vision of impersonal bliss is one of the faces of genius; a modified face it is true, but even so, one of the rarest beauty, illumined as it is, by the clear lantern of ultimate purity. Later in the present chapter we will consider the idea through which Leonardo adapted and modified this vision of perfection. First, we must consider the two remaining faces of genius. They are *distortion*, and *humanity*.

Both must rank below *vision* in the hierarchy of the universal values we are considering in their relation to the visual arts, since they are conceived within the framework of the conventional time scale, and are intimately bound up with the desire and striving peculiar to human existence, with its need of *myth*. Of that fantasy-producing myth which is the bedrock of faith, and belief; and of fear, too. Thus we have magic, and religious art, with the vast iconography of grandiose distortions that invest the magical and religious imagery of the ages with its ecstasy, and its fear invoking qualities.

Distortion in art, quite apart from its relation to the modern Expressionist movement, is vital for the success of a magical or religious iconography which must feed and sustain the philosophical myth, or legend, upon which it is founded. The less this system of imagery conforms to the normal, and natural appearances of everyday life, the deeper will be its meaning for the community, who have always delighted, irrespective of the particular mythology, in associating their beliefs with strangeness, mystery, and even terror. The highly imaginative distortions of Egyptian magical art are a clear example of the employment of the mysterious, and terrible, as the means of invoking a religious fear in the collective mind of the community. Baroque art of the seventeenth century sought, in its religious applications, to achieve a similar objective: an end which was already apparent in the dramatic terrors of Michelangelo's "Last Judgment".

In Christian art, throughout the whole of the Middle Ages, the severe, formal imagery of the Byzantine conception gave to Christianity that cold, stark, relentless and inhuman quality that was so much the part of a millennium of fear, and tyranny. In Greece however, between the years 530–320 B.C., when the golden, or classical age was in being, distortion worked in *reverse*. The deities of Greece were conceived in the image of man himself; of ideal, and perfect, *physical* man. Thus the striving for that ultimate perfection of bodily beauty, and grace, which distinguishes the sculpture of the period.

Distortion in the service of religion is also apparent in the painting and sculpture of India. The imagery of the Jain religion, for instance, a non-Brahminical doctrine with Buddhist affinities is marked by stylization. Figures are curiously angular, eyes and hands deliberately exaggerated in size. In sculpture we may take as an example the extravagant voluptuousness with which Siva[1] is often depicted. Particularly when the god is performing the dance that symbolizes the spirit of fertility, and the ecstasy of sexual union.

I have chosen Picasso to illustrate the element of distortion, not only because he is still the most controversial figure in modern painting but because he, perhaps more than any other contemporary painter, has used distortion with something of the awe-inspiring quality that imbued the art of Egypt with its magic, and terror. An important part of the imagery of Picasso is essentially an iconography of the awful; a pictographia charged with warnings, and portents, and at the least, with the deadliest satire. Here is a master who uses the idea as a means of focusing, not the face of sublime serenity, but symbolically, the twisted countenance of the human tragedy. He exposes, not only the calculated evils and brutalities of man, but also that grotesqueness of aspect which is now the inheritance of a species of life that has specialized over the centuries, in distorting, voluntarily, both its mind, and its appearance. Ages of so-called civilization, of conformity to a long succession of insane thought and behaviour patterns, have provided this penetrating artist with the rich material of his scourging satire. Do you really think, after serious reflection, that the imagery of an artist like Picasso is any more grotesque than man himself? Or than man's appalling record of grotesque brutalities: a catalogue of crime against his fellow men, in war, and peace, which sends the imagination shuddering and reeling in horror?

Why are we so indignant when a great artist like Picasso, or Goya[2], penetrates the masks of hypocrisy, and by symbolism, and distortion, present a remorseless

[1] The Hindu god held by some to be the supreme deity of the triad consisting of Siva, Vishnu, and Brahma. Siva, the great lord, is the destroyer, and creator of life: Vishnu, the Preserver: and Brahma, the Absolute, the universal and eternal soul.

[2] Consider the series of etchings "The Disasters of War" (1810–13), Goya's appalling commentary upon war. Here too, the idea of horror has been expressed through distortion.

picture of human loathsomeness? Only because our conscience, as a community, is guilty. (See pictures facing page 176).

Consider the history of those thought and behaviour patterns that have conditioned the life of Western society since the beginning of the Christian era. It is the story of remorseless superstitions, and insane taboos; of relentless tyrannies, and crippling conventions. In many ways the distortions of Picasso are the sum of all these monstrosities. If you think the imagery of Picasso grotesque, just look around you in the streets; the first bowler hat you see is as startling and grotesque a symbol, as any you will find, wilfully employed by Picasso to point a moral, or a truth.

The celebrated double portraits of the artist, in which two aspects of a face are made visible simultaneously—a profile and a three-quarter view for instance—merely symbolize the duplicity of personality: an idea which has clearly used distortion as the vehicle of expression. Granted such portraits look grotesque. They are intended, not to convey a mechanical likeness of any particular person, but *an abstract idea*. Now a *bowler hat* is an abstract idea—though an unscrupulous one. It is a symbol and, as such, a distortion, intended to convey the idea that the wearer, by virtue of the symbol, is necessarily a decent, clean living, respectable, trustworthy member of society, in every way to be relied upon; as a man who wears his cap on one side might not be. In the long run however, it is an artist like Picasso who raises the bowler, both literally, and figuratively, to examine the man, *or the society*, beneath. Later, I will consider that aspect of Picasso's distortion which is concerned with fundamental human evil. Here, the artist uses distortion to express the idea of human wickedness—of man's inhumanity to man.

It is with *humanity* that we are finally concerned. Humanity, with its twin tributaries of emotion and humility, is the remaining factor in the trinity of absolutes employed by the great artists of history. Curiously, it is a quality less frequently encountered in art—as in life—than either vision, or distortion. The reason? Simply I think that humanity is less interested in *itself*, and its ultimate well-being, than in chasing the red herrings of economics, politics, and religion. It sows the seeds of its own, immemorial tragedy in this curious paradox, and reaps, as might be expected, only a harvest of sorrow, and pain. The vision of the mystic may well be the ultimate reality, and distortion vital for the maintenance of myth, and legend, but mankind must still endure, even temporarily, the joys, and sorrows of earthly existence. Of toil for what? Of pain, to what end? Of joy, so fleeting.

The painter who can accept this riddle without qualification, as did Rembrandt—and of course Van Gogh—who sees in the humblest human situation the hand of divine majesty take shape, and transfigure, even the ghostly rags of beggar, or prodigal, into a priceless spiritual raiment, has seen the true wonder of mankind. The power to invest even the simplest things with glory, if *dignity* is preserved. Dignity in the face of suffering, and compassion for all things that suffer, these qualities are the true measure of man's greatness. He may fly to the moon, or colonize the planets, but if he loses these attributes, he is surely less than the dust. Dignity gives man the strength to shoulder the burdens of life. Compassion evokes the pure emotion, and the humility, which are the natural complements of human dignity. They inspire in man the love of his fellows without which the world is merely a jungle, or rather perhaps a ferocious market-place where *pride* has ousted dignity, and where compassion has been trampled underfoot by the violent emotions of greed, and the lust for gain.

Where the idea is used, as in Rembrandt, or again Van Gogh, to express the quality of universal humanity, the vehicle is almost invariably that of poverty, or at least, of the simple, humble life. For it is easier for the beggar and the outcast to achieve dignity and compassion, than it is for a king.

Having then established the nature of the three faces of absolute genius, seldom of course, if ever, combined by one master, let us take a look at Leonardo's "Virgin of the Rocks"[1] (between pages 24-5), painted between the years 1506 and 1508, for in this later of the two versions of the subject executed by the master, we have a clear indication of Leonardo's knowledge of the vision of ultimate bliss— the impersonal nirvana.

First however, let us consider some important facts about the painter. The many faceted genius of Leonardo has long presented a bewildering problem; how can he possibly be classified, or pinned down at any point? Of course he cannot. Scientist, anatomist, mathematician, engineer, technician, and incidentally, painter—he is the true explorer; restless, inventive, probing. Seeking in all things, whether the human face, the swift rhythms of water, the grace of plants and flowers, or the structure of geological formations, that fundamental *oneness* which permeates and unifies all the things of creation. Leonardo's pantheism is in fact a first step to nirvana, for if all things are one, it is first necessary to *know* that they are one. Leonardo is a far less baffling problem if we see his enquiries into the structure of living things, his thirst for empirical knowledge, not as a series of loose, independent studies, but as a search, *through* knowledge, for the oneness that is the ultimate truth. That he should have travelled by many roads to this goal is typical, not only of the many-sidedness of the man himself, but even more so, of his time. The Renaissance was essentially an age of adventure—of exploration and discovery, a period of energetic research, very like our own. It was a time in which the mind of man, freed at last from the fetters of medieval tyranny, was at liberty to

[1] An earlier version of this subject is to be found in the Louvre. It was painted between the years 1483-1490.

investigate the nature of the physical world, and to evolve those patterns of free thought, of doubt, and scepticism, that were later to be almost extinguished in the fires of the Counter-Reformation.

Leonardo's quest for oneness is fundamentally rooted in the multifarious researches so characteristic of his time; but it would be wrong to dismiss him merely as the greatest free thinker and scientist of his age. Where the Renaissance was interested in the bits, Leonardo was concerned with the bits only in so far as they were the reflections of an indissoluble unity.

"The mind of the painter", he said "should be like a mirror which is filled with as many images as there are things placed before him." Elsewhere he wrote, "Do you not see how many and varied are the actions which are performed by men alone? Do you not see how many different kinds of animals there are, and also of trees, and plants and flowers? What variety of hilly and level places, of springs, rivers, cities, public and private buildings; of instruments fitted for man's use; of divers costumes, ornaments and arts?"[1]

These are Renaissance sentiments surely; but they are also the key to the mystery of the man. In his apprehension of the diversity of phenomena, and of the painter's need to understand and embrace this teeming world, in its entirety, without prejudice, or bias, the master expresses his belief that ultimate truth must lay in the understanding of the force which unites all things. But first, all things must be understood. The painter was profoundly concerned with the nature of the life force. Yet there is something even deeper than this to be discerned in the art of Leonardo if we can understand the significance of the one feature that unlocks the door into the innermost recess of his personality—*the smile*. No aspect of Leonardo's work has been such a frequent subject of speculation as the so-called enigmatic smile popularly associated with the Mona Lisa. Whether the smile appears in "La Gioconda" (1503), "The Virgin, the Infant Christ and St. Anne" (c. 1499), "St. John the Baptist" (c. 1509), or in the "Virgin of the Rocks", its meaning, surely, is clear.

Leonardo's aesthetic smile was the idea through which he expressed both his understanding of the oneness of all things, and his knowledge of the vision of nirvana. The "Virgin of the Rocks" is in fact a harmony of those aspects of natural history that so absorbed the artist in the particular. Here, the water and the rock formations, the vegetation and the painter's knowledge of anatomy have been brought into a superb unity. It is a unity which emphasizes both the spirit, and the inherent structure of the order of nature. But it is in the *smile* of the virgin, and the angel—which are of course really *one* smile—that Leonardo unmasks his secret. The smile, wherever it appears in his work, is the symbol of knowledge: knowledge

[1] From the Notebooks of Leonardo da Vinci. See reference in *Classic Art* by Heinrich Wölfflin: page 21.

of oneness, and knowledge of vision. The perplexing impersonality of the Leonardo face which, like the smile, is always the *same* face; the strange sexlessness of his characters, whether drawn from life, or imagination, with their distant aspect, transfigured by a piercing, and disturbingly subtle beauty, all this is understandable if we seek in the master's work, not the particular, but the general. Every character in his painting is a synthesis of oneness, and vision, and the smile is the key to the mystery. The smile, in fact, is *the idea*.

That he chose basically conventional subjects through which to express this idea is perfectly understandable, since the propagation of an idea which may at first be unacceptable to a wide public because of its strangeness, or unorthodoxy, is best insinuated through an orthodox framework. Not that the true message of Leonardo's art is appreciated on any wide scale today; but then neither is the teaching of Christ. Humanity still tails far behind its sages.

Leonardo chose as a receptacle for his idea, the conventional theme of the mother and child, which even in *his* time, must have been something of a hackneyed subject. I say *chose* this subject, by which I mean, that he saw the possibilities of using it as the framework of his idea, *after* he had been commissioned to paint the subject by a group of monks. But no one will argue that this is a *religious* depiction in the sense that a Byzantine representation of the same subject was religious. For Leonardo, the subject was merely the excuse for the presentation of a pantheistic, and visionary conception. As such, it is by medieval standards, a profane and heretical work.

The painter's disinterestedness in the conventionally religious significance of the subject, can be judged from the fact that a work which was commissioned in 1483, was not in fact completed until 1490, much to the disappointment of the monks who had expressly requested an early delivery, as one of the terms of contract. But Leonardo worked only slowly, and with intense deliberation. Besides, he had a profound, oblique message to express through the medium of a subject which in its simple form, many a lesser master would have "knocked off", so to speak, in no time at all. The "Virgin of the Rocks" was to become for Leonardo, the point of maximum concentration, the vortex in which, after considerable effort, even for such a master (the two versions cover a period of some twenty-five years), all the separate rivers of his knowledge were to meet as one truth, in the ocean of the impersonal smile; the smile that symbolizes the knowledge of nirvana. . . .

This then is how one great artist dealt with the immutable quality of vision. Now let us consider how Rembrandt presented the case for humanity. Leonardo spoke with the tongue of an exalted silence, Rembrandt with the tongue of common man.

The acceptance of one's lot as a human being, without rancour or envy, taking in one's stride both the good, and the bad, success and failure, wealth and poverty, as they come, is the best to which man can aspire, at least in his attitude to the uncertainties of human destiny, and the caprices of fortune. This is true nobility, and nowhere is it better expressed than in the life of Rembrandt himself, who knew both great material success and, in his later years, extreme poverty. To know, as he did, that it matters not whether you stand in rags, or in riches, but only whether you stand in dignity, with compassion for humanity, and humility in the face of the glories of creation, that alone is greatness. Yet how seldom do we meet with this nobility of character in life. We are often ourselves guilty of corruption by the black forces of bitterness, and envy. Bitterness that life has not endowed us either with the riches or the successes we had *planned* for ourselves, and envy of those who *seem* to possess all the things we do not.

Rembrandt's message surely is that humanity consists in the acceptance of one's personal and social destiny, coupled with a deep concern for the condition of one's fellow men. A concern supported by compassion, and humility in the knowledge of one's ultimate littleness. But humility too, as I say, in the face of those marvels which the Creator reveals only to the truly humble in mind, and heart. The acceptance of the human situation, as it stands, is the key to revelations that no arrogance will unlock. Nor is this philosophy in conflict with the possibilities of evolution in human affairs. One accepts what is *unchangeable* in life, while at the same time striving for new achievements. Invention, and discovery may eventually bring about change, but they are not in *themselves* change.

For Rembrandt, the supreme miracle of creation was to be found, in aesthetic terms at any rate, in the glories of *chiaroscuro*. His message of humanity and compassion is bedecked in the priceless cloth of light and dark, a garment encrusted with the diamonds of highlights, and the golden bars of subsidiary lights. In the art of Rembrandt, *chiaroscuro* is not simply the division of a canvas into a pattern, or design, of lights and darks; the mystical and symbolic properties of the two were rallied to the full in his painting.

"He accosts with his dark lantern the world of the marvellous, of conscience and the ideal. He has no equal in the power of showing the invisible."

This is how the French painter-critic Eugène Fromentin (1820–76) described the mystique of Rembrandt[1], at the heart of which we find, not the implacable face of an impersonal truth—even though that is the ultimate—but the warm, familiar, intermediate countenance of mankind. Of a humanity, arrayed like the king of kings, in the jewels of pure light, while the darkness, laps close. It is a darkness

[1] The quotation is used by R. H. Wilenski in his *Dutch Painting*: page 97.

**THE MANTELPIECE** (*above*) **and
GIRL IN AN INTERIOR**
Edouard Vuillard (1868–1940)

Vuillard was originally a member
of the "Nabis" (see page 175), and
later of that small band, among
them Pierre Bonnard (1867–1947),
who became known as the "Intimists". In these two domestic
subjects Vuillard epitomizes the
main objective of Intimism: to
charge the familiar scenes of
everyday life with a pervading
sense of that inward beauty which
transfigures the ordinary, and imparts, even to inanimate matter, a
mystical and emotive significance. By the use of rich, glowing
colour and a profound sense of
the importance of simple, homely
things, Vuillard invested his subjects with a majesty that at one
time would have been thought
possible only in some vast
religious, or heroic subject.

**THE ARRIVAL** (c. 1914)　　C. R. W. Nevinson (1889–1946)

Perhaps the most original British artist of his generation, Nevinson gave stability to "Futurism" (see page 181). In this proud, towering design, the painter has employed the crisp, mechanical forms of Cubism as the basis of his composition. Through these he has symbolized the age of machinery and speed.

which symbolizes the mystery in which life is enshrouded—and a light which symbolizes the wonder and clarity of consciousness, and of conscience. At the centre of this mystique, is man. *Chiaroscuro* is the idea through which Rembrandt presents his conception of humanity, as essentially a nobility, poised at the heart of the dark and mysterious waters of the unknown, yet aware, with flashes of profound insight, that the only real merit in human conduct and behaviour is to be found in compassion and humility. The idea of light and dark is the foundation of his mystique of mystery and revelation. The revelation to *individual* man, of God's majesty, and glory.

The faces that appear in the painting of Rembrandt are pools of clear, and noble resignation; his hands, sweet with the healing touch of compassion. In the end, the light must triumph over the darkness. This is the faith which sustains the life of man—a faith, poignantly expressed in the idea of Rembrandt's *chiaroscuro*.

We cannot aspire, in our first few lives at any rate, to the sum of Leonardo's ultimate perfection; but we *can* take a step or two in the direction of perfection, by practising, here and now, something of the humanity which Rembrandt preaches in the gospel of his light and dark.

\*　　\*　　\*

No modern painter has used distortion with a more intense sense of its emotive and symbolic power, than has Picasso. Can you imagine any type of visual depiction which could symbolize more terribly, the awful suffering and degradation of the bull-ring, than the harrowing portrayal painted in 1934. (Facing page 176).

Those of my readers who are familiar with Spanish tauromachy will recognize, perhaps with a turn of the stomach, the central tragedy of the bull-fight. But even if you have never seen a bull-fight the message of the picture is clear. The average Spaniard sees only the central glory of the contest, the *moment of truth* when the torero, having successfully "dominated" the bull, despatches it with a single, swift thrust of the sword. But for many, the bull-fight—*corrida*, or *novillada*[1] —is dominated by the tragedy of the bull, and the final grotesque and grovelling degradation in a vile death, which this picture illustrates so movingly. A death which more often than not is far from swift and clean.

The position of the sword in Picasso's terrible painting suggests the inexpert thrust of the *novillaro*, the weapon having failed to penetrate the *cross*[2]. This bungling causes great suffering, and frequently a number of thrusts are necessary

[1] The *corrida*, or bull-fight proper, is one in which only fully fledged matadors (toreros) take part. The *novillada* is a novices bull-fight in which only apprentice toreros (novilleros) participate. It is important to appreciate this distinction especially if you propose attending your first bull-fight while on holiday. The technique of the *corrida* is of course far superior to that of the *novillada*.

[2] The *cross* is a space in the hump of the bull's shoulders leading straight through to the creature's heart.

o

before the wretched animal is finally despatched. Even so it may be necessary to resort to the *puntilla*, a dagger used for the *coup de grâce* when the torero fails repeatedly to finish the bull. To know all this, preferably at first hand, gives the deepest possible meaning to the agony of Picasso's dying bull whose sufferings are so powerfully intensified through the painter's grotesque distortion of form, posture, and expression.

During the years 1933–37, the bull features prominently in Picasso's work. A phase that was to culminate in the great mural of Guernica. During the preliminary period, the bull, and the idea of the bull-ring are used symbolically to suggest the arena in which the battle of life is fought out against the blind, brute forces of implacable, and remorseless evil. (See pictures facing page 176).

In 1937, when the Spanish civil war was at its fiercest, the Basque town of Guernica was destroyed by German planes in alliance with Franco. The mural "Guernica" which was installed in the Spanish Pavilion at the Paris World Fair of 1937, uses the tragedy of the German bombing as the flashpoint for Picasso's depiction of the tragedy of humanity, broken on the wheels of war. The idea behind the distortions involved in this portrayal, is simply that the crucial tragedy of human existence is not the suffering imposed upon man by fate, or fortune, over which he has no control, but the horror and madness of those monstrous evils he *wilfully* inflicts upon himself.

"Guernica" is painted completely in black, white, and grey, a colour distortion which in itself suggests the lonely agony of pain, and the bleak coldness of cruelty. It is a scene of carnage and destruction. At the right of the picture a woman can be seen falling from a blazing building, on the left, a mother raises her dead child. The anguish of the horse symbolizes human suffering (the horse is man's friend), the bull, the triumph of evil. The whole scene is illuminated by the relentless light of an electric lamp, symbolizing the eye of destiny, unmoved by the insanity of these self-inflicted wounds.

This is how a great contemporary master uses the timeless element of distortion to express *his* idea of the horror of brutality and evil.

Distortion, as I remarked earlier, was employed in ancient times by the Egyptians as the tangible support for an abstract idea; that of a religion steeped in magic, superstition, and fear. Some five thousand years later, distortion of a similar kind is employed by an artist of our own time to militate against the forces of evil that are no longer vested in religion—but in *man*.

Thus far we have travelled; man is now the sole remaining enemy of mankind. When we have conquered *ourselves*, we shall move, out of the barbarous jungle, on to the clean, sweet plains of true civilization. This, more than anything else is the message of Picasso's distortion, and of "Guernica".

# A Glossary of Technical Terms

THE following terms are commonly used by writers on art. Many will be found in the present volume, but the list contains others which the student is likely to meet with in his general reading.

ACADEMIC. In painting, sculpture, etc., conforming to established conventions: in the manner of an approved tradition. In the most restricted sense of the term, not original.

ADVANCING COLOUR. A warm colour, such as red, which appears to advance to the forefront of a painting.

AERIAL PERSPECTIVE. (Also known as ATMOSPHERIC PERSPECTIVE.) The creation of distant effects on a plane surface, by using colder, and paler colours, for the more distant features. Theoretically, objects tend to become colder in hue, and paler in tone, as they move into the distance. All colour is modified by the conditions of light, air, and distance.

AESTHETICS. The branch of philosophy which deals with the nature of the beautiful in relation to the work of art; its perception and appreciation. Theoretically, the purpose of aesthetics is the establishment of laws, criteria, etc. which will facilitate the appreciation and understanding of works of art.

ALLA PRIMA PAINTING. Direct painting. A painting which is completed by a single application of paint, as opposed to one which is produced in a series of stages, such as glazing and scumbling over an underpainting.

BAROQUE. The term used to describe the stylistic tendencies which accompanied the Counter-Reformation of the Jesuits. In painting and sculpture, dramatic and contrived composition, theatrical lighting effects, and the expression of violent emotion, are characteristic. In architecture, the fantastic and grotesque use of ornament is typical. The style prevailed during the seventeenth and eighteenth centuries, and the word *baroque* derives from the Spanish *barrueco*, meaning, a rough, irregular pearl.

BODY COLOURS. Paint, whether oil or water-colour, which possesses body or opacity, as opposed to paint which is transparent.

BROKEN COLOUR. A passage of colour which is varied by the introduction of hues, such as those reflected, or picked up, from the proximity of other hues.

CANVAS. A support for oil painting which was not brought into general use until late in the fifteenth century.

CAST SHADOW. The shadow cast by one form on to another.

CHIAROSCURO. The treatment of light and shade in painting. Contrast in light and dark.

CHROMA. See COLOUR.

CLASSICISM. In art, the opposite of Romanticism. Art which is based on established ideals of perfection, rather than upon the caprices of imagination. In the strictest sense, art which emphasizes the characteristics of the Greek and Roman style: i.e. objectivity, order, discipline, restraint. The classical style may be defined as an amalgam of simplicity, harmony, and proportion.

COLOUR. Colour possesses three qualities:

(a) *Hue*: The colour itself, e.g. red, yellow, blue, green.

(b) *Chroma*: The relative brilliance and purity of a colour, e.g. *bright* red, or *dull* green.

(c) *Value*: The degree of its modification by the prevailing conditions of light, air and distance. (See AERIAL PERSPECTIVE.)

COLOUR CIRCLE. The arrangement of the colours of the rainbow, or spectrum, in circular form, one half of which contains the *warm* colours, and the other, the *cool* colours. The colours which appear opposite one another, such as red and green, orange and blue, yellow and violet, are the contrasting, or complementary colours. If a colour circle is revolved rapidly, the colours will merge, and the disk will appear as white, so proving that white light is composed of the colours of the spectrum, a fact which formed the basis of Impressionism.

COLOUR PERSPECTIVE. An alternative term for AERIAL PERSPECTIVE (which see).

COLOURED GREY. A grey which is made by the mixing of complementaries, such as red and green, orange and blue, etc. As opposed to a neutral grey which is produced by the admixture of black and white. The degree of strength or paleness of a coloured grey is conditioned by the use of varying proportions of white.

COMPLEMENTARY COLOURS. Colours which exhibit maximum contrast, and appear opposite one another on the colour circle. When mixed they tend towards greyness.

COMPOSITION. The structural organization of a painting. The arrangement of shapes, forms, masses, contrapposto, etc.

CONTENT. The subject matter of the work of art as distinct from its aesthetic form.

CONTOUR. The outline, or external boundary of a form. The illusion of a line enclosing form.

CONTRAPPOSTO. (From the Italian, meaning opposed). In the broadest sense, the quality of contrast in painting: the opposition and contrast of masses, movements, rhythms, etc. In the more restricted sense it refers to the opposition of movements in the human body, such as the twist of the shoulders at an angle which opposes the horizontal alignment of the pelvis.

CONTRAST EFFECT. The intensification of colour which is caused by placing complementary colours side by side.

COOL COLOURS. The bluish colours which appear in the cool half of the colour circle.

DRAGGING. A process in oil painting which consists of dragging stiff colour, with little or no medium, over the tacky surface of a painting, in order to create a broken effect, or to add variety to the texture of the picture. Colour which is dragged skims the surface of the canvas without taking in its depressions.

EARTH COLOURS. Those pigments, such as the ochres, raw sienna, and the umbers, that are obtained by mining, and prepared for use by such processes as grinding, floating, and roasting.

ECLECTICISM. A theory taught by the Carracci at their Academy in Bologna. Lodovico (1555–1619), Agostino (1557–1602), and Annibale Carracci (1560–1609) founded the Eclectic school of painting whose work was based on the theory that the painter should select what he considered to be the respective merits of various schools, and masters, and combine these qualities in his own work. Such a theory is now generally considered to be decadent. In the more general sense, any type of painting which borrows freely from a variety of sources.

EMPATHY. Literally, "feeling into" the work of art. The feeling, or projection of personality into the object of contemplation. *Becoming one* with the work of art.

"EN PLEIN AIR". (In the open air; out of doors). An expression used to describe the practise of painting in the open, on location. The practice, common today, was first pioneered by the painters of the Barbizon School (members of which included Millet, Rousseau, Corot and Daubigny), and continued by the Impressionists.

EYE LEVEL, or EYE LINE. (Also known as the HORIZON LINE.) In perspective, the line which cuts the picture plane at the same height above ground level as the eye of the spectator. Parallel lines converge to meet at vanishing points on the eye level.

FORESHORTENING. The apparent shortening of forms in relation to the angle from which they are observed. The appearance of shortening becomes more acute as the angle between the alignment of the form and the line of sight is reduced. Thus one can observe the full length of a form— such as an arm, or a leg—only when it is set at an angle of forty-five degrees to the line of sight.

FORM. In painting, any mass, representational or abstract, which exhibits a three-dimensional appearance.

GESSO. Plaster of Paris, or gypsum. A ground or priming for wooden panels, or canvas. Gesso grounds have been in use since the earliest times and are referred to in the writing of Cennino Cennini, the Italian authority on the techniques of the Giotto Period. Cennini was born about 1372, and wrote a famous treatise on painting, called, *Il Libro d'Arte*.

GLAZE. A film of transparent oil colour applied over an underpainting. It is essential that a glaze should be of a darker tone than the underpainting it is to cover. Glazes are made by mixing colours with vehicles such as varnish, sometimes mixed with spirits of turpentine. They can be applied either with a soft brush, with the finger-tip, or with a cotton pad.

GOLDEN SECTION. A geometrical proportion which has long been regarded as a universal law governing the harmony of proportions both in art, and in nature. The proposition is formulated in two propositions of Euclid: "To cut a given straight line so that the rectangle is equal to the square in the remaining segment", and, "To cut a given finite line in extreme and mean ratio". A more common formula is "to cut a finite line so that the shorter part is to the longer part as the longer part is to the whole". The resulting section is described by Sir Herbert Read in *The Meaning of Art* as, "roughly in the proportion of 5 to 8 (or 8 to 13, 13 to 21, and so on), but never exactly so". In the simplest terms the proposition means the division of any given line at a point a little more than a third of its total length; as for instance in the case of the horizon line in Botticelli's *The Birth of Venus*. (See facing page 24).

GOUACHE. When transparent water-colours are made opaque by the admixture of white, they are known as gouache colours. Strictly speaking, any opaque water-colour, such as poster paint, is gouache.

GROUND. Also known as priming. The surface applied to a canvas, or other support, upon which a picture is painted. A coating of a material suitable to receive and hold oil colours: such as a white oil priming.

"HALF CLOSED EYES". The practise of looking at a subject with half closed eyes, so as to reduce the obtrusiveness of inci-

213

dental detail, and enable the painter to resolve its appearance into simple masses of light and dark.

HALF-TONE. Those values in painting that are midway between the extremes of light and dark. Sometimes referred to as middle-tone.

HIGH KEY PAINTING. A painting which has been executed in bright, or brilliant colours.

HORIZON LINE. An alternative term for EYE LEVEL, or EYE LINE, (which see).

HUE. See COLOUR.

IMPASTO. Solid colour. Paint which is applied with maximum thickness. Heavy impasto is usually confined to the lighter passages in a painting, such as the high-lights.

IMPRIMATURA. A coloured tint applied to a white ground before painting. Sometimes laid over an outline. Many painters find it disturbing to work on a glaring white ground which they prefer to "kill" before beginning to paint. Colours most favoured for the Imprimatura are pale shades of brown, green, and grey.

"L'ART POUR L'ART". Literally, art for art's sake. A French expression which gained currency during the second half of the nineteenth century. It reflected the desire of poets and painters to set themselves, and their art, apart from the phili-stine, and the bourgeois. It became a watchword of the English Aesthetic Movement led by Walter Pater, and Oscar Wilde. Nowadays considered to be a decadent philosophy.

LAYING-IN. The preliminary organization of the subject on the canvas. The arrangement of the composition, orchestration of light and dark, etc.

LINEAR PERSPECTIVE. The art of deline-ating solid objects, in depth, on a plane surface, by the exercise of the science of perspective.

LOADED LIGHTS. The application of lights, high-lights especially, with a heavy impasto.

LOADING. Painting with a heavy impasto.

LOCAL COLOUR. Theoretically, the actual colour of an object. Strictly speaking, local colour has no exact existence, since all things are subject to the special conditions in which they are seen, such as the prox-imity of other colours, the prevailing circumstances of lighting, viewpoint, and so on.

LOW KEY PAINTING. A painting which is executed in subdued colours.

LOW TONE. Colour which is subdued in tone.

MANNERISM. The excessive addiction by minor artists to the distinctive manner, or style, of a master. The superficial imitation of a creative style without the interior feeling of the original. Painting in the manner of a master from *without*, rather than from *within*. All mannerism is re-garded as decadent.

MASS. In painting, any large form, or group of forms, or any substantial area of colour, light, dark, etc. Composition depends largely upon the skilful organiza-tion of mass and space.

MATIÈRE. An expression used when referring to the intrinsic qualities of the physical surface of a painting irrespective of subject content.

MEDIUM. A term which can be used in three senses:

(a) The liquid with which pigments are ground during the process of being made into paint.

(b) The liquid used to render paint more easily workable during the process of painting, or to facilitate the mixing of colours.

(c) A term used to describe the particular material in which a picture is executed: such as, water-colour, oil, pastel, conté, pen and wash, etc.

MIDDLE DISTANCE. In landscape, the area, or plane, between the foreground and the background.

MODELLING. The process of representing form: in pencil, chalk, paint, clay, etc.

MONOCHROME. A painting in one colour. Underpaintings are sometimes executed in monochrome.

MOTIF. The dominant feature, or idea, in a composition.

NATURALISM. In art, realistic method; fidelity to appearances; exact imitation.

NEUTRAL COLOUR. A colour which has no positive hue, such as a grey.

NEUTRAL GREY. A grey mixed from black and white.

OIL. The medium which is used for the grinding of pigments during the preparation of paints, and also as a vehicle during the process of painting. Oils are divided into two main types: (a) Essential Oils (Volatile) (b) Fixed Oils. Essential oils, such as spirits of turpentine, tend to evaporate, whereas fixed oils, such as linseed, are permanent.

OIL COLOUR. Paint which is produced by grinding pigments with an oil, such as linseed, or poppy oil.

OILING OUT. After a while, the colours in an oil painting tend to "sink", either uniformly, or what is more likely, in patches. If it is proposed to repaint any such sunken passages, the colour may first be restored to its original lustre by rubbing in a spot of linseed oil. The method is purely temporary and of use only during the process of re-painting. The lustre of colours can be "permanently" restored by varnishing.

OPACITY. Non-transparency in certain colours. The characteristic of those colours that reflect the light from their surface, but do not transmit it to the surface below.

OPTICAL MIXING. (See chapter on Modern Art: Pointillism). The theory that if colours are placed side by side on the painting surface instead of being mixed on the palette, the spectator's eye will automatically do the mixing, and produce on the retina the *sensation* of those colours that would normally be produced on the palette before application to the canvas.

OVER-PAINTING. Any layer of paint which is applied over a dry underpainting.

PALETTE. A term which possesses two meanings:

(a) The surface on which an artist mixes his colours.

(b) The particular range of colours which an artist, or a school, employs.

Thus we talk of the restricted palette of an artist like Titian, or the spectrum palette of the Impressionists.

PIGMENT. The colouring matter, usually in powder form which is ground with oil to make paint.

PIGMENTS: *Their Classification.* Broadly speaking, pigments may be divided into two main groups, according to their source of origin:

(a) *Mineral Pigments.* Natural pigments such as the earth colours, and those which are artificially produced, for example, Cobalt Blue, the Cadmiums, Viridian, etc. Many artificial pigments are produced in high temperature furnaces.

(b) *Organic Pigments.* Pigments that are produced from animal and vegetable sources, such as the Madders, Sap Green, etc.

Pigments may also be classified in relation to certain other qualities: (a) Opaque and Transparent; (b) Fugitive and Permanent.

PERSPECTIVE. See AERIAL and LINEAR PERSPECTIVE.

PICTURE PLANE. The plane on which the artist works. This may be thought of as a transparent plane, such as a sheet of glass, set between the eye of the spectator and the subject, and upon which the artist projects images in perspective.

PLANE SURFACE. The two-dimensional surface, such as paper, or canvas, upon which the artist works.

PRIMARY COLOURS. Red, yellow, and blue; the three colours from which with white it is possible to mix the remaining colours of the spectrum—orange, green, and violet.

PRIMING. The preliminary coating which is applied to the support, such as wood, canvas, or card, to render it non-absorbent, and so suitable for oil painting. However, before applying a priming, it is first of all essential to seal the pores of the support with coatings of glue size.

REFLECTED COLOUR. Any colour which is reflected into the *hue* of an object from an extraneous colour source.

REFLECTED LIGHTS. Those lights in a subject which are collected from a secondary source of illumination, such as a mirror.

RETREATING COLOUR. A cool colour, such as blue, which appears to retreat into the distance of a picture.

ROCOCO. From the French, *rocaille*, meaning pebble, or rock work of the kind used to decorate artificial grottoes. A style, especially of interior design, closely associated with the French Court of the eighteenth century. It originated during the reign of Louis XIV, and was continued under Louis XV. The rococo style is characterized by profuse and fantastic ornamentation (François Boucher (1703–70) is a notable example in painting) though it is much lighter and more charming than the baroque. It was purely decorative, and not propagandist in purpose.

ROMANTICISM. Art in which imagination plays the predominant role. The tendency to put imagination before reason, or the ideal of classical perfection. Art which springs from the subjective personality of the artist, rather than from any objective aesthetic system. The term is used especially to describe the movement which flourished in France during the 1830s, when Eugène Delacroix (1798–1863) and Theodore Géricault (1791–1824) led the romantic reaction against the school of Neo-Classicism founded by Jacques Louis David (1748–1825) the leading painter of the Revolution. In literature, the poet Byron (1788–1824) would serve as an example of the romantic imagination in action.

SCUMBLE. The reverse of a glaze. The application of a film of opaque colour over a darker colour, to lighten it.

SFUMATO. The soft blending of light tones into dark.

SIGNIFICANT FORM. The significance of the aesthetic form of the work of art, irrespective of subject content. Thus the critic Roger Fry (1866–1934) wrote: "No one who has a real understanding of the art of painting attaches any importance to what we call—the subject of a picture— what is represented". This is of course an extreme, and limited view, since Fry was passionately concerned with significant form. The consummate work of art must possess both subject, and significant form.

SINKING-IN. During the process of painting, and especially after completion, oil colours are likely to sink, so that the painting becomes dull, and matt, either in parts, or throughout.

SPECTRUM PALETTE. The range of colours first used by the French Impressionists (see Chapter on Modern Art: Impressionism.) and restricted to those of the spectrum, viz.: red, orange, yellow, green, blue, indigo, and violet.

216

SQUARING, or SQUARING UP. A method of transferring a small, preparatory study, on to a larger surface. The process is based on the division of both areas into a series of numbered, proportionate squares.

STYLE. An artist's characteristic manner of expression. The term may be applied more generally to the characteristic manner of a particular period of art, or the manner of a school.

STYLIZATION. Conformity with the rules of a conventional style. Mannerism. In art, a tendency towards the academic.

SUPPORT. The material upon which, after suitable treatment, the artist paints his picture.

TACTILE VALUES. Those qualities in a painting that make it possible for the spectator to apprehend the special properties of solids (hard and soft, rough and smooth, etc.), and through their apprehension, to enjoy those intangible qualities, such as distance and space, warmth and coolness, in which solids have their being. The total experience, both physical and imaginative, of apprehending and enjoying the work of art.

TEXTURE. In relation to painting, the term possesses two meanings:

(a) The representation of the special physical characteristics of any particular surface, such as, skin, fabric, wood, metal, earth, etc.

(b) The character of the paint surface in itself: rough, smooth, etc.

TONE. The relative value of a colour in terms of light and dark, as distinct from hue, or intensity. In painting, the correct orchestration of relative tone values is of great importance.

TOOTH. The relative roughness, or grain, of canvas.

UNDERPAINTING. A preliminary painting in colour, over which the artist intends to glaze films of transparent colour. An underpainting may also be a preliminary study in monochrome, over which the painter intends to work in opaque colour.

VANISHING POINT. In perspective, the point on the eye level, or horizon line, to which parallel lines converge, and where they vanish.

VARNISH. A transparent coating, such as mastic varnish, applied to a painting to protect the surface against damp, and other forms of atmospheric attack.

VEHICLE. A term which can be applied either to describe the liquid with which pigments are ground during the process of being made into paint, or to the liquid, such as linseed oil, with which colours are rendered more workable during the process of painting.

WARM COLOURS. The yellowish colours which appear in the warm half of the colour circle.

WASH. A thin, transparent film of watercolour, usually applied over a relatively large area; thus the expression, "laying a wash". The term can also be used to describe a type of drawing, such as pen and wash, in which the main areas of shadow are applied in washes of ink or watercolour.

# Appendix

IN MARCH 1957 I presented an exhibition of paintings by spare time artists at the
South London Art Gallery, in Camberwell. The exhibition, entitled "Fire in The
Hold" (sub-titled: Pleasure Painting in the Mid-Twentieth Century) was organized
by myself for the local authorities, and I have included an extract from the Introduction
which I wrote for the exhibition, because I feel that while certain aspects of the argument
have already been broached elsewhere in the present volume, my most intense and compact feelings about the nature and significance of pleasure painting in our time, are best
revealed here. Perhaps I might supplement those feelings with two relevant thoughts from
M. André Malraux. In 1935 this distinguished Frenchman wrote that the novelist's duty
was to "make men aware of the greatness that lies unacknowledged within them". Since
then he has observed with great pertinence that today, people the world over, are now
looking to art "to fill an empty place for which they have no name".

The first argument is of course equally applicable to the function of the painter;
while the truth of the second observation was borne out by the Camberwell Exhibition.

\* \* \*

It is easier to let the mind die away like a cry on the wind, than to fan the core of
divine fire into a flame which can illumine the dark puddle of human potentiality. That
this spark is extinguished, or at least blindfold, even before a child leaves school, is a
challenging indictment of an educational system which makes few concessions to the
need for the training of creative personality. There is little provision in general school
curricula for the shaping of mind into an instrument that can forge creative action, from
the furnace of creative thought. So far as creativity is fostered at school at all, it invariably
follows lines of least resistance, happy in its pursuit of the phantoms of "free expression"
in dislocation from any system of discipline, and order. I am referring, of course, to
"child art" which is largely a fabrication of the artist-critic-educationalist *manqué*.

In the Western world where creative thought and action are limited to the specialist—
*good*, or *evil*—there is no incumbence upon individuals to think, or act, at all. Indeed,
the primary objective of political extremism has been the destruction of the core
of creative fire; while the decadent democracies of the West with their ceaseless carping
upon the freedom myth, without ever acknowledging the act of individual responsibility
which true liberty involves, have been content to sit back and watch the debasement
of the fire by the various mediums of mass entertainment.

It is tempting to squat in the sty of contentment, luxuriously appointed with every soul killing device, while the mind slips cosily into the slime of "entertainment," softening and crumbling beneath the dead caresses of radio and television, until we are left with a nation of cows at gates.

Yet where these mediums have been used to stimulate thought, and action, especially through television in the field of visual self-expression, the results have indicated very clearly, not only the passionate need for creative thought and action that exists throughout the structure of society—the participants in the present exhibition range from housewives to doctors—but in relation to the proliferation of people who can so easily be encouraged to paint creatively, just what that need, and its fulfilment really signify.

The late Professor Collingwood spoke of art as "the community's medicine for the worst disease of mind, the corruption of consciousness". Certainly this age has ample need for such medicine. The rise of the phenomenon of painting as an instrument through which society can challenge the forces of the materialistic oligarchy, is one of the few healthy signs of the time. The individual spirit is on the prowl, it is still, thank God, free to think, and to act, and the sheer act of creative doing, however inadequate or crude by professional standards, is what really matters. Provided, of course, this act is not merely imitative of debased standards in professional painting, such as the decadent illusionism still practised by the academies.

Pleasure painting today is a manifestation of the community's need to find a vigorous antidote for the grosser effects of materialism. The will to create is *the fire in the hold:* the conflagration below the decks of overt personality. Social psychologists of the future may well interpret the current popular enthusiasm for painting as the first tangible revolt against an era of soulless materialism. If humanity is to survive, and the future has never been endowed with such a sensational choice—that between glittering progress or total destruction—society must learn to think creatively in its individual elements. Ultimately, law and order must spring from the individual, and any step that leads to an increase in the practise of creative thought, and action, in the individual, is vital.

The moment people commence painting they start *thinking*—many perhaps for the first time—and if at the outset the thought is limited to problems of line, form, and colour, it will soon expand to encompass far more extensive horizons. The act of physical looking is often the springboard to more abstract considerations. In this exhibition you will find the process of creative thought at work in a variety of intriguing ways, and I have avoided, generally, only those types of pleasure painting that lack a core of personal creative fire. The genre of third-hand imitative academic illusionism has no place in the pattern of genuine pleasure painting. Models, and tricks of the trade, often in themselves debased, and represented by bad teachers and instructional journals as fixed scales of action for the spare-time artist, are extremely dangerous.

At the very least, pleasure painting today is a new folk art—intense, joyous, anarchical. Beyond the outmoded chimaera of economics, politics, and religion, it represents the real measure of human dignity—the individual will striving towards realization and fulfilment.                                                MERVYN LEVY.

# Index

# INDEX